Second Edition

Quick Degunking Sheet!

W9-CXS-726

The Degunking 12-Step Program

Here is the basic 12-step degunking process that you should follow to fully degunk your PC:

1. Get rid of the files you don't really need (Chapter 3).
2. Uninstall programs you don't need (Chapter 4).
3. Organize your files and folders (Chapter 5).
4. Clean up your Desktop and Start menu (Chapter 6).
5. Reduce your e-mail spam, and sort through and organize your Outlook mail (Chapters 7 & 8).
6. Install the latest upgrades (Chapter 9) and troubleshoot Service Pack 2 (Chapter 10).
7. Fix the media problems you're having with Windows Media Player and Movie Maker (Chapter 11).
8. Optimize your hard drive (Chapter 12).
9. Clean and fine-tune the Registry (Chapter 13).
10. Incorporate new hardware (Chapter 14), PowerToys and good shareware to help keep your machine clean and running efficiently (Chapter 15).
11. Improve security and set up a good firewall (Chapter 16).
12. Back up your system on a regular basis (Chapter 17).

Degunking with Time Limitations

To get the full benefits of degunking, we highly recommend that you complete all of the main degunking tasks in the order that they are presented. Performing all of these tasks will require a bit of time. If your time is limited, here are some suggestions for valuable degunking tasks you can perform in the time you *do* have—whether it's ten minutes, three hours, or a half day.

Ten-Minute Degunking

If you have a very short amount of time—less than half an hour, say— you should focus on archiving, deleting, and compressing some of your e-mail:

1. Move a large group of old e-mails to an archived folder and delete the e-mails from your current inbox (Page 135).

2. Empty the deleted bin of your emails (Chapter 8).

3. If you have any more time, look for large blocks of e-mails that you no longer need and delete them. A good place to look is any folder that contains e-mail more than six months old (Chapter 8).

4. Look in the Sent folder and delete all sent e-mails with attachments (Chapter 8).

5. Empty the Recycle Bin to free up space on your hard drive (Page 78).

6. Download and install Microsoft's new spyware utility.

Thirty-Minute Degunking

If you only have thirty minutes or so, we recommend you perform the ten-minute degunking plan listed above and then the following tasks to get rid of files and programs stored on your hard drive that you no longer use:

1. Remove the excessive junk in your default folders: My Documents, My Music, My Videos, and so on (Page 24).

2. Remove the temporary files on your system (Page 41).

3. Try to remove the programs you no longer use by utilizing the programs' uninstall options (Page 52). Because deleting a program might take a few minutes, you might need to focus on deleting five or so programs.

4. Remove unwanted programs that don't have an uninstall option with the Control Panel (Page 53).

5. Empty the Recycle Bin to free up space on your hard drive (Page 78).

6. Change Service Pack 2's security settings for better productivity and performance (Page 154).

7. Check manually for updates to your system both from Microsoft and from the manufacturer's Web site (Page 153).

8. Download and install TweakUI to get underneath the hood of Windows XP and make Windows XP more efficient (Page 265).

One-Hour Degunking

If you have an hour to degunk your PC, you can go a little deeper and remove more e-mails, files and folders, and programs you no longer need. Here are the tasks to focus on:

1. Perform the thirty-minute degunking plan.

2. Delete more unnecessary files by focusing on the following:

   • Remove the files you don't need from your root directory on your main drive (C:\) (Page 34).

   • Search for files you don't need on your default drive and remove them (Page 37).

   • Remove unused unzipped files and other duplicate files (Page 40).

3. Uninstall more unnecessary programs by focusing on the following:

- Remove extraneous Windows components from Control Panel (Page 54).
- Search for programs you didn't know you had and remove them (Page 56).
- Remove programs for hardware you no longer own or don't use any more (Page 60).

4. Empty the Recycle Bin to free up space on your hard drive (Page 78).
5. Look through the music you have stored in Windows Media Player's Library, and delete duplicate files or delete unwanted playlists (Page 186).
6. Look though the files you've created with Windows Movie Maker, and delete files you no longer need (Page 192).

Three-Hour Degunking

Because you now have a little more time to degunk your PC, with this plan you'll be able to:

1. Perform the one-hour degunking tasks.
2. Fine-tune the programs you regularly use to improve their performance (Page 61).
3. Organize the default folders by creating additional, embedded folders and moving files into them (Page 70).
4. Use the File and Folders tasks pane in Windows XP to rename, move, copy, or delete folders (Page 75).
5. Use Disk Cleanup and Disk Defragmenter to really complete the cleansing process (Page 81).

Half-Day Degunking

When you have limited time to degunk, your focus should be on cleaning up e-mails, files and folders, and unused programs. Having a half day to degunk allows you to clean up and tweak your Desktop and Start menu, as well as perform some additional e-mail degunking tasks:

1. Perform the three-hour degunking tasks.
2. Clean up and personalize the Taskbar so you can work faster and smarter (Page 88).
3. Remove items from the System Tray that use valuable system resources (Page 91).
4. Limit the programs that start when Windows starts (Page 95).
5. Personalize the Start menu by adding or deleting programs, reordering the list, and more (Page 95).
6. Personalize the Desktop with your favorite folders and shortcuts, and remove unused icons (Page 99).
7. Go through all of your media files, deleting media you no longer need or want (Chapter 11).
8. Set-up a separate spam filtering utility to help you reduce the amount of spam you receive (Page 122).

Spare Moment Degunking

There may be times when you are doing something with your computer and you discover that you have a few minutes to spare. To this end, we've created our top twenty list of degunking tasks that you can perform. These tasks do not need to be performed in any specific order. Simply select a task and perform it to help clean your machine.

Twenty Useful Degunking Tasks

1. Delete five icons off of your Desktop (Page 90).
2. Get rid of annoying pop-up messages with a useful utility (Page 272).
3. Empty the Recycle Bin (Page 78).
4. Uninstall one or more programs you no longer use (Page 50).
5. Remove annoying Spyware (Page 59).
6. Delete 10 of your top 30 largest e-mails (Chapter 8).
7. Setup Internet Explorer to better manage cookies (Page 290).
8. Remove extraneous Windows components from Control Panel (Page 54).
9. Add or remove default icons on your Desktop (Page 99).
10. Remove a program from your Start menu that you really don't need (Page 95).
11. Check your e-mail outbox and drafts folders to make sure gunk isn't accumulating there (Page 145).
12. Locate five one megabyte or larger files that you no longer need and delete them.
13. Empty your Deleted Items in your e-mail (Chapter 8).
14. Use the Windows Backup utility to back up important files and folders (Page 306).
15. Download and use the TweakUI PowerToy to customize Windows settings (Page 265).
16. Personalize the Windows default folders with folders of your own (Page 75).
17. Configure your virtual memory settings to fully utilize the memory you have (Page 240).
18. Unsubscribe from an e-mail newsletter you no longer read (Chapter 7).
19. Configure Internet options to protect, secure, and keep your private information private (Page 284).
20. Physically clean your screen or keyboard (Page 248).

Praise from Readers for *Degunking*™ *Windows*®

"[*Degunking Windows* is] a great new book that explains why computers lose their vigor over time. It offers easy-to-follow instructions for cleaning out your hard drive, tweaking programs, eliminating spyware, sorting e-mail and updating your system."
—*Parade Magazine*

"Do you own a PC or Mac computer and use it regularly? Then, it has gunk. Gunk is all the unnecessary junk on your computer that can slow down performance and ultimately cause system malfunction. It's those fuzzy photos that never got tossed, e-mail you've filed and forgotten, old programs you never use, hidden programs you don't want and too many programs that launch at startup. I found very useful advice from two books: *Degunking Windows* by Joli Ballew and Jeff Duntemann, and *Degunking Your Mac* by Joli Ballew."
—*Seattle Times*

"I once wrote a four-part series in *InfoWorld* about correcting what I called 'Windows arthritis.' This is the lethargy that seems to overtake the operating system as little as six months after it's installed.... Now Joli Ballew and Jeff Duntemann have compiled an entire book [*Degunking Windows*] on the subject, and it's a good one."
—*Brian Livingston*

"After all the worm news these days, when something goes wrong, users will often jump to the not-necessarily accurate conclusion that they have a virus or something like that. Maybe they do, but it's not usually the only problem they have. Joli Ballew and Jeff Duntemann have beaten me to a great idea for a book on this: *Degunking Windows* from Paraglyph Press. I really wish I'd thought of it first."
—*Larry Seltzer in eweek*

"The information found in *Degunking Windows* is exactly what the doctor ordered. Joli Ballew and Jeff Duntemann do an excellent job of helping you to find the things that are slowing down and cluttering up your system. They explain in plain-English what you need to know to remove unwanted programs and optimize your Windows machine for maximum performance."
—*About.com*

"I am impressed. [*Degunking Windows*] makes a very useful companion for step-by-step computer maintenance....My copy is filled of highlighter marks and 3M page markers."
—*Memphis PC User's Group*

"I thought I knew my way around a PC until I bought this book....I can heartily recommend *Degunking Windows* to any PC user and only wished it had been published sooner. Now I have uncovered many ideas, solutions and practical hints that I was totally unaware of."

—*Bits & Bytes*

"When explaining network security to your users, have on hand *Degunking Windows* by Joli Ballew and Jeff Duntemann. Chapters explain file cleanup and organization, spyware, spam, cookies and setting up a Windows XP Internet Connection firewall."

—*Network World*

"Only one word is needed to summarize [*Degunking Windows*]: terrific! The authors display an awesome knowledge of Windows XP and its workings, and tell us how to use them to good advantage. The information provided in the book is comprehensive and detailed, yet highly readable."

—*Sierra Vista (AZ) IBM PC User Group*

"The authors in nontechnical language can help you keep the registry clean, backup your critical files, organize your file systems, clean up your desktop, keep your hard drives from working too hard, clean up your e-mail program, work with the taskbar, remove spyware, prevent spam and a great deal more. Even if you never want to touch your computer in a maintenance kind of way, this book will help you understand why you should."

—*Billings (MT) Gazette*

"Just follow this book [*Degunking Windows*], chapter by chapter and you'll be amazed at how you can improve your PC. The targeted audience in this extremely valuable book includes all serious Windows users who are tired of the common gunked up result that is just what happens in a Windows machine, and who are willing to take charge of their machine and take control over these gunking aspects. While most all extant PC technicians are likely already to be savvy to many of these super suggestions, I bet most all will also find some ideas in this book they have not yet heard of."

—*Golden Triangle PC Club*

Second Edition

Joli Ballew

Jeff Duntemann

President
Keith Weiskamp

Editor-at-Large
Jeff Duntemann

Vice President, Sales, Marketing, and Distribution
Steve Sayre

Vice President, International Sales and Marketing
Cynthia Caldwell

Production Manager
Kim Eoff

Cover Designer
Kris Sotelo

Degunking™ Windows®, Second Edition

Paraglyph Press, Inc.
4015 N. 78th Street, #115
Scottsdale, Arizona 85251
Phone: 602-749-8787
www.paraglyphpress.com

Paraglyph Press ISBN: 1-933097-07-8
Bookclub Edition: 1-933097-12-4

Printed in the United States of America
10   9   8   7   6   5   4   3   2   1

PARAGLYPH PRESS

The Paraglyph Mission

This book you've purchased is a collaborative creation involving the work of many hands, from authors to editors to designers and to technical reviewers. At Paraglyph Press, we like to think that everything we create, develop, and publish is the result of one form creating another. And as this cycle continues on, we believe that your suggestions, ideas, feedback, and comments on how you've used our books is an important part of the process for us and our authors.

We've created Paraglyph Press with the sole mission of producing and publishing books that make a difference. The last thing we all need is yet another tech book on the same tired, old topic. So we ask our authors and all of the many creative hands who touch our publications to do a little extra, dig a little deeper, think a little harder, and create a better book. The founders of Paraglyph are dedicated to finding the best authors, developing the best books, and helping you find the solutions you need.

As you use this book, please take a moment to drop us a line at **feedback@paraglyphpress.com** and let us know how we are doing—and how we can keep producing and publishing the kinds of books that you can't live without.

Sincerely,

Keith Weiskamp & Jeff Duntemann
Paraglyph Press Founders
4015 N. 78th Street, #115
Scottsdale, Arizona 85251
email: **feedback@paraglyphpress.com**
Web: **www.paraglyphpress.com**

Recently Published by Paraglyph Press:

Degunking Your Personal Finances
By Shannon Plate

Degunking Microsoft Office
*By Wayne Palaia
and Christina Palaia*

Degunking Your PC
*By Joli Ballew
and Jeff Dunteman*

Degunking eBay
By Greg Holden

Degunking Your Email, Spam, and Viruses
By Jeff Duntemann

Surviving PC Disasters, Mishaps and Blunders
*By Jesse Torres
and Peter Sideris*

Degunking Your Mac
By Joli Ballew

As always, I'd like to dedicate this book to my family, for all their help and support.

—Joli Ballew

In memory of Chewy, 1982-1998, who chose the long life rather than the glorious one

—Jeff Duntemann

❧

About the Authors

Joli Ballew, MCSE, A+, is a full time writer and digital enthusiast who also teaches, creates Web sites, and consults from her home base of Dallas, Texas. Joli has written almost a dozen books on subjects ranging from digital photography to network administration. Several of her books—*Windows XP: The Ultimate Users Guide, Windows 2000 Server On Site, Degunking Your Mac*, and *Degunking Your PC*—are also available from Paraglyph Press.

Jeff Duntemann is an author, editor, programmer, lecturer, and technology columnist, with over a dozen books under his belt, including *Degunking Your E-Mail, Spam, and Viruses, Jeff Duntemann's Wi-Fi Guide,* and *Assembly Language Step-by-Step*. Jeff is the former editor-in-chief of *PC Techniques* and *Visual Developer Magazine*, and has been a blogger since before the word was coined—see **www.duntemann.com/Diary.htm.**

Acknowledgments

Quite a few people made our latest book together a success. First, a special thanks to Keith Weiskamp and Steven Sayre for giving me the opportunity to help with this book. I'd also like to thank team members Ben Sawyer, Jeff Duntemann, Cynthia Caldwell, and Kim Eoff for their help in producing this book in record time.

I'd also like to thank my agent Neil Salkind, who always finds something for me to do, and who always has a project up his sleeve. It's always a pleasure working with you.

Finally, I'd like to thank my family for all of their support and encouragement. First, my parents, who are the most wonderful and supportive people in the world; without you I wouldn't be who I am today. Also my daughter Jennifer, who is so beautiful, patient, and smart; how I wish I could be half as good a person as you. Finally, Cosmo, who is always there with words of encouragement, a laugh and smile, and who drags me out to the golf course when I get too stressed. I could not be surrounded by more beautiful and wonderful people.
—Joli Ballew

Many thanks to the whole Paraglyph crew, Keith, Cynthia, Steve, and Ben, for getting the project off the ground and keeping it going!
—Jeff Duntemann

Contents

Chapter 8
Cleaning Up E-Mail Gunk 133

Chapter 9
Installing Upgrades for Your System 151

Chapter 15
PowerToys and Awesome Shareware 261

Chapter 16
Improving Security 279

Foreword

For a long time, what we now call "Windows gunk" was The Problem That Had No Name. People knew that Windows got slow and weird over time, but couldn't quite put their fingers on what was going wrong. When we introduced *Degunking Windows* in January 2004, people just went, "Yeah, that's it! Gunk!"

Suddenly, everyone understood the problem, and the book became an instant sensation. It wasn't just the name. We had dared to assemble a 12-step program to help people recover from Windows gunk, and it just *worked*: "Hello. My name is Windows, and I'm a gunk magnet." We saved a *lot* of old PCs from the curb.

The authors found themselves in demand for radio shows, and scant weeks later were often back on the same shows, explaining the ways that Windows bogs down and offering tips on how to make things work again. Reviewers began to rave:

"The cheapest infusion of power to a Windows XP computer can now be had for a mere $24.99. It's not a faster processor or more memory but a well-done book titled "*Degunking Windows.*"
—*Miami Herald*

"The advice is elegantly presented with superb hand-holding from coauthors Joli Ballew and Jeff Duntemann."
—*Chicago Tribune*

"Get on board with this 12-step program, or rather processes, to clear out the cobwebs and garbage hiding in the chips of your computer. [*Degunking Windows*] makes me want to put on yellow dishwashing gloves and take the pink feather duster as I get to work. Be gone, crowded Favorites! Shoo, unused programs and files! When you finish the housework, take a load off and treat yourself to a TV dinner."
—*Lockergnome*

This long string of raves culminated in a July 4th review in *Parade Magazine,* which reached twenty million people and sent *Degunking Windows* all the way up to #4 on the *full* Amazon book sales rankings, right on the heels of Bill Clinton's autobiography and *The Da Vinci Code. Degunking Windows* received the "IPPY" award for Best Computer Book of the Year from *Independent Publisher.*

We were clearly on to something.

"Degunking" had quickly become an industry catchphrase and what computer geeks call a "meme," or an idea with a life of its own. What might once have meant "scraping the grease off a crankshaft" now meant "squeezing the chaos out" from almost anything. People were asking us, "What about the Mac? What about Linux? What about dust mice on my motherboard?" We got to it, and what had worked so well for Windows was soon working for other operating systems, email, and other technical topics. The Degunking concept even spread beyond the IT industry and gave life to a book titled *Degunking Your Personal Finances* that in turn become part of a set of television programs to help people with their own personal "money makeovers." As we write this, we're not sure how far Degunking will continue to go, but we're happy to see it help so many people combat clutter and all of those annoying things that get in the way of a full and efficient life.

The second wave begins here, with a completely revised and much expanded *Degunking Windows,* now in its second edition. Windows XP's Service Pack 2 injected a certain amount of gunk into XP systems, but XP also provided new features in media and backup that figure prominently in the degunking equation. It's all here, and as Windows continues to create new corners for gunk to gather in, we'll keep providing new ways of digging it out.

In the meantime, we're looking around to find new realms of gunk to conquer. Where would you like to see the Degunking broom sweep next? Do drop us a line and let us know!

—*Keith Weiskamp & Jeff Duntemann*
August 20, 2005

Introduction

Your brand-new PC is here, and you're in heaven. You tell all your friends how wonderful Windows XP is and how fast your new PC is. With all of the extra time you have, you start fixing up things around the house and catching up with old friends. You think to yourself, "Why did I wait so long to get a new version of Windows?"

Then weird things start to happen. Your PC starts getting a little slower. It starts crashing in situations where it never crashed before. You start to develop problems with your favorite applications and your Web browser. Another month goes by, and your PC gets even slower. The number of spam e-mails you receive is starting to increase dramatically. It seems as if every time you surf the Web, you're bombarded with more and more pop-up ads. It becomes difficult, sometimes impossible, to run your PC for a whole day (or even a few hours) without crashing. Then your PC becomes so slow and so unreliable that you wish you had a new computer again.

Of course, you don't really need a new computer. The actual problem isn't with the computer at all. The problem is with something we call "gunk." Think of it as software entropy, data chaos, or just too many bits lying around in all the wrong places. Gunk is disorder among your files, chaos inside your Registry, the fragmentation of your hard disk. It increases over time, no matter what you do—and it increases much more quickly if you're careless and become the victim of spyware, adware, viruses, and worms. To get your Windows PC back to the way it was when it just came out of the box, you need to *degunk* it!

Traditionally, a clean install of Windows is the best thing to do when a PC bogs down, but this takes *hours*. And that's just reinstalling Windows. You could spend days beyond that backing up all of your files and then reinstalling and reconfiguring all of your applications. If you're feeling rich, you could hire one of those high-priced consultants to clean the gunk out of your machine. But who are you kidding? You've got kids to put through college; bills are pilling up; Visa is calling. Besides, you just spent a bundle on this fast, new machine—why should you spend even more money degunking it?

There is a much better solution. You can degunk your PC in just a few hours yourself, using a set of tried-and-true techniques. With this step-by-step guide, *Degunking Windows, Second Edition*, you can quickly clean your machine, speed it up, secure it from dangerous hackers, worms, and viruses, organize your e-mail, reduce spam, and make your computer work as quickly and reliably as it did the day you brought it home. This book is not just another book on how to use Windows. It is an easy-to-read and concise guide showing you, step-by-step and in plain English, how to improve the performance of your PC after time, hard use, and less than optimal organizational habits have gunked it up. We'll show you how to reorganize files that are scattered all over the place, how to reduce or eliminate spam, what to do with a fragmented hard drive, how to fix improperly installed and uninstalled programs, and how to handle a host of other PC problems you may not even know you have.

Why You Need This Book

Without regular maintenance and careful work habits, *all* PCs running Windows will get gunked up over time. The goal of this book is to show you how to degunk your own Windows PC.

Degunking Windows uses a unique approach that can save you countless hours of valuable time, and a bundle of money on help and equipment that you don't really need. Here are some of the unique features of this book:

√   An easy-to-follow 12-step degunking process that you can put to work immediately.

√   Explanations, in everyday terms, of how to easily fix common problems that create gunk on your PC.

√   Information on how to save money with free degunking tools that are easily found on the Internet.

√   Helpful "GunkBuster's Notebook" sidebars in every chapter to help you solve specific problems while reducing the clutter on your PC.

√   Degunking maintenance tasks that you can perform on a regular basis to keep your machine in top form.

√   Instructions on how to degunk your e-mail and reduce the amount of spam you receive.

√   Advice on how to "work smart" and keep your PC gunk-free so that you don't eventually have to reinstall the operating system.

√   How to know when you have to do a clean install, or (as the very last resort!) buy a new PC.

How to Use This Book

Degunking Windows is structured around the order of the degunking process that you should follow. The book starts off by explaining the importance of degunking and why operating systems like Windows XP require degunking. Each subsequent chapter describes an important degunking task, explained in plain English with step-by-step instructions.

TIP: *This book is designed around a 12-step program (outlined in Chapter 2) that we recommend you follow, starting with Chapter 3 and continuing through the end of the book. We highly recommend that you follow the process in the order that it is presented here. This will result in the most benefit from the time you spend degunking your PC.*

Once you've completely degunked your PC, you should then perform different degunking operations at different times, depending on your needs, to keep your PC in tip-top shape. We expect that *Degunking Windows* will become one of your most-used computer books, and we'll bet that it will end up on your bookshelf right next to your PC.

A Note on Windows Versions

The degunking tasks presented in this book were written to work with the current versions of Windows XP Home Edition and Windows XP Professional Edition. Some of the operations presented, such as backing up Windows and using System Restore, are very specific to Windows XP. If you are using an older version of Windows, such as Windows 98, Windows NT, or Windows 2000, you can still benefit from many of the degunking techniques presented here. The degunking tasks explained here involve more general operations—such as removing files you don't need, organizing your hard drive, and cleaning up your e-mail—that you can easily adapt to the version of Windows you are using. Here are some of the more general (and less version-specific) tasks you can perform, regardless of the version of Windows you have:

√ Getting Rid of Files That Shouldn't Be There (Chapter 3)

√ Uninstalling Programs You Don't Need and Tweaking Those You Do (Chapter 4)

√ Organizing Your Remaining Files and Folders (Chapter 5)

√ Tweaking Your Desktop and Start Menus (Chapter 6)

√ Preventing Spam Gunk (Chapter 7)

√   Cleaning Up E-Mail Gunk (Chapter 8)

√   Optimizing Your Hard Drive and Startup System (Chapter 10)

You can also perform the tasks that are more version-specific (such as cleaning the Registry) by using the appropriate software. For example, if you are using Windows 98 and you want to clean the Registry, you can follow the general discussions presented in Chapter 13, but to actually clean the Registry, you'll need to use a Registry cleaning tool designed for Windows 98.

The Degunking Mindset

The more you learn about degunking your PC, the more you'll realize that degunking is a mindset, not just a set of technical skills. We view degunking as mostly psychology, not just technology. Rather than simply being a process that you follow when your computer becomes unusably gunked up, degunking involves a disciplined approach to managing your computer and organizing your work habits. If you follow the basic steps outlined in this book on a regular basis, you'll earn yourself a sort of Windows insurance policy and save yourself a lot of aggravation down the road. We also believe that *Degunking Windows* will make your time on your PC more time-efficient, more productive, and maybe even more enjoyable. Windows can be fun. With a little care and attention to detail, it can be as much fun three or four years down the road as it was the day you took your PC out of the box!

Why Is My Computer All Gunked Up?

Degunking Checklist:

√ Make sure you understand the four basic processes involved in degunking Windows.

√ Learn how files saved on your hard drive can gunk up your machine.

√ Understand why you need a strategy for dealing with pesky temporary files.

√ Learn that you can develop a plan to combat spam.

√ Understand why installing too many programs can really gunk up your machine.

√ See how your Desktop and menu system are two places where gunk can build up.

√ Learn how hard drive fragmentation and limited drive space can impact the performance of your drive.

√ Learn how Service Pack 2 (SP2) can cause gunk.

√ Understand how unorganized data files and Web favorites can gunk up your machine.

Because you've picked up this book, chances are you fall into one of three categories: You're a person with a Windows machine that is struggling to stay afloat; you're a person whose dad or mom just asked why their machine has run out of hard-drive space and won't function properly; or you're a help-desk clerk trying to show people how to save their machines from oblivion. Whatever the case, you're the victim of a fairly common problem—you have a gunked-up computer that you need to keep from falling apart (and driving you crazy). The hard drive works overtime to send or receive an e-mail with an attachment. The start-up process takes three times longer than it did the day you first bought your computer. When you shut down your PC, you can run down the street to get your latte and get back home before the machine finishes winding down. When you feel that your computer is ready to be put out to pasture, you're likely to ask yourself: What the heck happened? Where did I go wrong?

Don't let hardware vendors convince you that your hard drive has suddenly gone bad or that your computer processing chip has gotten too old and cranky. They want you to buy a new machine every year. You can probably see the magazine ads now: "You need the latest whiz-bang RX43210-75 chip" or "Our new micro-woofer, repeater, wireless, sub-atomic, low-heat hard drive will run circles around the competition."

The truth is, you probably don't need what these guys are selling. You just need a little experience, a little time, some degunking insight, and a copy of this book.

Our PCs are like our houses: Benign neglect usually leads to problems like leaky roofs and clogged drains. Through a combination of internal factors (forgetting to back up your hard drive, not closely watching what gets installed, subscribing to too many e-mail newsletters, and so on) and external factors (spam, viruses, and poorly programmed software), our PCs get really gunked up. Files get plastered all over like clothes in a teenager's bedroom, the Registry (the place where information about your files is stored) starts to go south, and your hard drive can barely support what's currently installed on it (let alone that new road atlas DVD you got for your birthday that you want to install).

It's hard to pinpoint exactly why your computer has gotten so gunked up. After all, every user's experience is a little different. "Getting gunked" involves a combination of many factors, though, and some of them will certainly match your situation. For instance, after a while (no matter who you are), with normal wear and tear, every computer will start to slow down. The hard drive spins longer, programs take longer to load, programs crash more frequently, and in general, a PC becomes harder to use. PCs don't last forever. Additionally, you likely continually acquire music, movies, data, and applications that you forget to properly organize or delete. Finally, updates, service packs, spyware/adware, and system-hogging programs use more and more valuable resources and your poor old PC can't keep up with the demands placed on it.

The good news is, there are solutions to overcoming these common factors that create gunk on every PC. In this book, we'll identify common PC gunk creators and how to manage them so your computer keeps running quickly and efficiently.

What the Experts Know

Hardcore Windows users and those geeky guys you hear on Sunday afternoon radio shows know how to keep their machines working well. And the good news is that most people can learn to do this, too. The problem is, until now, no one has put all this degunking information into an easy-to-follow book. What we're about to show you is really not that hard. By following these sequential steps, you can improve the operation of your machine considerably.

Our process is divided into four key areas:

1. *Basic computer housekeeping 101*: Here, we'll focus on how to get everything back in its place and rid yourself of all the gunk. (Just think about how good it feels to clean out your closet and throw away all of the stuff you don't need.) We'll start with data, such as files, pictures, movies, and music, and continue with applications and programs and services that run unnecessarily and hinder your PC's performance. You'll then spend some time organizing what you want to keep and personalizing Windows to suit your preferences.

2. *Repairing common problems*: Once you've culled down the programs and files on your machine, it's time to repair some basic and common problems. You can think of this as a basic tune-up of your system, and it can be the capstone to a core cleaning and improvement process.

3. *Improving preferences and settings to maintain things better.* Once you've officially degunked your machine, you'll want to tweak the operating system and key programs so you don't end up back where you started. You can make improvements by setting preferences to improve the chances that files go where they should, or by scheduling automated tasks such as hard drive optimizations, and creating simple shortcuts that make it easy to remove unwanted files. Another final set of improvements involves incorporating some programs that improve security, virus protection, and the overall optimization of system performance. Consider this step as putting the wax on a newly cleaned car.

4. *Improving security and backup*: In this area, you will take steps to improve the security of your PC, thus keeping it save from hackers, viruses, spyware, and thieves. You'll also learn ways to back up your data so you'll always feel safe.

Understanding How You Got So Gunked Up

You understand now that it is common for your system to run more slowly than it once did and that you haven't done anything wrong. Things in your computer might be, well, a bit disorganized. Let's review how most users end up in this predicament.

Files Are Saved All over the Hard Drive

Novice users, and even some savvy ones, will have document files, downloaded files, and other programs saved in many different places on their hard drive. This happens all the time. For example, the program used to open an attachment from Outlook or Outlook Express stores a copy of the file in a temporary directory in your Windows directory system. If you don't resave the file in your My Documents or other designated document folder, the document will remain in the temporary directory. This is an example of gunk.

Other users will also casually save stuff to their desktop or the C: root directory of their drive without giving it any further thought. Files received from IM (instant message) services usually end up in completely different directories. The point to all of this is that if you don't pay attention to where your files are going, you could end up with a situation in which you easily jam up your hard drive with a lot of data you don't need or even know how to find again.

Temporary Files Aren't Always So Temporary

Windows has a fascination with temporary files. The problem is that when computers crash or files are improperly saved, temp files like to stay around and gunk up your system. It's like temporary tax hikes—they somehow become permanent fixtures. The result is that you can find hundreds, if not thousands, of files stuck in obscure places, with obscure filenames, throughout your hard drive. To make matters worse, some of these files can't even be located unless you really understand how to find them. Getting these files off your hard drive is not always easy.

Of course, there are automated utilities that locate and delete your temporary files, but they don't typically clean out all of the files. In some cases, you have to resort to some hand-cleaning to get rid of all of the temporary files you don't need on your hard drive. Thus, it helps to know where they hide and how they get there in the first place.

Spam, Spam, Eggs, Bacon, and Spam!

Spam is the bane of anyone with an e-mail account. We all hate spam. Spam is like weeds in our gardens. The more we try to get rid of it, the faster it comes back. Eventually, it overwhelms us one way or the other. We end up with e-mail repositories teaming with irrelevant files, adding to a bloated hard drive, one that is slow to respond to searches, deletions, sorts, and more. Spam is also the most common source of viruses and worms on ordinary people's PCs.

You might have convinced yourself that there is nothing you can do about spam. But as you'll learn in this book, there are strategies you can put to work right away to greatly reduce your exposure to spam. Many users we talk to simply throw in the towel when it comes to spam, and some spend up to 30 minutes or more per day sorting through their e-mail and deleting their spam. If you take a more proactive approach by using different e-mail addresses, setting up spam filters, using different e-mail clients, and avoiding activities that trigger spam in the first place, you could save a lot of time.

Installing Too Many Programs

We are all guilty of this sin. You hear about some cool utility or you need a neat game to keep the kids occupied. Worse yet, your kids find 18 games to keep themselves occupied. You download a couple of media programs, 5 instant messaging systems, and more. You install the gardening CD-ROM in the spring, use it once, and then forget about it. And what about the genealogy CD you put in last Christmas and totally forgot about until we just brought it up? Caught you! Remember the 50 screensavers you're downloaded over the last four years? Maybe, if you're lucky, you uninstalled some of them. The problem is, your idea of uninstalling them was to drag them into the trash and ignore the warnings that these were installed programs. Windows technically thinks you still have them.

When you install a program, you're doing more than just copying files to the hard drive. Programs can make physical changes to the Windows operating system, including something called the Registry, which is sort of like a street map or rulebook on how programs work in Windows. Gum up your Registry and it can be like driving in New York City without the traffic lights working.

We've done this before, and believe us, it's not fun.

Your Menu System Is Overrun

As you add and remove programs, they each tend to add program icons to your Start menu. Eventually, given enough time and lack of upkeep, you'll end up

Figure 1-1
Too many items in the Start menu is one of the first signs of gunk.

with tons of separate folder entries on the Start menu (like the one Figure 1-1), making it unmanageable. Worse yet, some of the icons might not even work anymore. Your system is probably still functional, but you can make Windows quicker to load and easier to use by cleaning up the Start menu. If your Start menu looks like the one in Figure 1-1, you picked up the right book.

Your Desktop Is Overrun with Icons

Does your Desktop look like the one shown in Figure 1-2? Okay, we admit it. This is a screen capture from one of our computers once upon a time. We saved it to show you that even the most experienced geek needs some degunking help from time to time. A bloated Desktop is similar to the Start menu problem just discussed, and it can be even worse because not only are some program icons put on the Desktop when programs are installed, but users often put other junk on their Desktop as well. The result is a Desktop that looks like it contains the contents of your entire drive. Every piece of junk that you found while using your computer is out there for the world to see. It's like a closet without doors. The background image on Windows is so obscured you probably don't even recognize it anymore. Your friends walk by and think you are a

Figure 1-2
Too many items on the Desktop is another sure sign of gunk.

power user because you have all these icons on your Desktop, when in fact, you just never thought about cleaning it up.

Segmented Hard Drive

As a computer utilizes its hard drive, it stores programs and files in bits and pieces all over the place. Big data files and large programs aren't stored in one contiguous stretch; they are stored hopscotch style, with a piece here and a piece there. As a result, the reader on your hard drive has to physically move back and forth multiple times to read the data in one file. This slows down the hard drive and causes more wear and tear on it. And the more wear and tear on your hard drive, the higher the likelihood that it will crash, misbehave, or wear out more quickly.

Users who install and uninstall lots of programs, create and delete lots of files, and construct large e-mail files (and don't delete them when they should) can suffer from this disk access problem. By optimizing the hard drive correctly, you can speed things up and keep your machine running better and longer.

Low Hard Drive Space

Windows utilizes the hard drive to keep the operating system running, to keep open programs running, and to perform basic tasks, in addition to storing temporary files, running scheduled operations, and a myriad of other tasks.

Windows also uses the hard drive to serve as an extension of working memory and to perform other core operating system functions. Thus, if your hard drive runs very low on disk space, you can create a problem that causes Windows to crash more frequently or slow waaaaay down. This is less of a problem nowadays because more people have machines with gigantic hard drives and loads of memory. However, by increasing the number of video files, music files, big Internet downloads, and digital photographs they store, people are filling up their hard drives much faster and they aren't keeping up with their cleaning and organization tasks. Laptops and PDAs fall victim to this a lot because they tend to have smaller hard drives. By learning to keep only what you need on your drive, organize what you do keep, and clear out files expertly, you can ensure that you don't fall victim to the dreaded "low hard drive space" syndrome.

Unorganized Data Files

Some people put their files all over the place. There are a few people who at least put files in a few core folders. But wouldn't it be nice if you not only had your data files in the right folders, but you also named them correctly? While you are at it, you could even get rid of duplicate files (making folders easier to search) and get rid of files you don't need anymore.

Here's a pop quiz: How many digital photos do you have on your computer that aren't worthy of printing (much less keeping) and you've failed to delete them? How easy is it for you to find that great sunset photo from two years ago when most of your photos have filenames like SNR062500b.jpg? Look at the file directory in Figure 1-3 and tell me it doesn't look like one of yours. Consider how hard it is to locate files when they are stored in a directory with tons of ambiguous filenames.

Our computers get gunked up because we're flooded with new files all the time. We're not just dealing with word processing documents and a few spreadsheets anymore. We're downloading MP3 files for music; we're ripping our CD collection to the hard drive; we're taking hundreds of digital photos and videos; we're adding PDFs and PowerPoint slides, JPEGs and GIFs, and Photoshop collages. Somehow, we need to do more than just dump this stuff in folders without having some type of organization.

Unorganized Web Favorites

If you surf the Web a lot, you probably have a long list of bookmarks or Web Favorites. Chances are that you've discovered a quick-key for saving Web Favorites (Ctrl+D in Internet Explorer), so you may have a long list, as shown in Figure 1-4. Even if you've tried to organize them before, there are always additional favorites hanging around the bottom of the list (see Figure 1-4). I'll

Figure 1-3
Data is harder to find when it isn't organized.

bet you don't need many of them either. Don't worry; we'll show you how to clean all of that up!

Spyware Boogeyman

Spyware is a catchall name for products that, once installed, essentially report back information on your Web surfing habits or help bombard you with pop-up ads and other advertising, including spam. Spyware has also become synonymous with installed programs that don't show up in your installed programs directory. This makes them hard to find, hard to deal with, and, worst of all, hard to uninstall. In truth, some spyware is pretty harmless—it won't raid your hard drive or report the balance of your bank account to hackers—but some is not so harmless. Spyware these days can track keystrokes and thus potentially steal passwords and account numbers. Either way, since these programs can eat up available memory or resources, slow down your machine, and/or interfere with other programs, you'll want to get rid of them.

The Dreaded Cookie Monster

Cookies are not programs. They're basically tiny pieces of text data that Web sites place in a special directory on your machine. For example, a site like Yahoo! might place a small cookie on your machine with the contents

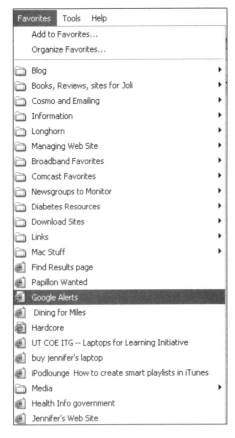

Figure 1-4
You can try to clean up your Favorites list
with folders, but if you're not careful, you'll
just gunk it up again.

"xu44$@dncsdlk3," which is a unique string of characters that it uses to recognize your computer. Unless you log in to Yahoo!, that string doesn't serve any purpose; it is used only by Yahoo! to recognize you when you visit their site. Cookies can also store more specific data, such as the date of your last visit.

Overall, Cookies are fairly harmless. They usually eat up only 1 KB (Kilobytes) to 2 KB of hard drive space, and they usually don't give a site much information other than that you have visited before. However, many people like to get rid of them because, after a while, you can have a few thousand of them and about 99 percent of them are useless. In addition, if you ever accidentally stumble onto a gambling or porn site, you might find cookies from them on your machine, which can be disconcerting for some people. Imagine searching for all text files on your machine and seeing a small 1 K file named cookie:www.tripleXfunland.net.txt.

Some people set their browsers to avoid accepting cookies altogether, but some very legitimate sites use cookies to make your experience better and more customized. (Ever wonder how Amazon recognizes you when you visit? Cookies.) Disabling cookies can sometimes lead you to throw the baby out with the bathwater, so to speak. It can prevent you from accessing a Web site that requires it. It's your call, and in the end you'll probably decide to accept cookies, so it is worthwhile to know how to clean them out by hand.

Service Packs and Updates

Finally, while we'll preach that you should always get the latest fixes, patches, updates, and upgrades for your system, as you'll find out, some can cause problems. Service Pack 2, for instance, will disable your ability to open attachments in Outlook Express. It may also offer up new and irritating error messages regarding your anti-virus software, claiming it isn't installed or configured properly. Even the new SP2 firewall can cause problems for gamers and networked computers.

Installing Movie Maker or Media Player upgrades can be trying, too. Where are the old features, and what are the new ones? You'll have to play around to find out. Are these new versions sending any personally identifiable information about you to Microsoft or third-party sites? It's hard to keep up.

So, part of degunking is not only getting updates, but managing them. You need to know how to recover from a bad or corrupt update, get update "updates," and configure updates so you can do what you want and when—we're guessing you'll still want to be able to open e-mail attachments!

You're Gunked Up!

Chances are that if one of these things is happening on your computer, nearly all of them are. But if you commit yourself to degunking, you can get most or all of your computer programs and the operating system itself back running the way it used to. The problems we just discussed will only get worse with time, and that's why your entire computer can get so bogged down.

Ready for Degunking?

The most difficult part of getting your machine back to where it should be involves dedicating a little time. As we move on and look at the different degunking techniques, we'll arrange the tasks in the order that will likely get you the most results in the shortest amount of time. Our approach will be to show you not only how to fix things, but how to get yourself on a maintenance program so that your computer *always* runs well. Throughout the book, after introducing tasks, we'll tell you how often to do it. We'll even show you how to automatically schedule tasks. If you're new to the world of degunking, don't worry. It's much easier than putting together a barbecue in the backyard with those ridiculous instructions they provide.

Degunking Your PC

Degunking Checklist:

√ Make sure you understand that the best degunking results can be obtained by performing cleanup tasks in a specific order.

√ Understand how you can manage the limited resources in Windows.

√ Learn why good file management is a critical aspect of degunking Windows.

√ Understand why the Desktop and Start menu are two places that attract gunk.

√ See how your e-mail can get really gunked up.

√ Learn degunking procedures such as Registry cleanup, hard drive optimization, and security setup.

√ Learn how Service Pack 2 (SP2), Movie Maker, and Media Player can all gunk up your PC.

√ Understand what you can do when your PC doesn't respond to the standard degunking procedures.

√ Learn the degunking 12-step program.

We could have called this chapter "Degunking: The 12-Step Program to Success," because our final goal is to introduce our proven 12-step program, which can really help you improve the performance of your PC. But to get there, we need to focus on the strategy behind the degunking process and then introduce you to the critical Windows activities that relate to degunking. This chapter is designed to help you get into the mindset for degunking. In the following chapters, we'll show you, step-by-step, how to roll up your sleeves and complete the 12 essential steps of our degunking program. The best part is that even if you have limited time, any step you perform will go a long way in helping you make your machine run better.

The most important thing to understand about the degunking process is that you will get the best results if you just follow the process we outline in this book. For example, defragmenting your hard drive (also known as optimizing the hard drive) is typically worthwhile only after you've deleted the files you no longer need. You shouldn't defrag your hard drive and then delete files because the process of deleting a bunch of files will simply fragment your drive again. Similarly, cleaning out the Registry before you've uninstalled and cleaned out all the installed programs (or uninstalled remnants) that you no longer need doesn't make good sense.

You might feel tempted to skip around in this book. If you do, you probably won't see the best results. Of course, there are some processes that could be performed at any time to solve specific problems. But in our experience, we've found that it's best to have an organized strategy the first time you do a "major degunk" so that you get the best results out of our degunking routines.

The Strategy Behind Degunking

The strategy behind degunking is based on how Windows operates in the first place:

√   How Windows stores certain types of files in specific folders (directories)

√   How Windows provides default directories, such as My Music and My Pictures, for specific types of files

√   How data is stored and retrieved on your hard drive

√   How Windows installs and removes programs on your computer

√   How main programs and other utilities can be set up to automatically load when you start Windows

√   How Windows uses an internal database, called the *Registry,* to store critical information about your computer

√ How Windows uses different types of memory (disk space, RAM, virtual memory) to store and process data

√ How basic services such as e-mail, security, and backing up data work

√ How SP2 works to protect you and your PC

√ How Windows' built-in tools, such as System Restore, can be used to repair your system when things go wrong

As you'll learn in this book, the more you understand about the basics of how Windows operates, the better you'll get at degunking and improving the performance of your PC. Of course, you don't need to be an expert on operating systems to make your machine run better. A little bit of knowledge and common sense goes a long way.

Windows needs lots of free memory and system resources. Windows also needs lots of hard drive space, but most Windows computers nowadays have ample amounts of free hard drive space to offer. The big challenge with Windows is that there are many components, such as files, programs, and system utilities, that aggressively compete for the available resources. When too many resources get used up, your machine really starts to bog down. You have to configure your PC so that as many resources as possible are ready when Windows needs them.

Your basic degunking and ongoing maintenance strategy is to ensure that the resources you have are used wisely. If you have too many files on your hard drive because you never remove any, your computer will slow down. If you have too many programs installed on your computer (or you try to run too many at the same time), your computer will take a long time to start up and will run very slowly. Of course, you can add more memory to your computer (we'll cover this later in this book) and increase the size of your hard drive, but you'll eventually run out of resources unless you monitor the ones you have and regularly get rid of the things you don't need.

Important Questions to Ask Yourself

As you use your computer on a regular basis, you need to ask yourself some of the following questions:

√ Does it seem that my computer is running slower and slower with each passing month?

√ Do I put a lot of new files on my computer but rarely remove any old ones?

√ How often do I look at my personal data directories, such as My Documents, to see if I'm storing files I don't need or keeping my system organized?

√   Do I really need all the programs on my computer? (When was the last time you even looked at all the programs you have installed?)

√   Do I use all of the programs and utilities that load automatically when Windows starts up? And by the way, what programs *do* start up when Windows boots?

√   When was the last time I went through my e-mail and deleted the messages I no longer need?

√   When was the last time I ran a third-party utility such as PC Cleanup or a Windows utility like Disk Cleanup to remove the temporary files on my hard drive?

√   When was the last time I defragmented my hard drive?

√   Do I have third-party software set up to keep viruses and other nasty programs from gunking up my machine?

√   Did I configure SP2 after it was automatically installed on my computer? Do I even have SP2?

√   Have I ever delved into Movie Maker 2 or Media Player, personalizing these applications so they work their best?

√   Do I know what to do if something goes wrong with my machine because it has gotten really gunked up?

Let's continue by putting together a degunking strategy that first explores the important system-level components of Windows. Once you are familiar with how Windows works, you'll be able to see how our 12-step degunking program (which we'll introduce at the end of this chapter) will help improve the speed and performance of your computer.

File Management 101

The biggest initial problem with a gunked-up PC is that it is probably overrun with files. Personal data files and installed programs take up a lot of space, and your computer likely won't have enough free hard drive space for Windows to run well. Even if it has enough hard drive space for Windows to function properly, if the files are fragmented (not stored contiguously on the hard disk), it'll take Windows much longer to find them and offer them up to you when you ask for them. Degunking a machine for the first time can be a real challenge because it's likely that data files and programs have not been saved in an organized fashion either. And you can't just step in there and start deleting files. You must first go through all the directories on the hard drive and take an inventory of what you have. Then you'll need to reorganize the data so that you get a clear picture of what to keep and what to get rid of. In the next chapters, you'll see a set of strategies to help you quickly deal with hard drives that need serious degunking. These chapters will walk you through the beginning of our 12-step degunking program.

Another aspect of file management is that there are often numerous small utilities and Taskbar programs running on your system that aren't needed. This alone can really gunk up your machine. Often these programs get set up accidentally, and before you know it, your system starts to slow down. You'll especially notice this if your system takes a very long time to boot up. In Chapter 6, we'll show you how to eliminate unwanted Taskbar programs and other utilities.

Finally, within the file reorganization process, you'll find a number of programs to uninstall, which will help clean up the Registry. To ensure an even cleaner Registry, we will also run some utilities that automatically clean it up, which in turn makes it run smoother and helps protect it from getting corrupted.

So as part of your overall degunking strategy, the first thing you'll need to do is reorganize your entire file system and delete as much stuff as possible in the process. The best part is that after you complete this work, you'll feel as if you've really accomplished something, and you'll notice that your PC runs better than you would have thought possible.

Desktop and Start Menu

Once you've cleaned up the programs and data files on your drive, you will need to turn your attention to the Start menu and Desktop. These components usually need to be cleaned up for a few reasons. First, you may have uninstalled a program but didn't delete its shortcut from your Desktop or Start menu. There are also other data files on your Desktop worth disposing. Finally, everyone's Start menu can use some better organization. The fewer programs in your Start menu, the easier it is to find what you want—and the menu will load faster, making your computer more responsive overall. In Chapter 6, we'll show you how to fix your Desktop and Start menu by using some easy-to-follow processes that work wonders.

E-Mail Degunking

After you've completed the file system and Desktop overhaul, you'll need to turn your attention to the next culprit that eats up a lot of hard drive space—your e-mail system. E-mail programs store e-mail in a relatively similar fashion; that is, all e-mail is stored in a database. Unfortunately, each e-mail program stores its data in a different database system, so it's not a one-size-fits-all situation. The good news is that no matter what e-mail program you use, you can apply some general principles to manage your e-mail better, reduce the amount of spam (junk e-mail) you receive, and better organize the e-mail you receive and send out.

The e-mail program we're going to focus on in this book is Outlook Express, since it's the program that comes with Windows XP. We'll touch on other e-mail programs, though, to provide you with some alternatives to reducing the amount of spam you receive. While Outlook, Outlook Express, and other e-mail programs store data differently, the degunking process is the same for all of them. First, you want to delete as much e-mail as possible, and second, you want to compress the remaining e-mail to reclaim some disk space. At the same time, we'll show you how to set up rules and other filters in Outlook Express to make it easier to delete stuff and keep the volume of your e-mail down and more manageable going forward. Because of the importance of e-mail, we've devoted two chapters (Chapters 7 and 8) to it.

Clean Up Those Program Remnants

In an ideal computing world, you could install and remove as many programs on your PC as you wanted without any repercussions. Unfortunately, our PCs operate like our bodies. If we just stuff ourselves with food all of the time, we'll likely pay the price—gain too much weight and slow down. Eating is fine as long as we have a good exercise program to back up our passion for food. With your computer, you can install as many programs as you want and later remove them, but you'll need to perform some important maintenance tasks to keep your internal system from getting too bloated.

Windows is designed around a central database system called the *Registry,* which keeps track of just about everything under the sun related to your computer, including the programs that have been installed and removed. You could compare the Registry to your heart. It must work properly and be in good condition to offer up a healthy PC. To keep your computer in top shape then, the Registry needs to be placed on a regular maintenance program (just as you do). In Chapter 13 you'll learn how to really clean the Registry and maintain it well. As you'll learn, the Registry needs to be cleaned on a regular basis to remove all of the program remnants that can get left behind, which in turn can cause your computer to boot slowly and run inefficiently.

Hard Drive Optimization

With your file system cleaned and organized and your e-mail reclaimed, you'll need to focus on optimizing your hard drive. This process, called *defragmenting your hard drive,* takes all the files on the drive and stores them as close to the center of the drive as possible. It will also organize files in a way that speeds up access and load times for programs. Depending on the size of your drive and the amount of data you deleted during the degunking process, the defragmentation or optimization step could take a while. The good news is that the optimization process is fairly automatic.

Once you've optimized your hard drive, you'll be well down the degunking road. Your machine should be running faster, with better response and fewer problems. Unfortunately, that doesn't mean you're done just yet…

Patch Things Up

After working through the first half of the book, you'll need to upgrade the software on your machine and patch up the programs you use most often. This can benefit you in two ways:

√   It reduces exposure to bugs that could crash the machine. Crashes are often indications of the need for degunking, but they can also contribute to adding more gunk.

√   It reduces exposure to viruses and security problems (leaks). If your software isn't fully up-to-date, nasty viruses can easily get into your machine and attack your computer when you least expect it. Viruses and security leaks are the bane of diligent degunkers.

CAUTION: Microsoft releases patches (fixes) for all its programs, including Windows and Office. However, the savviest users, despite wanting to keep their systems up-to-date, usually wait to update their machines. This happens because some newly issued patches and service packs actually do more harm than good. What we recommend is that you upgrade minor patches and security patches quickly, usually within a week. On the other hand, you should wait a month or so to upgrade with larger, all-encompassing service packs.

With your machine patched and the basic degunking steps completed, you can move on to more preventative tasks. This includes improving how your installed programs run, putting stuff in the right place, setting up e-mail filters, and installing programs that will improve your security.

Speaking of Patches…

As noted in the Caution earlier, some of the full-fledged service packs can actually cause you problems. Such is the case with the largest of all service packs offered for Windows, SP2. After installing SP2 (which now happens automatically if you have Automatic Updates enabled), you'll see noticeable differences and functionality problems with your e-mail, among other things. To deal with this, we've devoted an entire chapter, Chapter 10 to recovering from this installation. You'll need to tweak SP2 so you can once again open e-mail attachments and learn how to use SP2's interface to configure the new firewall and other options.

Security

Security is a key degunking issue, and that's why we've devoted an entire chapter to this topic—Chapter 16. Without proper security on your machine, you're at serious risk of getting viruses and other menacing programs that can be directly harmful or take up power and resources. This could cause your computer to run slower or crash more often. A good security plan has three pieces:

√   Anti-virus/anti-spyware software: This software will help prevent malicious computer programs from getting installed or otherwise affecting your system.

√   Firewall: Installation or activation of a firewall will protect your computer from unwanted intrusion by hackers or programs. (SP2's firewall is sufficient for most users.)

√   Pest protection: Installation of a Trojan horse or pest protection system is sometimes built into firewall software. Trojan horses and pest programs may not be malicious, but they could install themselves on your computer and eat up resources. One example is Gator, a small system program that installs itself and shares information about your computer and past browsing history with advertisers. The Gator applet provides little benefit to you. Aside from sending out information about you, it also takes up bandwidth and processor time.

Thankfully, all three types of security software are readily available and easy to install. There are even several free options. As part of our plan to secure your computer, we'll show you how to remove unwanted programs and prevent new ones from entering your system.

Backups

Your best electronic friend in the universe is your most recent system backup, which you've stored in a safe place. If you're reading this thinking, "I don't need to back up regularly because I've never lost anything," you're missing an important lesson here. Tempting fate with your computer and all of your valuable data is not a good idea.

Developing a regular backup procedure is a must, not only because it will keep you from losing valuable data but because it will save you from losing all of the setup information and critical programs that are essential to the operation of your computer. As you'll learn in Chapter 17, creating backups on a regular basis using proper procedures will allow you to quickly get your machine back up and running in the event your suffer a major setback, such as a hard drive crash.

If you're still not convinced, consider this: a curious child with a cup of red Kool-Aid could really mess up your hard drive, especially if that Kool-Aid spills into the open air vents of your tower. An unfortunate lightning strike could also bring down the heartiest of machines. It's like insurance: you may never need it, but when you do, you'll be glad you paid the premiums.

Doing a Clean Start

The best part about degunking is that you can easily extend the life of your PC by performing the set of tasks presented in this book. But there may come a time when your PC simply won't respond to the basic degunking operations—the first 11 steps of our 12-step program. So if you're at the end of your rope and you're tempted to throw in the towel, you can first try a few lower-level options such as getting rid of incompatible hardware devices, fixing hardware drivers, and restoring your system to an earlier state using the System Restore feature. You can also use the Repair option on the Windows XP CD-ROM to repair your computer. As a last resort, you can either install a new version of Windows or you can give up completely and get a new machine.

Whatever option turns out to be the best one for your situation, you'll want to proceed carefully and apply a smart approach to help save time and money. For example, if you decide to sell your computer to the highest bidder and purchase a new PC, there is a set of procedures you should follow to safely move all of your personal data and applications over to your new setup. If you purchase a new machine, you'll need to degunk it before you even start using it. New PCs come with all kinds of gunk, from ISP offers to mounds of trial software. You'll learn the quick way to degunk a new PC in Chapter 14. You'll still want to work through this book when you get a chance though, going chapter by chapter, to learn how to find and uninstall this unnecessary and unwanted data, software, and trial applications, so you can get that brand new machine in tip-top shape. Of course, you'll also want to create a backup program, make sure your Internet and e-mail settings are secure, get anti-virus software, and more. If you're planning on getting a new PC, spend some time with it and this book to degunk it.

The Degunking 12-Step Program

Here is the basic 12-step degunking process that you'll follow in this book:

1. Get rid of the files you don't really need (Chapter 3).

2. Uninstall programs you don't need (Chapter 4).

3. Organize your files and folders (Chapter 5).

4. Clean up your Desktop and Start menu (Chapter 6).

5. Reduce your e-mail spam, and sort through and organize your Outlook mail (Chapters 7 & 8).

6. Install the latest upgrades (Chapter 9) and troubleshoot Service Pack 2 (Chapter 10).

7. Fix the media problems you're having with Windows Media Player and Movie Maker (Chapter 11).

8. Optimize your hard drive (Chapter 12).

9. Clean and fine-tune the Registry (Chapter 13).

10. Incorporate new hardware (Chapter 14), PowerToys and good shareware to help keep your machine clean and running efficiently (Chapter 15).

11. Improve security and set up a good firewall (Chapter 16).

12. Back up your system on a regular basis (Chapter 17).

These steps are straightforward and easy to follow. If you set aside time to follow them, you'll save yourself a lot of time, money, and aggravation in the long run.

Summing Up

If you follow the degunking process in the way that we've described and you perform certain tasks on a regular basis, you'll be surprised at how your PC will respond. Even though you may think your computer is ready for the trash heap, we'll show you that (in most cases) you can squeeze more life out of it. So don't throw in the towel too soon. Just take the time to perform the tasks that we've outlined and you'll begin to see results.

Getting Rid of Files that Shouldn't Be There

Degunking Checklist:

√ Remove the excessive junk in your default folders: My Documents, My Music, My Videos, My Pictures, and so on.

√ Remove the files you don't need from your root directory on your main drive (C:), as well as from other partitions on your hard drive.

√ Clean up your root directory by moving files (and folders) to more appropriate locations.

√ Remove unused zipped and unzipped files and other duplicate files.

√ Remove the temporary files on your system.

√ Remove the unused files from unused user accounts.

Welcome to Basic Housekeeping 101. You know the drill: *Your mother doesn't live here, so please pick up after yourself!* You have to sweep the floors, put away the laundry, stack the dishes, and vacuum the floor. You have to keep things from getting too cluttered by taking out the trash regularly. You also need to clean out your closets once or twice a year and throw away things you no longer need. These are chores you do to make your home livable, and if you don't do them, your house won't function as well as you'd like.

Just as you take out the trash when you clean your house, you have to clean up the trash you've accumulated on your computer occasionally, too. *Therefore, getting rid of unnecessary files is the first step in degunking your computer.* If you're a pack rat, this could be painful, but we'll help you get through it! We'll take a look at what you've accumulated on your computer in the last few months (or years) and get rid all of the gunk you've added and don't need—music files, digital pictures that didn't make the cut, files you unzipped and viewed but never deleted, temporary files, documents you've created and mailed (or e-mailed), and anything else you don't need.

Clean Up the Default Folders

Hopefully, you've been saving files to the default folders. You've likely seen them around as you've been using Windows:

√   My Documents folder

√   My Music folder

√   My Videos folder

√   My Pictures folder

If you have or haven't been saving to these folders, if you've created folders of your own, or if you've simply saved everything to the C: drive or some other partition, you should start the cleaning process here. That's because when you first get your new XP computer, XP prompts you to save pictures to the My Pictures folder, documents to the My Documents folder, music to the My Music folder, and videos to the My Videos folder. If you accept the default saving options at any point, you'll have files in these default folders.

Deleting superfluous files might not seem necessary if you have an 80 GB hard drive, but it is. When XP looks for a file, it has to search the *full* hard disk for it. The more stuff on your hard disk, the more stuff it has to look through. Additionally, deleting unnecessary files is certainly essential if you've received the dreaded "low on disk space" error. Either way, we'll bet money that you've got some files you can throw out!

TIP: *Cleaning out files usually means that you'll have to open some of them to see what they are. Be careful! If you see an unfamiliar .exe file and double-click it, the file will run, and you may execute a virus on your PC. Other files with other extensions (Including .scr, .vbs, .pif, and quite a few others) can carry hidden malware. It's always safe to open .TXT files, and almost always safe to open image files like .gif and .jpg. To be safe, keep your anti-virus utility updated on a daily basis, and run a virus check immediately before spending any serious time "going hunting" for files to delete. If you have any doubts about a particular file, you can often right-click on the file and select a "check file for viruses" item, depending on your anti-virus software. (NAV does this, as does AVG and most other major AV products.) Better to spend a few seconds checking a file than releasing a virus to wreak havoc and create more gunk!*

Documents

Windows XP provides a My Documents folder where many users store all of the documents they create. This folder serves as the default location until it is changed. Stop reading for a minute and take a peek in there and see what you can find. If you see something you don't like or you don't need, delete it. Here's how:

1. Double-click the My Documents folder. It should be on the Desktop, but if it isn't, you can find it on the Start menu. A gunked-up My Documents folder is shown in Figure 3-1.

Figure 3-1

This My Documents folder is a mess, with pictures, Word documents, a Movie Maker 2 file, client artwork, and files that don't have associations.

2. Right-click any file, and choose Delete from the shortcut menu.

3. In the Confirm File Delete dialog box, click Yes to delete the file.

TIP: If you prefer using the keyboard over the mouse, hover the mouse over the item to highlight it and then press the Delete key on the keyboard. When prompted to confirm the deletion, press the Enter key. You can also drag the item to the Recycle Bin.

Delete to your heart's content, but don't delete files if you don't know who they belong to or what they are used for. For now, let's just concentrate on taking out a bit of the garbage that *you've* created.

Media Files

Let's now take a look at some other folders. Windows XP also provides default folders called My Pictures, My Videos, and My Music for storing other types of files. If you have a digital camera, for example, you might find that you have a lot of files in the My Pictures folder. If you make a lot of movies with Movie Maker 2, we'll bet you've got some files in the My Videos folder you can delete as well. If you are a music hound, we'll bet your My Music folder is really scary!

My Pictures

Look at Figure 3-2 and you'll see an example of one of our My Pictures folders. It's pretty gunked up, although you can see that some prior attempt at organizing the images has been made. There are folders for the various image subjects, but there are lots of images haphazardly placed in the My Pictures folder. These need to be moved to the appropriate subfolders. If you look closely, you'll also see old client artwork, a screen shot, and a folder with only one image, all of which should likely be deleted. Deleting pictures from this folder is just the same as deleting from the My Documents folder. You simply right-click, choose Delete, and be done with it!

TIP: Don't delete any pictures you've used in Movie Maker 2 project files, office documents, or similar applications. When the file or program calls on them and they aren't there, you'll certainly hear about it!

My Videos

Deleting video files is a little trickier. With Movie Maker 2, 2.1, or future versions, you capture the video files (raw footage) to your computer, and you create a project using those files. These project files are given a .MSWMM file name extension, as shown in Figure 3-3. You tweak the project file and then

Figure 3-2
You can organize the My Pictures folder with subfolders, but you still have to
put the pictures in them.

you create a movie, and the movie files are given a .wmv extension. The movie
is the final product, so if you've turned a particular project file into a movie, you
can delete that particular project file. However, if you think you'll need any of
those files later, if you want to save the raw footage for posterity, or if you are
planning to use those files in another movie, you shouldn't delete them. Figure
3-3 shows an example of a pretty gunked-up My Videos folder.

In this example, we can delete many of the project files because most have been
turned into movies. We can also delete duplicate movie files and any sound files
we don't need. As you can see in Figure 3-3, we have deleted a lot of files. Windows XP comes with a Windows Movie Maker sample file, too, and we've even
deleted that. (Delete as usual: select and press the Delete key on the keyboard.)

TIP: *Remember, though, a movie (the final product) is uneditable. So, if you think you*
might need the project files at another time, don't delete them.

Figure 3-4 shows a My Videos folder that has been cleaned up a bit. We've
deleted a lot of files, and we've even deleted the Windows Movie Maker 2
Sample File that came with Windows XP. The files are arranged by type, too

Figure 3-3

Projects have a .MSWMM extension, while completed movies have a .wmv extension.

Figure 3-4

When deleting items from the My Videos folder, be careful to keep any project files you might need later.

(View>Arrange Icons By>Type), so we can easily tell the difference between project files and completed movies. Later, we might even go back and create subfolders for these files.

My Music

Ah, your music. We bet that you have quite a lot of files stored here if you're a music enthusiast. Not only can you literally have thousands of files, but if you've subscribed and unsubscribed to various online music sources, you probably have a lot that you can't even play because you don't have the proper licenses. Deleting music files is just as simple as deleting anything else described so far: simply right-click and delete. You can also highlight the song or folder and click Delete This Folder or Delete This File in the File And Folder Tasks pane, as shown in Figure 3-5. (If you hold down the Ctrl key to select multiple files or folders, the option will change to Delete The Selected items.)

Figure 3-5

Select songs or folders to delete; consider deleting the contents of Windows XP's Sample Music folder if you don't listen to anything in it.

GunkBuster's Notebook: Saving Space by Spotting Duplicate MP3s

If you're like most people who collect MP3 music files, you gather them from wherever you can and then toss them into a designated MP3 directory somewhere on your (huge) hard drive. If you do this, chances are excellent that you have duplicate MP3 files in that directory—and since each MP3 file is several megabytes in size, you can waste a *lot* of disk space that way.

Most of the problem stems from inconsistent file-naming conventions. If you get MP3s from newsgroups, file sharing services, or your friends, their names may be arranged very differently. Even if they are the very same file, Windows will not catch your duplicates if they have different file names!

Here's an example. The following four files are identical. Only the names are different:

Beatles – If I Fell 3330 KB Winamp Media File 1/5/2005 10:05 AM

If I Fell – Beatles, The 3330 KB Winamp Media File 7/1/2004 10:05 AM

The Beatles – If I Fell 3330 KB Winamp Media File 4/17/2003 11:18 PM

If I Fell – Beatles 3330 KB Winamp Media File 8/29/2004 10:05 AM

It's easy to spot the duplicates, *if they're one after the other in Windows Explorer.* Unfortunately, if they're mixed in with hundreds of other MP3s, you may not know they're all there. Most people sort files in a Windows Explorer window by file name. In this case, the first file would be up with the *B*s, the second and fourth would be with the *I*s, and the third would be down with the *T*s.

The easiest way to spot duplicates like this is to click on the Size header in a Windows Explorer display to sort the files by *size.* That will bring all files of identical size together (here, 3330 KB) in the display. As you scroll down through your files in the Windows Explorer pane, look for multiple adjacent lines with the same file size, and you'll discover that many of those are duplicates with slightly different file names.

This isn't a complete solution, of course. Ultimately, eliminating MP3 file dupes requires that you decide how you will name your MP3 files. Band name first? Album? Or cut? It's good practice to impose a file-naming convention on your MP3 files as you gather them, so you don't have to go through 1,000 MP3s and change 1,000 file names. As you rename your files according to your file-naming convention, Windows will object when you try to give a duplicate file the exact same name as an existing file.

Watch out for band names beginning with "The" and either eliminate the word entirely or make sure it's *after* the first significant word in the band name (e.g., "Beatles, The"). A lot of duplicates happen that way. Also, look for underscore characters (which are not obvious at a glance) between words in a file name. Even a few duplicate MP3s can hog 40 or 50 megabytes of disk space. Nuke 'em till they glow!

NOTE: You can find more information about degunking your media in Chapter 11.

Shared Folders

If you share a computer with another person (or with several people) and you don't belong to a large corporate network, you might have used the Shared Documents folder to pass along information or documents to others who access the computer. You might have also employed the Shared Music or Shared Pictures folder. These shared folders contain files that anyone who logs onto the computer can view (even guests), and they are just as susceptible (if not more) to getting gunked up as any other folder on the computer.

You can locate and clean the Shared Documents folder using Windows Explorer:

1. Log on as an Administrator.
2. Right-click the Start button and click Explore All Users.
3. Locate the Shared Documents folder. It's at C:\Documents And Settings\All Users\Shared Documents. This is shown in Figure 3-6.
4. Browse through each folder, deleting items as needed.

If you take the time to clean out these default folders, you'll be well on your way to getting your machine running smoothly again. This is a good first step. Now, let's take a look at some of the other places you could have saved your files.

CAUTION: Don't empty the Recycle Bin just yet. Leave the files in there for a week or so, just to make sure you aren't going to miss anything you've deleted.

Figure 3-6
Don't forget to delete unwanted items in the Shared Documents folder.

GunkBuster's Notebook: Use the Shared Folder to Your Advantage

If you have multiple users with multiple accounts on your PC, you can use the Shared Folder to decrease how much data is stored on your hard drive. For instance, you can move all music to the Shared Music folder and then everyone who accesses the PC can listen to it. That will eliminate lots of duplicate gunk because multiple users won't have a need to copy tracks to the hard drive that are already there. Additionally, you can save all Movie Maker files to the Shared Video folder and all pictures to the Shared Pictures folder. Instead of each person storing the vacation photos and videos in their own personal folders, they'll be stored in the shared folder (and only once). You can even create subfolders inside the Shared Documents folder to personalize it for your family or your workplace.

When you move data around like this, though, you have to tell your applications where to look for the data the next time it's required. In Windows Media Player 10 for example, you'd use Tools>Options and the Library tab to tell Media Player 10 to search for media in your Shared Music folder. In Movie Maker 2, you'd need to browse to the new folder to save and retrieve files.

Consider the following for subfolders to further personalize your Shared Folder:

√ A Homework subfolder where junior can save his homework and you can check it.

√ A Team Project subfolder, so every employee on a project team can access and edit data stored there.

√ A Family First folder where everyone has access to a shared calendar, address book, events schedule, wills, important documents, and other pertinent information.

√ An Internet Downloads folder where downloads can be stored and accessed by everyone.

√ A Zipped folder where zipped files can be stored and universally managed.

√ An Attachments folder so users can save e-mail attachments so they aren't e-mailed to other users, gunking up each user's e-mail program.

√ A Recipes folder with subfolders for each member of the family. Junior can find out here how long to put a hot dog in the microwave or a pizza in the pizza oven, while the hubby can learn how to boil water.

√ A Teams folder that holds schedules, team rosters, rankings, and phone numbers.

Clean Up Your Main Drive

Go ahead, admit it. Sometimes you just save files randomly to whatever folder they open in. Sometimes you simply click Local Disk (C:)—or some other partition—in the Save In dialog box, and save all of your stuff to the root directory on your main hard drive. (We won't make you admit that you sometimes can't find that stuff later.) Saving randomly or leaving the files in a jumbled, disorganized mess in your root directly is just going to make things uglier as time passes; it's time to clean out the garage and do a little organizing. In this section, we'll show you how to both clean and better organize your root directory and remove unwanted files that have been randomly saved on your hard drive.

GunkBuster's Notebook: Be Careful What You Delete

As you begin exploring the C: drive and removing files, you'll notice lots of folders. Windows XP has specific files it needs to function properly, to boot up, and to run effectively, and they are stored on this drive. Windows files are stored in the Windows folder (makes sense), which contains many other folders, including Drivers, Downloaded Installations, Fonts, Profiles, Repair, and Resources. You certainly don't want to delete anything from that folder (at least not yet)!

Another folder you'll notice on the C: drive is the Program Files folder. In this folder, you'll find subfolders that contain the files for the programs you've installed. We have folders entitled Adobe, Canon, Corel, Emusic Download Manager, Microsoft Plus!, and Lexmark. However, you'll find built-in folders as well, including Internet Explorer, Messenger, Movie Maker, Outlook Express, and Windows Media Player. You certainly don't want to delete any of these folders or their files either.

TIP: If you want to delete a program, you don't do that by right-clicking and deleting the folder that contains the files anyway. Deleting programs is done from Control Panel. We'll talk about that in the next chapter.

So, what can you delete, and what should you look for? For the most part, you can delete anything *you've created* and no longer need: pictures you've saved to the hard drive; movies you've made; music you've downloaded; PDF files you've opened and saved; zipped and unzipped files; Excel, PowerPoint, FrontPage, and Access files; and documents you've written. You can also delete temporary files that Windows has saved all on its own.

Delete Files from the Root Directory (C:)

Your root directory is likely to be a place where you are storing files inappropriately or storing files that you don't need. Let's quickly get rid of the unwanted files and then we'll move some files to better organize this directory. Open wide; let's take a look:

1. Right-click the Start button and choose Explore.

2. Expand My Computer and click Local Disk (C:).

3. If you see any files you created that you no longer need, right-click and choose Delete. These should be personal files you've created, not folders. You

do not want to delete the Windows folder, the Program Files folder, or the Documents And Settings folder! Keep an eye out for zip files, movie project files, picture files (.jpg, .bmp., .gif,. and .tif), documents, music, PDF files, PowerPoint and Excel files, or similar gunk you've created.

Once you've finished deleting what you no longer need from the root directory in the C: drive, you might still have some stuff there that you want to keep. Take a look at Figure 3-7. Even though we've deleted most of the stuff we don't want in the C: directory, there are still things we want to keep. There is a movie file, a driver zip file, a few installation application files (.exe), an MP3 file, and others. The next task is to move them to a better location.

Figure 3-7
First, get rid of what you don't need, and then follow that up with organizing what you want to keep.

TIP: *If you want to know more about what should be in the C: directory and what shouldn't, refer to the GunkBuster's Notebook earlier.*

Better Organize Your Root Directory by Moving Files

You don't want to leave these remnants hanging around in your root directory. You want to move them to a more suitable holding area. Leave the folders that belong there where they are, like the Documents And Settings, PerfLogs, Program Files, Unzipped, and other system folders. *If you don't know what it is—don't move it!* However, you will want to move the extraneous files, like those stray music files, zip files, pictures, or folders you've created there by accident.

To move these files to a better location, follow these steps:

1. Starting with something similar to Figure 3-7, and select a file to move by hovering the mouse pointer over it.

2. Click the View menu, point to Explorer Bar, and select Folders if is not checked already (this will place a check mark by it.) Locate, in the left pane, the My Documents folder. It will be located at the very top of the list on the left side. If you have a partitioned drive, where C: holds only the operating system and program files and you store your documents elsewhere, locate that folder in the left pane. It might be on the D: drive (or E: drive). Do not select the drive, though; only locate it.

3. Back at the C: partition (or D: or E:), locate a file to move. Right-click the file, and from the shortcut menu, select Cut.

4. Expand My Documents in the left pane. (Remember, you might have configured My Documents on the D: drive.) Locate the folder to move the file to, right-click in that folder, and select Paste.

5. Click the C: drive again and repeat the process. When you're finished, the C: root directory should contain only folders that are necessary for the operating system and its programs to function. Don't move any folders created by other programs (like your instant messaging program), and don't move applications or system or hidden files.

There are other ways to move files, though, besides cutting and pasting. You can drag a file from one folder to another in Explorer, or you can open My Computer along with Explorer, resize the windows so you can see both, and then drag the files between them. Figure 3-8 shows this setup, and is a popular way to go because moving files this way is quite easy once you've made the windows the correct size. Remember when dragging to right-click first and choose Move Here when you drop. If you just drag and drop, you'll create a copy of the file. Figure 3-8 shows a drag and drop in progress.

TIP: When you move a file like a picture or a song and some application needs it later, it might not be able to find it. You'll have to tell that program where the file has been moved. This might take a few minutes out of your day for the next few weeks or so, but take our word for it: you'll be glad you did!

Figure 3-8
Dragging and dropping is another way to move a file.

TIP: *If you have a folder named Online Services in the Program Files folder, delete it. It contains files to help you get set up with AOL, MSN, and similar online services. Chances are, you're already online and you don't need to keep these files.*

Delete Unused Files in Other Locations

Your root directory is an easy target to look at for removing unwanted files. But what about the rest of your hard drive? It is likely that you have unwanted files hanging out on your entire drive, hiding in places you haven't even thought to look. Fortunately, you can use the Search option to locate files on your main hard drive that you no longer need. For instance, if you know you have lots of JPEG files from your digital camera still stored on your computer but you haven't run across them yet while degunking, you can search for them using the Search command. If you have created art files in Photoshop, Arts & Letters, Corel, or a similar art program, you can locate those files by searching for their file extensions as well. For instance, Arts & Letters is a program we use to create artwork. These program files all end in a .ged file name extension. Those files aren't stored in the usual My Pictures folder and are hard to find. The same goes for Photoshop and Corel files. You can also manually locate and delete misplaced music or video files simply by searching for them. Let's give this a whirl:

1. Click Start, and click Search. (If you don't see the Search option on the Start menu, right-click the Taskbar, choose Properties, click the Start Menu tab, choose Start Menu, click Customize, click Advanced, and check Search. Work your way out of the boxes by clicking OK as needed.)

2. From the Search dialog box, perform independent searches for *.jpg and *.jpeg to locate missing digital camera files and pictures; *.psd to locate missing Photoshop files; *.gif, *.tif, *.bmp, and *.tiff to locate art files; *.midi, *.mp3, *.wav, *.avi, and *.wma to locate music files; *.doc for Word documents; and *.pdf to locate PDF files. Of course, there are hundreds of other file types to search for; this is only the beginning, but it will probably keep you busy for a while.

3. If you find files you don't need that you created, opened, or imported yourself (these don't include program files), you can delete them from the Search window by right-clicking and choosing Delete. There are several ways to delete files if you find you have a lot to delete. We'll talk about that in a minute.

4. You can also move the files by dragging and dropping. To do this from the Search window, click View, point to Explorer Bar, and check Folders; then drag and drop to the correct folder or cut and paste to move them as detailed in the previous section. This might not be necessary, though; the files might already be in the right location! To see where a file is stored, right-click it and choose Properties, or view the files using Details view.

Figure 3-9 shows a Search result for *.jpg files. We've chosen View>Details so we can see where the files are stored, and we've expanded the In Folder section so we can see the entire folder name. Without counting them, it looks like there are thousands of JPEG files.

Scrolling through the files, which are sorted by their In Folder location (just click the In Folder icon in the Search Results window to do this), it's easy to see that there are lots of JPEG files stored in the Recycle Bin, in the Documents And Settings\Joli Ballew\Local Settings\Temp folder, and in the Documents And Settings\Joli Ballew\Local Settings\Temporary Internet Files folder. While some of these files are ours, some are created by Internet Explorer and Windows XP. Anything in the Temp or Temporary Internet Files folder can be deleted.

If you're really serious about degunking, though, as you scroll further you'll see additional unnecessary JPEG images. A few are in the Windows\Help\Tours folder (if you don't want to ever take Windows XP tours), in various applications' sample folders (such as Program Files\Incredimail\Data\LetterCreator\ISamples), and in similar areas.

Figure 3-9
Searching often yields hundreds, if not thousands, of files you can delete.

You can sort files in other ways, too. For instance, clicking once on the Name title sorts the files alphabetically; clicking once on the Size title sorts the file by its size. You can also right-click on any title to remove it or to add a different title to the interface.

Now, choose the items in the list you want to delete by selecting them separately, selecting them in nonsequential groups by holding down the Ctrl key, or selecting them in sequence by holding down the Shift key. Press Delete on the keyboard to delete the selected files.

Here is a list of other files types to look for:

√   ASA or ASP—Active Server documents

√   ASF—Windows Media Audio/Video files

√   CHK—Check Disk files

√   COV and CPE—Fax cover page files

√   FRM—WordPerfect 10 documents

√   MPA, MPE, MPEG, MPG—Movie files

√   PPT and PPS—PowerPoint files

√   SCR—Screen saver files

√   TXT—Text files

√   XLS—Excel files

You can see all of the file types stored on your computer from Windows Explorer by clicking Tools and then Folder Options. Select the File Types tab. Remember, you're looking for files *you* created.

TIP: *Although you can search for temporary files from the Search command window, you can also use Windows XP utilities. We like a utility called Disk Cleanup. We'll talk about that shortly, and we'll also give you more insight into temporary files. However, if you are so inclined and want to remove your temporary files manually, search for *.tmp. You can safely delete files that are more than a week old.*

Clean Up the "Unzipped" Folder

If you use WinZip (a popular program for compressing files), the Unzipped folder is where your unzipped files are stored so that you can open them, read or look at them, and then save them if needed. When you download a file from the Internet or get it from another source, it will have an extension of .zip if the file is compressed. Once you uncompress this file and save the unzipped files to your hard drive in another folder, you've got two copies! You probably don't need much of what you've got saved in the Unzipped folder. Let's take a tour:

1. Right-click the Start button and click Explore.

2. Locate the Unzipped folder and click it. It's generally located near the bottom of the list of folders on the root drive. (If you can't find it, you can always use Start>Search to locate it.)

3. Browse through what you see there, and delete any item you don't need.

In addition to simply looking in the Unzipped folder for unnecessary zip files, you should also use Search to locate ones you've created or ones that you saved in different places. Doing a search for *.zip on one of our test computers yields an additional 135 zip files, several of which were stored in a very full Recycle Bin.

Locating Duplicate Files

Locating duplicate files is a little more difficult than simply locating a JPEG or PDF file. Some duplicate files end in extensions such as .001, .002, and so on, and you can search for them using the Search utility. This usually isn't a very productive way to go, though. The best way to get rid of duplicate files on your system is to download, install, and/or purchase a disk cleaning software program. There are many on the market, including several free ones.

Enter the words *Windows XP Remove Duplicate Files Freeware* in a search engine in IE 6 and see what you get. Even some shareware utilities are free for 10 days or so, and that might be all the time you need to clean your system. Consider this if you can actually see duplicate files, you might not have a problem in that regard.

Figure 3-10 shows the interface for a program called Duplicate File Finder, a free duplicate file checking utility found on the Internet. The home page for the software is **http://srhoda.250free.com**. We like this program because it compares more than just text and image files; it can look for duplicates for many file types, including those with the extensions .bmp, .dll, .dic, .exe, . guf, .ht(ml), .jpg, .pas, .php, .phg, .psd, .tiff, .txt, and .wmf. It took only three or four minutes to download and install, and it's easy to use. As you can see in Figure 3-10, it's working hard to find instances of duplicate files.

Figure 3-10
Duplicate File Finder is free and effective.

Get Rid of Those Pesky Temp Files

If your computer is like ours, you likely have temporary (*.tmp) files hiding in every nook and cranny. You learned a little about finding temporary files using Search earlier in this chapter. If you've never taken the time to clean up your temporary files, though, or if you did a search for them earlier, you no doubt got (or will get) a big surprise! You can free up lots of hard drive space quickly and easily simply by deleting these unnecessary files.

There are lots of reasons temp files are created. When Windows locks up or crashes, or if you have to use Ctrl+Alt+Del to restart, some temporary files get left on your hard disk. Some installation routines also leave temporary files. Temp files can be files that the computer creates to use as backup files for office programs like Microsoft Word so that if something happens and the program shuts down unexpectedly, a saved copy will be available. Programs create temporary files, too, to store frequently-needed information in an easily retrievable folder. Temporary files are also created when you surf the Internet, and these files store information about the Web sites you visit. Most of the time, these files are created to save you time, but after a while, their buildup can cause a hard disk to bog down.

It's best to clean up your temporary file folders occasionally, just to make sure you aren't causing the hard drive any unnecessary strain. There are several ways to do this, and using Disk Cleanup is the easiest.

Use Disk Cleanup

Disk Cleanup is a utility that ships with Windows XP and can be used to delete temporary Internet files, temporary (computer) files, offline Web pages, the files in the Recycle Bin, and more. Temporary files aren't needed, and if you've used offline Web pages, they're taking up space, too. Disk Cleanup is easy to use, but this first time, you might want to lay off emptying the Recycle Bin, just to be safe.

Here's how to use Disk Cleanup:

1. Click Start, point to All Programs, point to Accessories, point to System Tools, and click Disk Cleanup.

2. Select the drive to clean up (if prompted), and click OK.

3. In the Disk Cleanup dialog box, select the items to delete. I suggest leaving the Recycle Bin unchecked, but the others you can leave checked as shown in Figure 3-11. Click OK, and then click Yes to tell XP that's what you really want to do.

TIP: *If you have multiple partitions, run Disk Cleanup on each of them.*

Figure 3-11
Check everything except Recycle Bin, and click OK to run Disk Cleanup.

Cleaning Up What Disk Cleanup Has Missed

You might have noticed that there weren't options in Disk Cleanup to remove cookies, browser caches, Internet Explorer history, recent documents, and similar items you might want to get rid of. In addition, if you use Search to locate the temporary files on your computer after running Disk Cleanup, you'll notice there are still some there. Here's how to clean up these additional temporary files:

1. Use the Search option and search your drive for *.tmp files to delete temporary files left on your machine. Make sure you've configured the Search Look In box to search all partitions and drives.

2. Right-click Name in the Search window and verify that Date Modified is checked.

3. Click Date Modified in the Search window to sort the remaining temporary files by date.

4. Hold the Shift key and select the first file that is more than a week old. Click again on the last file in the list.

5. Click Delete on the keyboard. (Not all files will be deleted.) We found 2,327 items, even after running Disk Cleanup on all drives!

Just for fun, search for and delete any files with the following extensions: *.dmp (dump files created when your computer crashes) and *.fts and *.gid (files that make searches faster; if you don't use Help a lot, delete these).

TIP: *To clear the Recent Documents list, right-click the Windows Taskbar, click* Properties, *click the Start Menu tab, and click* Customize. *Depending on the theme chosen, click* Clear *or* Clear List. *Click* OK.

GunkBuster's Notebook: Cleaning Out Your Web Browser Gunk

If you are an avid Web surfer (and who isn't these days?), you probably have accumulated a lot of gunk that you are not aware of. Web browser clients such as Internet Explorer, Netscape, and AOL save a few types of temporary files, which you can delete to free up space on your hard drive. Depending on how often you use your browser to access the Web or how many new sites you visit, you should manually clean your browser fairly often.

There are basically two main types of extraneous files that your browser keeps around—temporary cookies and temporary Internet files. (When we discuss security in Chapter 16, we'll cover cookies in more detail.) For now, all you need to know is that cookies are little bits of data stored as text documents that a Web site places on your computer when you visit it. The more sites you visit, the more cookies (and temporary ones at that) will be saved on your computer. Temporary Internet files are various navigation files that your Web browser saves from time to time.

In addition to cleaning up the temporary cookies and Internet files, you can get rid of offline content that is stored, browser caches, and browser history by following these steps:

1. Start the browser you use to access the Web, such as Internet Explorer or AOL.

2. If you use Internet Explorer, click Tools and click Internet Options. If you use AOL, click Settings, click Preferences, and then click on Internet Preferences from the list of options that is displayed.

3. Using the dialog box shown in Figure 3-12, make sure that the General tab is selected. (This same dialog box is used for all Web browsers, including AOL and Netscape.)

Figure 3-12
Clear Temporary Internet Files by clicking Delete Files.

4. To delete your temporary cookies, click the Delete Cookies button. To delete the temporary Internet files, click the Delete Files button. Be careful when deleting cookies, though; I don't usually delete them. Cookies store preferences and passwords for Web sites you visit and you might have trouble recovering those passwords if you need them again, especially if you don't have all of your passwords written down for each site you visit.

5. From the same tab, click Clear History to clear references to Internet sites you've visited.

6. To stop Internet Explorer from automatically using AutoComplete to finish entries for Web addresses, forms, or usernames and passwords, click the Content tab, click AutoComplete, and remove the check marks for AutoComplete settings. You can also clear forms and clear passwords, as shown in Figure 3-13.

7. Click OK until you have exited the dialog box(es).

Figure 3-13
Use the AutoComplete Settings dialog box to clear forms and passwords used by Internet Explorer.

As for Outlook Express, for now, deleting the items in the Sent Items folder and the Deleted Items folder can be somewhat helpful, but there are a couple of chapters on Outlook Express later, so we'll save the nitty-gritty for then.

TIP: Norton SystemWorks provides tools to optimize the hard drive, remove unnecessary files, and clean up the computer in general. We highly recommend a program like this.

Deleting User Files from Unused User Accounts

If you've ever created a user account for someone else so that they could access your computer, you'll have user account files for that person stored on the hard disk. If that person no longer accesses the computer and doesn't need the files they created, you can safely delete both the account and the files.

Here's how:

1. While logged on as an administrator, open Control Panel and click User Accounts.

2. Take a look at the user accounts on the computer. You'll want to keep yours, of course, and hopefully the Guest account is disabled, but if you see additional accounts you don't need listed there, you can delete them. Click the account to delete, and from the resulting window, click Delete The Account.

3. In the next window, Do you want to keep *<username>*'s files? (shown in Figure 3-14), click Delete Files.

4. In the next window, click Delete Account if desired.

Figure 3-14

Delete unused user accounts and their associated files.

TIP: You may be tempted to empty the Recycle Bin and run Disk Defragmenter now. However, wait a little bit to make sure you haven't deleted anything you want and make sure the computer boots properly. Once you're ready, delete the items in the Recycle Bin. Later, we'll talk about running Disk Defragmenter.

Summing Up

Deleting files and folders *that you've created* can be quite helpful in speeding up or improving the performance of your computer. If you took this first step seriously, chances are good your computer is now running better than it was before. Our gunked-up test machine is really screaming now, and we've only just begun!

Before you go to bed tonight, do a quick backup and run Disk Cleanup. In about a week, empty the Recycle Bin.

Uninstalling Programs You Don't Need and Tweaking Those You Do

Degunking Checklist:

√ Remove the programs you no longer use by utilizing the program's uninstall options.

√ Remove unwanted programs that don't have an uninstall option with the Control Panel.

√ Remove extraneous Windows components from Control Panel.

√ Search for programs you didn't know you had and remove them.

√ Remove programs for hardware you no longer own.

√ Fine-tune the programs you regularly use to improve their performance.

If you've deleted all of the unnecessary documents, temporary files, pictures, movies, and music from your PC, you've taken a gigantic step forward in reducing the amount of clutter on it. As you've learned, when you reduce clutter, you improve the performance of your system because your PC's hard drive doesn't have to sift through unnecessary data to find what it needs and the information you want. The next step in the degunking process is to remove *programs* you don't use and their related files. As with removing data files, removing program files frees up hard drive space; however, by removing program files, you sometimes get even more bang for your buck. Some programs start automatically each time you boot up and run in the background without your knowledge. This is the worst kind of gunk, and those programs should be removed if they aren't being used.

In addition to removing programs you don't use (or don't want), though, you can remove programs that you *can't* use, like programs that you installed with your first Web cam, applications for a printer you no longer own, or programs for an older digital camera or scanner you no longer have.

Finally, besides what you've installed, some components you might not need, like MSN Explorer or Games, may have been installed automatically. And you could have chosen to install some additional XP components yourself, like Windows Fax Services. Windows Fax Services isn't necessary if you've recently purchased a dedicated fax machine, so you can remove this Windows component.

CAUTION: *You should perform a comprehensive backup and create a System Restore point before starting this chapter.*

Remove Programs You Don't Use

Take a look at your All Programs list to see some of the programs you have installed on your computer. You can do this by clicking on the Start menu and pointing to the All Programs option. All of the programs installed on your computer won't be listed here, but many will. If anything strikes you as odd or if you don't know what a program is, open it up and take a gander. If it's a program you don't need or one that doesn't open, make a note of it. We'll uninstall it next. You should also make a list that includes programs you are not sure you use. You might encounter some programs that have names that are so cryptic or shortened that you might not be able to easily determine if the program is needed. Later, we'll show you how to play detective and uncover the mysteries of your installed programs.

GunkBuster's Notebook: Locating a Program's Uninstall Option

Programs that are installed on your computer are generally installed to the C: drive, and their files are usually located in the Program Files folder. If you accept the defaults while installing, chances are good most of your programs are installed there. When searching for an uninstall program, check there first.

Sometimes, though, you'll find programs and their uninstall commands in the Windows folder. This is especially common when the program or application comes with a computer that already has XP installed and has bundled software. For example, Corel's WordPerfect was found in one of our test computer's Windows folder and we didn't even know we had it! And right there, when no other uninstall command could be found, not even in the Control Panel, was an uninstall icon!

Another place installed programs might be hanging out is in folders that were automatically created by the programs themselves. Generally, these folders are in regular places like the Program Files folder, but sometimes they're in more obscure places, like the Windows\System 32 folder.

If you've purchased a computer that had Windows preinstalled, look in the Windows folder for other telltale signs, like folders with names created from a variation of the manufacturer's name. There, you're likely to find programs or shortcuts for subscribing to online services, help and support programs, and more. Don't delete anything yet, though; you have a little more to learn.

NOTE: *Applications that you use regularly will move automatically to the left-hand column of the Start menu. You can also put shortcuts on the Desktop by right-clicking any program name in the All Programs list, accessing a program from the All Programs list, or running the program from its program icon in its program folder.*

TIP: *Before uninstalling any program, close all running programs.*

When choosing what to uninstall, don't uninstall any program if you aren't sure what it is used for. In addition, shy away from uninstalling Microsoft Updates, your computer manufacturer's help and support programs, or Hotfixes, as well as any programs that were upgraded from one version to another. If your computer came with XP preinstalled and included several programs with it and all you got was a recovery disk, you shouldn't uninstall any of these programs unless you are positive you don't want them anymore. Many times, the only way to get these programs back (without the application's disks) is to format the drive and use the computer manufacturer's recovery disks.

NOTE: *If all you got was a recovery disk, and not an actual Windows XP CD and application CDs, call the computer store where you bought your computer and complain. There is a slim chance you can get "real" disks if you bark loud and long enough.*

Using a Program's Uninstall Command

Once you make a decision to remove a program, you should always check to see if the program has an uninstall option. The uninstall option is the best way to go because it will usually take care of a number of important cleanup and "book-keeping" tasks, such as updating the Windows Registry. This helps ensure that your system doesn't keep any junk around that's related to the program you're removing. The best way to see if a program you want to remove has an uninstall option is to check the All Programs list, as shown in Figure 4-1. The uninstall option is usually pretty complete and generally removes all instances of the program on the All Programs list and from the Program Files folder. Figures 4-1 and 4-2 show the Uninstall choice and an uninstall in progress.

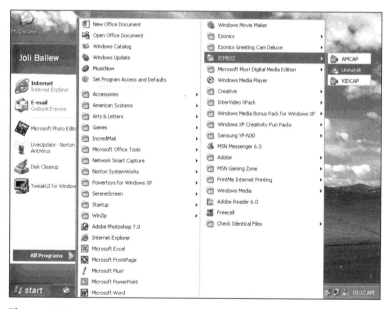

Figure 4-1

Look for an uninstall option first when uninstalling applications.

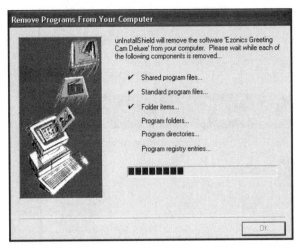

Figure 4-2
You'll be able to watch the progress of the uninstallation.

TIP: If you receive a message that you are going to uninstall some shared files when uninstalling, be sure to choose the option to not delete them. These files don't take up much room, but uninstalling one that is needed by another program can cause problems.

If you see any programs on the All Programs list that you want to remove but offer no uninstall choice, you'll need to remove them using the Control Panel and the Add Or Remove Programs option.

Using the Control Panel to Remove Programs

The Control Panel offers the Add Or Remove Programs option for uninstalling any program on your computer. If there's no uninstall option for a program, do this:

1. Open the Control Panel. If it isn't on the Desktop, open My Computer and look for it there. You can also access the Control Panel by clicking on the Start menu, selecting Settings, and then selecting the Control Panel option.

2. Double-click the Add Or Remove Programs option.

3. In the Add Or Remove Programs window, locate the program to uninstall.

4. Click Change/Remove, as shown in Figure 4-3.

5. Click OK if required, and wait while the program is uninstalled. Figure 4-4 shows an example of a Remove Shared File? dialog box. Selecting No To All is generally the best choice.

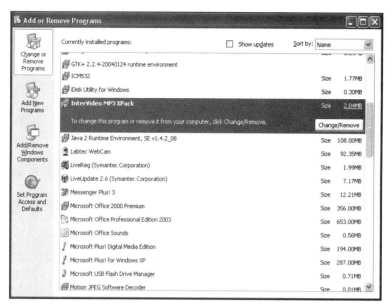

Figure 4-3

Choose programs that you don't use or need when uninstalling.

Figure 4-4

Choosing No To All is the best way to avoid problems when uninstalling programs.

Removing Extraneous Windows Components

You can also clean up your hard disk by removing or uninstalling Windows components you don't use. Earlier, we mentioned Windows Fax Services, MSN Explorer, and Games, but there are others as well. Figure 4-5 shows some of the available Windows components.

Figure 4-5

Remove unwanted Windows components.

To see what Windows components you have installed on your system and to uninstall the ones you don't need, follow these steps:

1. Open the Control Panel. If it isn't on the Desktop, click Start and look for it there.

2. Double-click Add Or Remove Programs.

3. Click Add/Remove Windows Components in the left pane of the Add Or Remove Programs window.

4. When the Windows Components Wizard opens, scroll down the list, click on the components you have installed one at a time, and read what they are used for in the description under the components list. If you have Internet Information Services installed but you aren't planning on creating your own personal Web server, you can uninstall it. You might also consider uninstalling MSN Explorer if you use IE6, Outlook Express if you use Incredimail or another e-mail client, Windows Messenger if you don't IM, and Games (under Accessories And Utilities) if you don't play. Select the item(s) to uninstall and click Next.

5. Wait while the Windows Components Wizard completes.

Cleaning Up the Start Menu

After uninstalling unnecessary programs, you might also need to remove references to them from the Start menu. This is pretty easy:

1. Click Start, point to All Programs, and from the list, locate the item to delete.

2. Right-click the item and choose Delete, as shown in Figure 4-6.

3. Click Yes to verify.

Figure 4-6

Right-click any program name and choose Delete to remove it from the All Programs list.

Keep in mind that deleting an item from this menu does not delete the program. You should have already done that. This command simply removes the shortcut to the item on the Start menu if it still exists. If you have any other shortcuts you'd like to delete from the Start menu, even if they are for programs you still have installed, you can remove them in the same manner. But remember, removing them from the Start menu does not uninstall them.

Find Programs You Don't Even Know You Have

Some of the items in the Add Or Remove Programs window might have looked a bit unfamiliar. We found one named PicoPlayer, one named Open MGSecure Module 3.1, and one named Network Smart Capture. Of course, we didn't dare uninstall them, not knowing what they were, but we'd certainly like to find out. You might have run across a similar issue.

There are several ways to find out what a program does. You can search the Internet for the application's name, you can open the Program Files folder and launch the EXE file, or you can see if there's a matching item in the All Programs list. If you can start the program, you can decide if you'd like to keep it or not. As it turns out, the computer manufacturer installed all of the items we had questions about, and thus, we uninstalled them.

Check Out the Program Files Folder

You'll be surprised what lurks in the Program Files folder. There are programs that aren't listed on the All Programs menu, that aren't shown on the Desktop, and that aren't listed in Add Or Remove Programs. To find out what you've got hiding in there, follow these simple steps:

1. Right-click the Start button.
2. Click Explore, and browse to the Program Files folder.
3. Click the program folders to see what files are in each one.
4. If you see a folder for a program you've deleted, right-click the folder and choose Delete. It shouldn't have any files in it other than perhaps an uninstall log.
5. If you see a folder that is named Online Services that has only files for selecting and signing on to an ISP, delete it.

If you find programs you don't want or need, there are really only three ways to get rid of them:

1. You can hope to find an uninstall option in the program folder.
2. You can visit the manufacturer's Web site for uninstallation instructions.
3. You can delete the entire folder by right-clicking and choosing Delete.

Use #3 as a last resort; deleting entire program folders can be hazardous to your computer's health!

About deleting program folders: Our test computer had a folder that contained several graphics-related program icons and EXE files. It was full of applications that weren't used, and there was no choice in the Control Panel to uninstall them. There was also no uninstall option that we could see in any of the Program Files folders. The only way to get rid of this folder and its contents was to delete it entirely. After a successful reboot, the deletion was not hazardous to the computer's health. However, you won't always be that lucky, and this isn't meant to imply that the computer won't have problems at a later date. Delete program files with care (and keep a good backup)!

CAUTION: *Don't delete program file folders unless you are really, really sure you understand the consequences. For instance, don't delete the Photoshop 6 folder after upgrading to Photoshop 7! You might find later that you needed those files.*

Finally, if you get errors at bootup after uninstalling programs, either you can use System Restore and start over or you can locate the offending Program Files folder and delete it. On one of our test computers, we kept getting bootup error messages related to a third-party shareware application we'd installed. After deleting the program folder, that error message went away.

GunkBuster's Notebook: Centralizing Storage of Install Suites

Windows provides ready-made folders for storing documents, music files, video files, and digital photo files. What it does *not* provide is a folder for "install suites," which are files that you download for installation as programs under Windows. When you download a utility from the Web somewhere (whether free or something you paid for), you're downloading a file. This may be a zip file (or some other type of compressed archive file, like a RAR file) or it may be an EXE (executable) file.

Whatever its format, this install suite file must be stored somewhere. Windows typically dumps it into your My Documents folder, and that's where it will remain unless you move it somewhere else. Some people move an install suite file from My Documents to the folder created when the utility is installed, somewhere under Program Files. Others move install suite files to the Program Files folder, above all the program-specific folders. Our advice is to create a separate folder for install suite files.

But first, why keep them at all? Once you've installed the utility, you don't need its install suite. That is, you don't need it...until you buy a new machine and need to install it on the new machine, or until your old machine crashes hard and must be reformatted and everything must be reinstalled. If you try a piece of software and don't like it (and then uninstall it), deleting its install suite is just good housekeeping. If you *do* like it, keeping the install suite file is essential.

Keeping install suites in one folder rather than scattering them "willy-nilly" across your hard drive is important for two reasons:

√ If all install suites are together, you can spot duplicates and old versions that are no longer needed and delete them.

√ If all install suites are together in one folder, you can back them up very easily by burning the folder to a CD. Backing up installed programs is pointless—you can't reinstall them just by copying them from a backup CD. That being the case, backing up install suites is essential.

What you name the folder is up to you, but something like "Install Suites" or "My Install Suites" works well.

One final note on install suites: Programs that you purchase by downloading from a Web site generally require an "unlock code" to make them fully functional. It's a good idea to create a document file that details all your unlock codes and the programs to which they apply. Store this document file in your install suites folder, and also print it out and keep a hard copy in your desk drawer, in case your computer crashes. An install suite without its unlock code is useless!

Remove Spyware

Spyware is another item you might not know you have on your computer. Spyware is a program that is installed on your computer either with or without your knowledge, and advertising companies use them to track what you do online, including what sites you visit. Sometimes they add new toolbars to your Web browser, change your home page, or cause excessive pop-up ads to appear on your computer. Other times, they can be more dangerous and do things like steal your passwords, credit card numbers, or other forms of identification. Illegal Internet music download sites can be culprits, as can unscrupulous businesses such as pornography sites. Xupiter was on our computer once, and we had no idea how it got there. Besides being an invasion of your privacy, though, most of these programs are poorly written, causing your computer to act buggy or respond slowly.

If you think you might be infected because you've visited or downloaded software from a risky Web site, or if all of a sudden you are experiencing problems such as a change to your home page, you might want to have your system scanned. You can get a free scan from many Web sites, including **www.spywareinfo.com** and **www.spychecker.com**. Visit **www.spychecker.com/software/ freeware_antispy.html** for various choices. We tried X-Cleaner Free, a free spyware checker (and more) and found it to be quite easy to use as well as functional. We also tried SpyHunter, **www3.enigmasoftwaregroup.com**. It scanned the system for free, found no spyware (although it did find some cookies it felt were of "medium" danger as well as a couple of files), and displayed protection options.

Our favorite, though, is Ad-Aware SE Personal by Lavasoft, **www.lavasoft.com**. This program scans your entire computer for data-mining traces, including your RAM, Registry, hard drives, and external storage devices. It's free too, although we've purchased the upgrade to Ad-Aware SE Plus for even more protection. This interface is quite comprehensive and is shown in Figure 4-7.

Figure 4-7

Lavasoft's Ad-Aware SE Personal (or in this case Plus) provides comprehensive adware/spyware protection.

Remove Programs for Hardware You No Longer Own

Take a look around the room and make a list of all of the hardware you currently have connected to your computer. Include printers, scanners, speakers, CD and DVD burners, and Web cams, and don't forget items like MP3 players, PDAs, and digital cameras that you connect intermittently. Next, take a look at the boxes that hold your dead hardware, like that pen/camera/Web cam/ coffeemaker your mom got you for your birthday last year. Now, return to Add Or Remove Programs in the Control Panel and see if it includes any items in your list of hardware that you no longer own or use. We'll bet you'll find a few printers, maybe a scanner, and probably an old Web cam.

Old printer software is the worst because printers generally come with programs for enhancing photos, cropping them, publishing or e-mailing them, and performing similar tasks. If you use a different program (such as Photoshop or Photoshop Elements), or any of the available Microsoft tools (like Publisher, Photo Editor, Paint), or any of the newer software available in Office 2005, you probably don't need this additional software at all.

Keep uninstalling! Our test machine is running faster than ever, and we've only just begun!

Tweaking Programs You Do Need

Now that you have only the programs you want installed on your computer, let's tweak those and the Windows components for ultimate performance. There are several options for increasing performance, including having the program open in a specific window size, having a program run in a different operating system environment (using Program Compatibility Mode), configuring System Restore to use minimal system resources, tweaking Performance options, and working with virtual memory settings.

Right-Click Your Program Icons

Right-clicking any program shortcut icon brings up a deluge of choices. Choose Properties to see the properties for the program, as shown in Figure 4-8. Here, you can tell the program what to do when you click the shortcut icon. We like our programs to start in Maximized mode. You can also change the icon, set compatibility options, and more.

Figure 4-8

Configure properties to set options for opening programs, among other things.

Program Compatibility Mode

If you find that an older program that worked fine on your Windows 98 machine doesn't run so well on your new Windows XP machine, you can tell

Windows to run it in Program Compatibility mode. When you choose this option, Windows XP changes the operating environment for the program and creates an area for the program to run in its native environment. While you can use the Program Compatibility Wizard, you can also configure it manually:

1. Locate the program icon on the Desktop or the program name on the All Programs menu. The program has to be one that you've installed; you can't set compatibility options for Windows XP applications like Outlook Express, Internet Explorer, Paint, or similar programs.

2. Right-click and choose Properties.

3. Click the Compatibility tab, and check Run This Program In Compatibility Mode For, and notice that the options in the drop-down list become available. Choose a mode for the program from this drop-down list. See Figure 4-9.

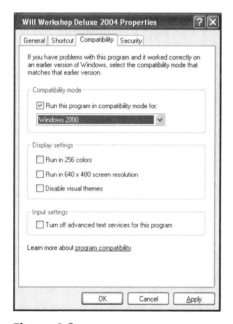

Figure 4-9
Program Compatibility Mode is a properties options for programs you've installed.

TIP: For best results, don't run anti-virus software in Program Compatibility Mode.

If the program still seems buggy after configuring it to run in Program Compatibility Mode, check the manufacturer's Web site for updates or patches, check Windows Update for program fixes, or if the program is a game that uses DirectX technology, ensure that you are using the latest version of DirectX (see the next section).

Make Multimedia and Games Run Better

Multimedia and games use DirectX, a tool that enhances the multimedia capabilities of your computer. DirectX enables programs to determine the hardware capabilities of your computer and then sets program parameters to match, thus making sure the program can access and use all of the high-performance options available. You can tweak DirectX using the DirectX Diagnostic Tool: Click Start, click Run, and type *dxdiag*. Then, click OK. Figure 4-10 shows the interface.

Figure 4-10

The DirectX Diagnostic Tool window offers options for tweaking and enhancing DirectX on your system.

If you are familiar with DirectX terminology and tools, or if you just want to see if there are any problems, you can work through the tabs of the dialog box. Each offers information on various problems and features. You can also perform tests to see if the hardware and software are functioning properly, including tests on your display, sound devices, music devices, input devices, and more. As shown in Figure 4-11, we've tested the music devices on our system. You can see in the Notes section that all DirectMusic tests were successful.

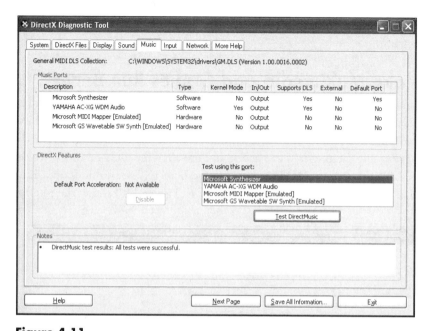

Figure 4-11
The music tests were successful on this machine.

If you do find problems, or if DirectX sounds like a planet in a sci-fi movie to you, you'll be better off using the options under the More Help tab. There, you'll find various troubleshooters that will walk you through solving any problems you've found. You can also click Help from any tab to get more information.

Performance Options

Keeping in mind that entire books could be written on enhancing performance options, let's go over the basics of the basics. Locate My Computer, right-click, and choose Properties. Click the Advanced tab. Performance options are available by clicking the Settings button in the Performance section. Figure 4-12 shows both the System Properties and Performance Options dialog boxes.

Notice that in the Performance Options dialog box, you can choose Let Windows Choose What's Best For My Computer. That's the default, but it can be changed. For instance, if you're interested in getting the best appearance from your computer, select Adjust For Best Appearance; if you want best performance, choose Adjust For Best Performance. You can also select Custom and check or uncheck anything you desire. We've checked Custom and have configured the options to suit our preferences.

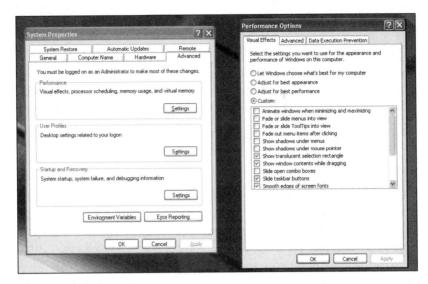

Figure 4-12
You can enhance performance via My Computer's Properties options.

Although adjusting the PC for best performance may seem like the best answer to getting the best performance, and it probably is, the problem with this setting is lack of appearance features! No fading or sliding of menus, no smooth screen fonts, no visual styles on windows and buttons. Your best bet for enhancing performance is to choose Custom and uncheck as many boxes as you're comfortable with.

The Advanced tab from the Performance Options dialog box also offers some other performance tweaks:

√   Processor Scheduling can be configured to use a greater share of process time for either programs or for background services. By default, the computer uses a greater share of its resources on running programs, but if you'd rather have XP focus its attention on running background services, you can change the default. Generally, the default is fine.

√   Memory Usage can be configured to use a greater share of memory, either to run programs or for system cache. By default, the computer uses a greater share of available memory on running programs, but if you'd rather have XP focus its attention on system cache, you can change the default. Generally, the default is fine.

√   Virtual Memory Settings can be configured for the paging file. The computer uses a specific area of the hard disk as if it were RAM, and XP sets a default paging file size. If you need to, you can click Change and set this manually. Chapter 12 introduces virtual memory and gives suggestions for configuring this option.

TIP: There are several sites on the Internet that offer performance-enhancing software. Just make sure you don't type in Enhance performance when looking for it! Instead type Windows XP improve performance. There are lots of cool tips at www.tweakxp.com.

System Restore

System Restore is a hard disk space hog. By default, System Restore is enabled on all drives when you first get Windows XP, unless you have less than 200 MB of free hard disk space. System Restore saves data on the hard drive so that if you have a computer problem, you can revert back to a saved state easily. It's an important feature, mind you, and we are not going to suggest you turn it off, but we are going to tell you how to tweak it, just in case you want to save a little (or possibly a lot of) hard drive space.

Let's check out your System Restore settings, and take a look at how much hard drive space is being used:

1. Click Start, point to All Programs, point to Accessories, point to System Tools, and click System Restore.

2. In the Welcome To System Restore dialog box, click System Restore Settings. (You can also access this dialog box through System in Control Panel.)

3. In the resulting System Properties dialog box (this should look familiar), notice that the available drives are listed and System Restore status is showing. In Figure 4-13, you can see that System Restore is monitoring both drives.

4. Select a drive, and click Settings. Figure 4-14 shows how your System Restore settings might be configured.

5. You can reduce the amount of disk space System Restore uses by moving the slider to the left. For the most part, 1 GB certainly suffices, and with 1 GB set aside for System Restore, you'll always have several restore points to choose. This will be a welcome relief if and when you need them. Reconfigure the slider if you'd like, and click OK.

6. Reconfigure any additional drives, and click OK. Close the System Properties dialog box.

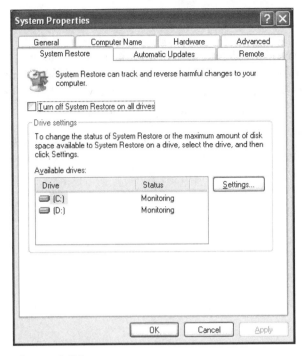

Figure 4-13

Configure System Restore to monitor all drives.

Figure 4-14

Most of the time, System Restore only needs 1 GB.

Summing Up

By now, you should have deleted your unnecessary documents, pictures, music, and movies, as well as uninstalled unnecessary programs. Hopefully, your machine is running better than ever! Keep in mind that we've only just begun; there are plenty more things we can do to degunk your computer!

Before going to bed tonight, do a quick backup and run Disk Cleanup and Disk Defragmenter. Wait a while before deleting the items in the Recycle Bin too, just to make sure you won't need anything you deleted today.

Organizing Your Remaining Files and Folders

Degunking Checklist:

√ Organize the default folders by creating additional, embedded folders and moving files into them.

√ Use the File And Folder Tasks pane in Windows XP to rename, move, copy, or delete folders.

√ Create folders on partitions configured for data only.

√ Empty the Recycle Bin to free up space on your hard drive.

√ Use Disk Cleanup and Disk Defragmenter to finalize the cleansing process.

Now that you've deleted unnecessary files, applications, and program files and folders, it's time to organize what you have remaining on your hard drive. Comparing this to our housecleaning analogy, this part of degunking is like cleaning out the garage: You need easy access to all of the stuff you have stored there, even if you don't use it very often. (You probably don't fertilize the lawn more than twice a year, and you likely only need access to the holiday decorations in the winter.) And while you want quick access to items when you do need them, you don't want to trip over them each time you need to use the car. Organizing your possessions for long-term storage and quick access can be a difficult task.

In this chapter, you'll learn how to organize your stuff, except in this case, your "stuff" will be the data on your hard drive. We'll walk you through how to create folders and how to move files and folders into them. You'll also learn some techniques for getting organized (and staying that way). Once this bit of organizing is out of the way, we'll run Disk Cleanup one more time and hold our breath and empty the Recycle Bin. Last but not least, we'll defragment the hard drive. Once all this is done, your PC should be zipping along at breakneck speed.

Better Organize the Default Folders

The simplest way to organize your files is to create personal folders inside the default folders. As we discussed in Chapter 3, the default folders are My Documents, My Pictures, My Music, and My Videos. You can create subfolders inside of those and move data into them to further organize what you want to keep. These default folders make great storage areas and can be used to organize everything from your accounting files to your zoo pictures. Hopefully, you've moved some of your files there already.

Because the default folders are generally located on the C: drive, you might encounter a common problem when using them—they tend to get really disorganized, really quickly. That's because in this age of large hard drives (80 GB or more), we tend to save everything, even things we don't need. Beyond that, though, many computers are partitioned into two drives: the C: drive, which holds the system files and programs, and the D: drive, which is supposed to store personal data. This sounds good in theory, and it's an easy way to organize data, but unfortunately, many people store personal stuff in the default folders on drive C: and completely ignore drive D:. One day these people wake up and realize that their 16 GB C: drive is full, and their 64 GB D: drive is empty! What a mess.

It's likely that your system is set up in one of three ways:

√ You have a single partition and use the default folders. (Partitions are sections of a hard drive that are created to hold specific types of data, like system files or personal data.)

√ You use a second partition or you have more than one hard drive and you create your own folders for storing personal data.

√ You have partitions beyond C: and D:, perhaps E:, F:, G:, or others.

You'll need to look at My Computer to see which way yours is configured. Figure 5-1 shows an example of a PC with two partitions (in the section Hard Disk Drives here), C: and D:. Fortunately, no matter what your particular set of circumstances, we can get it all straightened out. The techniques we'll introduce will apply to everyone.

Figure 5-1

Open My Computer and view the Hard Disk Drives section to see how your computer is configured.

TIP: *The icons Windows XP chooses for your drives do not always depict what they are. In Figure 5-1, drive D: is shown as a USB flash drive, but it is not. It is actually a partition on an 80 GB hard drive.*

Where Should You Put Your Data?

Because computers come in all shapes and sizes, you have to look at your specific setup and decide where you want to store your files. In the preceding section, you opened My Computer and took a look at what you had. If you found you had a single hard drive that contains a single partition, C: for instance, you should store your files in the default folders on that drive. If this is the case, skip to the section "Personalize the Default Folders with Folders of Your Own" later in this chapter. If you found you had two or more hard disk drives or hard disk partitions, you'll need to take a few extra steps. If your setup looks anything like the one shown in Figure 5-1, you'll know you have more than one hard drive or partition.

If you have a setup like this, you probably won't want to save to the default folders on the C: drive. That's because the C: drive is usually smaller than the D: drive. On the computer shown in Figure 5-1, the C: drive is 16 GB with a little less than 5 GB free. The D: drive is 58 GB with almost 55 GB free. It would make much more sense to save data such as images, videos, music, and data files to the larger drive, and leave the C: drive for programs, applications, and Windows files.

To see how large each of your drives (or partitions) are, follow these steps:

1. Open My Computer.
2. Hover the mouse pointer over any drive to highlight it (or click once if highlighting does not occur).
3. Expand the Details column in the left pane.
4. View the data there, as shown in Figure 5-2.

Figure 5-2
Select a drive or partition and then view the details to see how large the drive is and how much free space is available.

GunkBuster's Notebook: Creating Default Folders for Hard Drives with Multiple Partitions

If you have multiple partitions or drives, you should create some new default folders on a drive or partition other than C: and move your personal data over there (if it isn't there already). You won't have the luxury of having the standard default folders such as My Documents, My Pictures, or My Music. Thus, you'll need to set up your own organization system. Here are the steps to help you:

1. Open My Computer and open the drive where you want to place your data. On the computer shown in Figure 5-1, that would be the D: drive. Yours might have a different letter assigned.

2. Right-click an empty area of the folder window, point to New, and click Folder. Name the folder My Pictures. (If you think you'll get confused having a folder named My Pictures on both drive C: and D:, name this folder My Pictures on Drive D.)

3. Repeat step 2 and create three more folders: My Videos, My Music, and My Documents. You might also want to create My Webs if you create Web pages, My Current Projects to hold work in progress, or similar folders. Figure 5-3 shows an example.

Figure 5-3
Create folders on the larger drive to organize the data you need to move.

4. Close the window that shows the contents of the D: drive.

5. Open the My Documents folder on the C: drive, or open any other folder that contains data you'd like to move.

6. Select the items to move either by using the Edit menu and Select All or by selecting the files manually (The goal is to move your existing data—data you've created yourself—from the smaller drive to the larger one. When you're finished, the folders containing data on the C: drive should be just about empty.)

7. From the File And Folder Tasks pane, select Move The Selected Items.

8. In the Move Items dialog box, browse to the D: drive, locate the folder to move the data to, and click Move. The files will be moved automatically.

CAUTION: *Don't move program file folders, downloaded installation files, or any file that you did not create yourself. Doing so could cause system instability.*

The next time you need to open a file, picture, project, or music, make sure you browse to the D: drive! You'll also want to tell applications like Windows Media Player if you've moved your files. To do this, just open the player, click Tools, and click Search For Media Files. In the Search On drop-down list, choose the new drive.

Once you set up a new set of folders like this, you should take special care to ensure that your files are saved in the new location whenever you use applications like Word, Excel, and so on. Because the new default folders will have the same names as the ones that Windows XP sets up for you (they are now just stored on a different drive or partition), you could easily save to the wrong drive or partition if you are not careful. You might want to regularly check the default folders on your C: drive (My Documents, My Music, and so on) and move the files found in these folders to their proper corresponding folders on the drive or partition you are actually using to store your personal data.

Personalize the Default Folders with Folders of Your Own

Once you've decided where to store your data, whether it's on the C: drive or some other drive, you can begin personalizing the folders by adding your own touches. For starters, open the My Documents folder and categorize the documents in there. Perhaps you might organize what's in the folder by projects you need to finish, projects completed, and projects yet to be started. You could also take a different approach and organize by the document type, like budgets, health, taxes, or letters. You can repeat this practice for each of the default folders. Figure 5-4 shows a fairly organized My Pictures folder.

Figure 5-4
Organizing what's in each folder with personalized subfolders is the best way to get organized.

With ideas for folder names selected, create and organize your folders by following these steps:

1. Open the folder to organize. In the File And Folder Tasks pane, click Make A New Folder. If you can't see this pane, right-click an empty area of the folder's window, point to New, and click Folder.

2. Name the folder and press Enter.

3. Click and drag items from the folder into the new one you just created.

4. Repeat these steps until all of the items are neatly organized in folders.

> **GunkBuster's Notebook: Change the Default Location of Your My Documents Folder**
>
> Windows XP places your My Documents folder in a default location:
>
> C:\Documents And Settings\>*user name* \My Documents.
>
> Here C is the drive in which Windows is installed, and *<username>* is the currently logged-on user. (Remember that each user who uses your computer and has a logon name will have their own My Documents folder.) As you are moving your folders around, trying to better organize your hard drive, you might come up with a better location for your My Documents folder. The good news is that you can change the default location of this folder by following the simple steps presented here.
>
> Here's another scenario to consider: If you have a computer that has two partitions, perhaps one for the operating system files (C:) and one for data (D:), you may have already moved the documents you've stored on the C: drive to the D: drive by using the Move command. While you can copy, paste, and/or move data from your old My Documents folder on the C: drive to the larger partition on the D: drive manually, changing the default location of the My Documents folder is sometimes much easier. If you want to change the default location to the D: drive, for example, follow these steps:
>
> 1. Close all running programs.
> 2. Right-click the My Documents folder and select Properties.
> 3. Click the Target tab, and click Move.
> 4. In the Move dialog box, browse to the location to which you want to move the file. If the folder doesn't exist, browse to the location, and in the Select A Destination dialog box, click Make New Folder. Click OK.

Rename, Copy, and Delete Folders

You can rename, copy, and delete folders by right-clicking them. You can also change the default folder names (for instance, if you would rather have the folder named Pics instead of My Pictures). Just select the task from the list after right-clicking.

Move Data into the New Folders

While it's easy to drag and drop a file from inside a single folder into a new folder created there, it's a little more difficult to drag and drop a file between folders that are completely separate. As mentioned in the GunkBuster's Notebook "Creating Default Folders for Multiple Partitioned Hard Drives," Windows XP offers options to move folders and files in the File And Folder Tasks pane. We'll go over it again in case you skipped that tip.

Assume you have some videos that you took with your digital camera on the memory card instead of the tape and you saved them in the My Pictures folder. After seeing that they are videos, you want to move them to the My Videos folder. You could open both folders, resize them so you can see each, and then drag and drop the files manually. The better method for doing this would be to use this simple command:

1. Select a file or folder to move. In this example, we'll be moving the Videos From Camera folder from My Pictures and putting it in My Videos.

2. In the File And Folder Tasks pane, click Move This Folder, or if appropriate, Move This File. See Figure 5-5.

Figure 5-5
Use the File and Folder Tasks pane commands to move files.

3. In the Move Items dialog box, browse to the location to save the files and click Move. Figure 5-6 shows an example. The folder (or file) will be moved automatically.

Figure 5-6
Browse to the new folder in the Move Items dialog box to relocate the files.

Empty the Recycle Bin

In the first half of the chapter, we focused our efforts on organizing the data you have left on your hard drive. During this process, you might have found more junk to throw away. And of course, we still have all of the data and programs that we threw away in Chapters 3 and 4. Now it's time to take that serious step of emptying the Recycle Bin.

You might not be aware that when you first delete files, folders, or programs, they are not actually physically removed from your hard drive. They are simply marked for deletion and placed in a location called the Recycle Bin. This sort of gives you a second chance in case you actually delete something that you later realize you might need. In order to physically remove data from your hard drive, you must go to the Recycle Bin and remove it. Once it's gone from there, it's gone for good. So, before you right-click, let's make sure of a few things first, including that the computer can be restarted without errors!

Restart the Computer

Before deleting the items from the Recycle Bin, restart the computer. If you get any errors, you'll need to seriously look into what's going on before you do any deleting. There are several types of errors you can get on boot-up, including the following. I've also offered a few solutions, so read the list carefully:

√   Errors related to installed or uninstalled software: These errors can usually be repaired by reinstalling the application causing the error. You might also have to reinstall so you can successfully uninstall. Sometimes you can get rid of these errors by deleting the folder that contained the files for the program you uninstalled, but use this as a last resort. Figure 5-7 shows an example of a computer that has recently had several programs uninstalled, and not successfully.

Figure 5-7
Programs that are uninstalled incorrectly because you didn't use the uninstall option or go through Add Or Remove Programs in Control Panel can lead to errors on bootup.

√   Missing DLL files: DLL files (files with the .dll extension) are Dynamic Link Library files and are shared files used by many programs installed on the computer. A shared DLL file could have been deleted when a program was uninstalled. Visit **http://support.Microsoft.com**, type in the error message, and follow the directions given for repairing the problem. You might also solve the problem by doing a repair installation using the XP CD, using a program like Norton's WinDoctor to replace the missing files automatically, or recovering the files from the Recycle Bin yourself.

√ Stop errors: Stop errors occur when the missing file is a much-needed one. Stop errors are generally caused by missing device drives or damaged system files. SYS files and DLL files can cause Stop errors. **http://support.Microsoft.com** offers solutions to repairing hundreds of different stop errors. Many solutions include recovering the damaged or missing file from the i386 folder of the XP CD.

√ Missing Windows program files: "Windows could not start because of an error in the software" and "Load needed DLLs for Kernel" are caused by missing Windows program files. When a problem occurs as serious as this one, you'll need to "upgrade" to XP again and perform a reinstallation.

TIP: For unknown errors that can't be solved simply, read the Knowledge Base article #308041 on the Microsoft site. This article summarizes many different troubleshooting techniques.

In addition to repairing errors using the Knowledge Base articles, recovering from the Recycle Bin, performing a repair installation or upgrade, or copying the missing files from the i386 folder, you can also solve many problems with System Restore. Be sure to weigh all of your options before doing anything drastic, like formatting and reinstalling!

Make a Final Pass

Before deleting items from the Recycle Bin, make one final pass. Use Disk Cleanup to remove any unnecessary files that might have accumulated since the last time you ran it. Start each program that you have installed, and verify that they open and run correctly. If you find any errors, reinstall the program or recover the missing files from the Recycle Bin. Take a look at My Documents, My Pictures, My Videos, and My Music and make sure there isn't anything missing that you need. Additionally, verify that your anti-virus program is working and is up-to-date. You should always have current, up-to-date, running anti-virus programs and firewalls and have the programs set to automatically collect and install virus definitions. Finally, do a backup of your most important files.

Ready? Empty!

If everything looks good (or after you've repaired any items mentioned in the list of errors earlier), right-click the Recycle Bin and click Empty Recycle Bin. In the Confirm Multiple File Delete dialog box, click Yes to delete. If you have

Norton or some other anti-virus software, you might have a "protected" Recycle Bin, too. If you'd like to delete the files there, follow the directions for your software. Generally, it's as simple as right-clicking the existing Recycle Bin and choosing the appropriate item. See Figure 5-8.

Figure 5-8
Right-click the Recycle Bin to see what options are available to you.

Use Disk Defragmenter

You can count on one thing: If you've deleted a lot of files, moved files from one partition to another, deleted programs and applications, and emptied the Recycle Bin, your hard drive will be a mess. When we say "a mess," we don't mean it's disorganized by our standards. We mean that the files on the actual hard drive are *fragmented,* or disorganized by Windows standards. There are files and parts of files stored everywhere, and they aren't stored contiguously. That causes problems and degrades the performance of your hard drive.

Here's basically how a hard drive works: A hard drive is a circular disk, kind of like an old LP record. As data is written to the hard disk, it is written sequentially using the first open space it finds. If you installed a program on that hard disk the day you purchased the computer, it would be located near the beginning. As time passes, files are saved after it and the disk begins to fill up. If you uninstall that same program a year later, you'll have a big gap on the hard disk where that program once was (at the beginning of the disk). The next time you install a program or save a file, Windows will begin writing that data to the first open space it sees, most likely this gap where you uninstalled the program and freed up some space. This means you could have part of a file stored at the very beginning of the hard drive, another part stored in the middle, and the rest of the file saved at the end. When you open that file, Windows has to search the entire hard drive to put the pieces together.

When Windows has to piece together a file in this manner, the computer slows down because it simply takes longer to find the data. The disk might have to spin several thousand more times than it should have to, which not only causes a slow response but also causes unnecessary wear and tear on your computer. After a computer is *defragmented,* the files are stored (more) contiguously and the computer's hard disk has to spend less time spinning around and looking for files. This makes for better performance and less stress on the computer. The problem is worse if *program files* are stored in a noncontiguous manner. See Figure 5-9 for a visual representation of a hard disk.

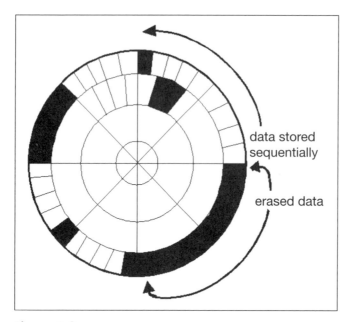

data stored sequentially

erased data

Figure 5-9
A hard disk holds your data, but not always contiguously.

Fortunately, Windows provides a utility called Disk Defragmenter that is designed to clean up the fragments in your hard dive. When you run this utility, Windows rearranges the files it knows should be placed together so that the disk will operate more efficiently. You'll see a huge difference after defragging your drive.

Are you ready to do some defragging? Make sure it's almost bedtime and you won't need your computer for a while and then follow these steps:

1. Close all open programs.

2. Turn off screensavers.

3. Turn off anti-virus software and disconnect from the Internet. (This is an important step.)

4. Click Start, point to All Programs, point to Accessories, point to System Tools, and click Disk Defragmenter.

5. Highlight a drive to defragment and either click Analyze to see whether or not the disk needs defragmenting or click Defragment to begin the process immediately. Figure 5-10 shows a disk being defragmented.

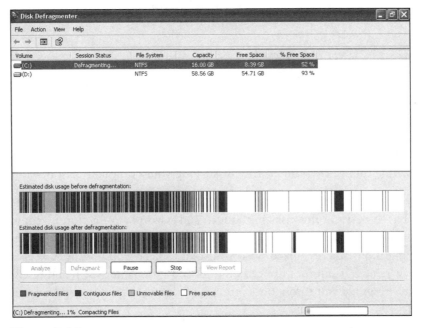

Figure 5-10
Defragmenting is the last step to organizing the data on your drive.

Some final notes about defragmenting: You should analyze your hard disks once a month to see if another defragmenting session is in order. Just click Analyze and see what Windows suggests. This is important because how often you need to defragment depends on how active you are on your computer. If you turn the computer on once a week to e-mail your kids, you probably won't need to defrag for a long time, but if you use your computer a lot and install and uninstall lots of programs, or if you create and delete lots of files, you'll need to defrag a bit more often.

The length of time it takes for Disk Defragmenter to complete depends on the size of your hard disk and how fragmented it is. It also depends to some extent on how fast your PC is. It's best just to let it run while you're asleep because it can take several hours on slow or extremely gunked-up machines. Make sure to disable screensavers and anti-virus programs, too; sometimes they interfere with the process. And finally, if for some reason you can't get Disk Defragmenter to run correctly or to complete, try running it in Safe mode or purchase a third-party utility like Norton SystemWorks.

Disk Defragmenter is one utility you should make a point to use regularly. Once defragmented, a drive will perform better, and you can expect noticeable performance improvements. It's well worth the time it takes!

Staying Degunked

Keeping your PC degunked is hard, we'll give you that. In fact, it's just as hard as keeping a sparkling-windowed, newly mopped, freshly dusted, vacuumed, trash-free home unsoiled. You can't. However, you can put your dishes in the dishwasher after you're finished eating, take out the trash every other day, and stay on top of the dusting and vacuuming by cleaning one item a day and rotating rooms. The same is true of keeping your computer pristine.

After working through Chapters 3, 4, and 5, you may be wondering just how often to perform the tasks introduced and what plan of action is required to remain degunked. Now that you've rid your PC of unnecessary files and applications and organized what you want to keep, you'll want to keep it that way. Table 5-1 outlines the tasks introduced in Chapters 3, 4, and 5. Use this table to guide you through the process of staying degunking and organized.

Table 5-1   Schedule for Staying Degunked and Organized

Task	How Often to Perform	Tips for Remaining Degunked
Clean up the default folders like My Documents and My Pictures.	Once a week	Put data in the correct subfolders each time you save a file and always delete items you know you do not need.
Clean up data in system folders like Unzipped and drives like C: or D:.	Once a week	Delete zipped files after unzipping and saving their contents and save files to their correct subfolders as they are obtained.

continued

Table 5-1   **Schedule for Staying Degunked and Organized** *(continued)*

Task	How Often to Perform	Tips for Remaining Degunked
Use Disk Cleanup and Disk Defragmenter.	Once a week and once a month, respectively	Create a scheduled task for these events in Control Panel.
Clean up Internet Explorer.	Once a week, or at least monthly	Remember that you are acquiring cookies and temporary files each time you surf the Web. Configure Internet Explorer options for best performance.
Uninstall unwanted applications.	Once a month	Do not install freeware or shareware unless you're sure it's from a trusted source, and only install third-party software you know you'll use.
Keep unwanted data off your computer.	Every day	Purchase, configure, and automatically run third-party anti-virus and anti-spyware software. Do not save data you know you don't need.
Create subfolders.	Whenever necessary	Create a new subfolder every time you upload pictures from your digital camera to your My Pictures folder, create a new movie, or obtain a new hobby, client, or work project. Keep files in their proper folders.
Empty the Recycle Bin.	Monthly	Restart your computer before emptying the Recycle Bin, especially if you've recently uninstalled an application.

Summing Up

In this chapter, we completed the optimization of the hard drive by organizing the files we decided to keep, moving them to their proper places on the hard drive, emptying the Recycle Bin, and running Disk Defragmenter. All of these things, especially running Disk Defragmenter, are "must do" items if you want your computer to run at its best possible and peak performance. Since the hard drive is an extremely important part of any computer system, it's important to regularly perform the tasks detailed here.

Tweaking Your Desktop and Start Menu

Degunking Checklist:

√ Clean up and personalize the Taskbar so you can work faster and smarter.

√ Remove items from the System Tray that use valuable system resources.

√ Limit the programs that start when Windows starts.

√ Group running applications, use Quick Launch, and employ AutoHide.

√ Personalize the Start menu by adding or deleting programs, reordering the list, and more.

√ Personalize the Desktop with your favorite folders and shortcuts, and remove unused icons.

√ Use non-system-intensive screensavers and themes to enhance performance.

√ Personalize folder options.

In Chapters 3, 4, and 5, you learned how to remove and organize a lot of data and programs that reside in your folders. You might not realize it, but there are also a number of personalization and organizational tasks that you can perform on your Desktop to make Windows run much better. Personalizing XP might not seem like a big deal, but it is. You can tell XP how you want the Taskbar and Start menu to look, what should or shouldn't appear on the Desktop, and how you want to interact with it when you need information (as with setting folder options). By personalizing Windows XP, you can work faster and smarter and perform tasks more efficiently than if you didn't personalize it at all. You can put what you need where you need it, making it a snap to open a program, locate a file, or perform a task. This is the fun part of degunking!

Clean Up and Personalize the Taskbar

The Taskbar is that little blue bar across the bottom of your screen. You can use it to immediately find out what programs are running, what programs started automatically when you booted Windows, and what programs you have configured to launch quickly (see Figure 6-1). The Taskbar is full of information and, by its very nature, a busy place that tends to get more than a little cluttered.

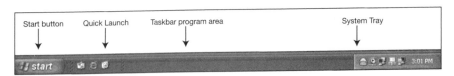

Figure 6-1
The Taskbar offers a lot of information.

The Taskbar contains four main components: In the bottom-left corner, you'll find the trusty Start button. To the right of the Start button is the Quick Launch toolbar (assuming you have this feature selected), which contains a set of program icons that you can click to quickly launch the programs they represent. The area to the right of the Quick Launch toolbar is the area of the Taskbar that lists the programs currently running on your computer. Finally, the section to the far right is the System Tray. The System Tray shows the programs that started when Windows did, and each runs automatically and in the background. The System Tray is where we'll focus our energies first; we bet you don't even know what you have in there! Every item in the System Tray is slowing down the boot process and bogging down your computer, and it's time to do a little cleaning.

Look at Figure 6-1 again and you'll see that the Taskbar's Quick Launch area is configured to display the icons for the programs Outlook Express and Internet Explorer, and it also includes the Show Desktop icon. Notice also that icons for an anti-virus program and network connections, an Incredimail icon, the system clock, and even a little icon for Windows Media Player are all located in the System Tray. With these items on the Taskbar, they can be accessed easily. You might have similar icons.

In this section, you'll learn all the tips and tricks you need to know to clean up and personalize your Taskbar, including adding or removing icons, adding or removing toolbars, using AutoHide, locking the Taskbar, grouping applications, and configuring Quick Launch, just to name a few! There is a lot that you can do to clean up and personalize the Taskbar, but we'll start with the System Tray feature first, because that is a likely place where you can do some serious degunking!

 If you want the icon for Windows Media Player to appear in the System Tray as shown in Figure 6-1, you'll need to get the Windows Media Player Tray Control. It's available in the Windows Media Bonus Pack for Windows XP here: **www.Microsoft.com/ windows.windowsmedia/download.bonuspack.aspx**.

Managing the Taskbar's System Tray

The System Tray in the Taskbar can be used to hold icons for items that we deem important for work or play. However, it seems as if we spend most of our time removing stuff from it. Programs, especially those downloaded from the Internet, like to place their icons there without our permission. If you don't monitor your System Tray regularly, it could become really cluttered. Very often, when you download a new program, it asks whether you want an icon placed in your System Tray. Many people don't think twice about clicking Yes to these requests. Most times now, though, the downloaded programs put themselves there without our permission at all. There should be a law against that!

You should also be very selective about what *you* place in the System Tray. When an icon is showing in the System Tray, the program it represents runs in the background all the time and uses valuable system resources. You don't want a lot of icons there for that reason, because besides cluttering up the System Tray, their programs hog valuable RAM. It's best to have as few items as possible in the System Tray.

Some of the items you might want running in the System Tray include icons for programs you regularly use or want access to (such as an anti-virus program) and icons for applications that you use daily (such as music download software or Media Player). You can also configure your network connections so that when they are connected, an icon shows in the System Tray. Using the connection's icon, you can disconnect, view properties, and make configuration changes quickly. Some items you probably don't want there are icons for programs you downloaded, tried out, and didn't like, such as RealPlayer, Napster, any instant messaging programs, and programs like wallpaper changers or jukeboxes. You should also remove the icon for any program you like but simply don't use that often. There's no reason to leave a program that you don't use running. That program will use system resources and slow down your computer. Remember, in this case, less is best, so don't gunk up your System Tray with unnecessary icons! Let's now look at how to both add and remove an item.

Add Program Icons to the System Tray

Some programs have a built-in feature that adds an icon to the System Tray. You can also instruct a program's icon to stay in the System Tray by checking an option from inside the desired program, as shown in Figure 6-2. This example shows a Norton Anti-Virus option, and it is checked so that the program's icon will be displayed in the tray. Different applications offer different ways to do this. I am just showing one example here to get you started. (Obviously, you

 Show the Auto-Protect icon in the tray

Figure 6-2
Some programs offer the option to put an item in the System Tray or remove it.
In the case of anti-virus software, it's best to leave it in the System Tray.

would uncheck this option to remove the program.)

Locating a program's System Tray option can be difficult if not downright impossible though. You can't just choose any program and instruct it to place a representative icon in the System Tray (or remove one). The developer who created the program must manually put in this feature, and unfortunately, many don't. Fortunately, freeware and shareware utilities are available that can help you take control.

TIP: It's a good idea to have icons for your anti-virus and firewall applications in your System Tray. That way, you can always make sure that your Internet connection is secure.

One application for setting up the System Tray is the Tray Minimizer. You can get the evaluation version at **www.trayminimizer.com**. This application lets you minimize items to the System Tray instead of the larger Taskbar area. This unclutters the Taskbar and lets you locate and find things more quickly than if you had to sort through various grouped icons. Figures 6-3 and 6-4 show the Taskbar before and after using this utility.

Figure 6-3
Before using the third-party software Tray Minimizer.

Figure 6-4
After downloading, installing, and configuring the third-party software Tray Minimizer.

Remove Program Icons from the System Tray

As mentioned earlier and shown in Figure 6-2, some programs offer a choice so that you can remove their program icons from the System Tray. To find these options, right-click the program's icon and choose Properties, Preferences, or any other choice that will allow you to set the program's configuration. Look around and you might find what you are looking for.

If you can't find an option to remove the icon and you see icons in the System Tray for items you don't need or use (like instant messaging, Napster, RealPlayer, jukebox or other music software, or programs you've downloaded but don't use), you can tell Windows you don't want those programs to automatically start and you don't want their icons to appear in the System Tray when you start Windows. Here's how:

1. Click Start and then click Run. In the Run dialog box, type *msconfig.exe.* Click OK.

2. Click the Startup tab. Figure 6-5 shows an example. Here, an application we downloaded from the Internet is selected.

3. Uncheck items that you recognize and don't want to start automatically. In the screen shown in Figure 6-5, notice that several items are unchecked. If we want to use these programs, we'll start them manually! Don't uncheck anything you don't recognize, though. If you are unsure about an item, jot down the path to the program and see if you can figure out what it is by

Figure 6-5
After downloading a program, you may decide you don't want it to start up each time Windows boots; to stop this behavior, make changes in the System Configuration Utility.

  browsing there and starting the program. If that doesn't work, you can look up the program in question on the Internet.

4. Click OK and restart your computer.

5. On reboot, read the information and click OK in the System Configuration Utility dialog box. You'll notice fewer icons in the System Tray.

TIP: *If you get error messages on startup, find out what program those errors are related to and uncheck that item in the System Configuration utility. You might find that those error messages go away on the next boot up.*

Hide Inactive Icons in the System Tray

Now that you've decided what items you want in the System Tray, you can choose to hide them when the programs they represent are inactive, always show them, or never show them. With AutoHide, you can hide the icon without getting rid of it completely. This is a great way to unclutter the Taskbar and System Tray without actually having to remove items from it that you'd really like to keep.

Here are the steps to follow:

1. Right-click an empty area of the Taskbar, and choose Properties.

2. From the Taskbar tab, verify that Hide Inactive Icons is selected, and click Customize.

3. Under Current Items, click to set the options. The options are Hide When Inactive, Always Show, or Always Hide. Hiding icons will leave them accessible but will hide them in the System Tray under an arrow. Selecting Always Show will tell Windows to always show the item and never hide it. Click OK twice. Your System Tray will now look like the one shown in Figure 6-6. You can access the hidden icons by clicking the arrow.

Figure 6-6
Choose to hide inactive icons in the System Tray
behind the arrow.

Here's a summary of programs you might want to keep running all the time, and thus keep in the System Tray, and those you might not:

√ If you use an instant messaging program, by all means, keep it in the System Tray; if not, remove it. Consider using the AutoHide feature here.

√ If you use music software and a download site often, keep the software and connection to it in the System Tray. If you tried out the program, didn't like it, and don't use it, remove it.

√ If you don't recognize a program in the System Tray, remove it.

√ Leave items you access regularly in the System Tray, like Power Management on a laptop, anti-virus software, the volume icon, a firewall icon, or network connectivity status. Remove items that don't need to run all the time, like QuickTime, Napster, or video or music managers.

Add Quick Launch Icons

As you've seen, Quick Launch is an area of the Taskbar that is located just to the right of the Start menu and enables you to start applications quickly and with a single click. In addition to (or instead of) the default icons, though, you can add your own specific icons to start your favorite programs. This feature makes it easier to load frequently used programs; you don't have to go to the Start menu and search for the program you want each time. Turning on Quick Launch does not start the programs or cause them to run; it only creates a shortcut to them. It isn't like the System Tray, where valuable resources are sucked dry by programs that run in the background; Quick Launch only offers a place to access programs quickly.

So, turn on Quick Launch, add icons for your favorite programs, and then remove the shortcuts to those programs and other unnecessary icons from the Desktop if you desire. Doing so unclutters your Desktop while still offering quick and easy access to your most-used programs. Figure 6-7 shows an example of a customized Quick Launch toolbar.

Figure 6-7
Customize Quick Launch to hold your favorite icons.

You can use and/or customize Quick Launch by doing this:

1. Right-click an empty area of the Taskbar and click Properties.
2. From the Taskbar tab, check Show Quick Launch.
3. Click OK.
4. To add a program to the Quick Launch menu, locate the program from either the All Programs list or Windows Explorer.
5. Right-click and drag the program to the Quick Launch area.
6. Let go and choose Copy Here. (Don't choose Move or the program will no longer be available from the All Programs menu.)
7. To remove a program from the Quick Launch area, right-click the icon. Then click Delete, and click Yes to verify.

Some people prefer to keep their Taskbar cleaner and just rely on placing their favorite programs in the Start menu, with Quick Launch hidden. This is a good technique if you usually have three or four programs running simultaneously with multiple documents open at one time and you want to see them all on your Taskbar.

Lock, AutoHide, and Group Options in the Taskbar

You can lock the Taskbar so that it cannot be moved or resized, or you can configure it to hide when inactive. You can also configure it to group files opened by the same program in the same area of the taskbar. If you choose to group files, when the Taskbar becomes crowded, the buttons for the same program are collapsed into a single button. Figure 6-8 shows an example. To use AutoHide, to lock the Taskbar, or to group items, right-click the Taskbar, choose the Taskbar tab, and select the appropriate boxes.

Figure 6-8
Group similar icons to save Taskbar space.

Customizing with TweakUI

While there are a few other things you can do with the Taskbar, we'll move on to some really cool tweaks. Are you tired of seeing those balloon tip pop-up messages? Would you like to group files in a specific order? How about getting a warning in the Taskbar when you're low on disk space? You need TweakUI, a free and extremely powerful PowerToy.

FREE INFORMATION Download and install TweakUI from **www.Microsoft.com/windowsxp/ pro/downloads/powertoys.asp** and use its simple interface to tweak the Taskbar to your heart's content.

Personalize the Start Menu

In order to work faster and smarter, you need to personalize the Start menu so the things you need are readily available and the things you don't need or no longer have installed aren't taking up unnecessary space. There's nothing worse than having to wade through a disorganized Start menu looking for some program you think should be there, but isn't! As you can see from many of the screen shots in this book, we prefer the XP theme and default look. Figure 6-9 shows our Start menu. Yours could look much different than this. Notice that our most-used programs are showing on the left and My Computer has an arrow beside it. Pointing to this arrow or any other on the Start menu opens another menu with the item's contents.

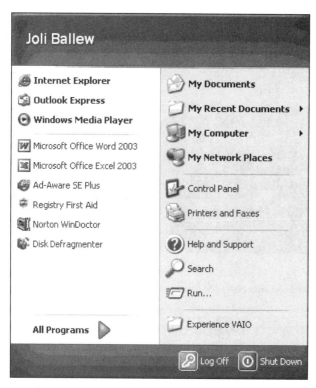

Figure 6-9
We prefer the default look for the Start menu.

You can customize your Start menu, too; right-click the Taskbar, choose Properties, and click the Start Menu tab. Click the Customize button for your particular Start menu style. There, you'll find almost everything you need.

XP Start Menu

If you're tweaking your XP-themed Start menu, after opening the Start Menu tab as detailed in the preceding section, you'll see what is shown in Figure 6-10. (You can also right-click an empty area of the Start menu, select Properties, and then click Customize to get to this dialog box.)

From the General tab, you can do the following:

√   Choose the icon size.

√   Choose the number of programs on the Start menu or clear the list.

√   Show or hide Internet and e-mail programs, and choose between them.

Figure 6-10
Tweak the XP Start menu with this dialog box.

Here's what you can do from the Advanced tab:

√ Choose to open submenus by pausing on them with the mouse pointer.

√ Highlight newly installed programs. (This is highly recommended because newly installed programs might be installed under a nondescriptive name and be difficult to find. For instance, one of our favorite programs, EZ Macro, is listed in the Start menu under the American Systems option.)

√ Show, hide, and display as a link or a menu Control Panel, My Computer, My Documents, My Music, My Pictures, Network Connections, and System Tools.

√ Show or hide Favorites, Help And Support, My Network Places, Printers And Faxes, Run, Search, and Set Program Access And Defaults.

√ Enable dragging and dropping from the Start menu.

√ Enable Scroll Programs, which shows the programs list as a scrollable, single-pane list instead of horizontal pages.

√ List or clear most recently opened documents.

Configure the items as you like them and OK your way out of the dialog boxes.

With the Start menu configured, you can perform several additional tweaks.

√ Right-click any item in the left pane to pin it to the Start menu, remove it from the list, or rename it.

√ Right-click any item in the right pane to rename it, view its properties, or see other information.

√ Reorder the items in the All Programs list by right-clicking any program and clicking Sort By Name, rename or delete any items from the list, or see an item's properties.

Adding Items to the Start Menu

If you have the dragging and dropping option enabled from the Advanced options in the Customize Start Menu dialog box, you can drag and drop to add items to the Start menu or reorder them. (Although there are other ways, this is the easiest.) To add an item to the Start menu, follow these steps:

1. Locate the item using Windows Explorer, right-click, and drag the executable file to the Start menu.

2. Drop the file in the All Programs menu or the left pane of the Start menu.

3. Choose Copy Here if prompted. Figure 6-11 shows an example. Always remember to choose Copy; you don't want to move the file.

Figure 6-11

Drag any executable file to the Start Menu to copy it there.

In addition to adding programs to the Start menu by dragging and dropping, you can move programs around to reorder them. Just drag and drop!

Classic Menu

If you're using the Classic menu, you'll see different options when you customize the Start menu's properties. (Remember, right-click an empty area of the Taskbar, choose Properties, click the Start Menu tab, and then click Customize.)

Customizations are similar to those listed earlier for the XP Start menu:

√ Display Administrative Tools, Favorites, Log Off, and Run.

√ Expand the Control Panel, My Documents, My Pictures, Network Connections, and Printers.

√ Enable dragging and dropping, scrolling the Start menu, using personalized menus, and selecting icon size.

√ Add or remove a program from the Start menu, or sort or clear items.

As with the XP Start menu, you can right-click any item on the Classic Start menu and delete it, sort the items by name, use drag and drop to add programs or reorder them, and right-click see an item's properties.

TIP: *TweakUI, mentioned earlier, offers one really nice option for tweaking the Start menu. You can select which items can or cannot appear on the Most Frequently Used Programs section of the Windows XP Start menu. You can do it in the depths of XP, it just isn't easy to do.*

Clean Up and Personalize the Desktop

There's really only one more item we're going to clean up and then personalize with our own touches, and that's the Desktop. You can make the Desktop look however you want it to. It can have lots of icons or none at all; it can show My Computer, My Network Places, Internet Explorer, and/or the Recycle Bin; it can have shortcuts to programs you use a lot, folders you access daily, networks you connect to, and more. You can also choose screensavers, although for the purpose of degunking, we'll talk about non-system-intensive ones as well as non-system-intensive themes.

You can add anything you want to what normally appears on all Windows XP Desktops. This makes it quite easy to gunk it up. There is no worse productivity zapper than a really messy Desktop. Over the years, we've looked over the shoulders of friends and family, only to discover a Desktop that looks really scary. Let's face it: Most of us simply drop applications and folders on our Desktop until we can't tell what the background screen is supposed to look like anymore. Then, we search the screen whenever we are looking for a specific program to start up or folder to use. Not only that, but we'd venture to guess some of the links don't even work anymore. There must be a better way!

Our recommendation is that you develop a strategy for what you will allow to be displayed on your Desktop. You should be very picky—if you're right-brained, think of your desktop as really valuable real estate, like beachfront property—you don't want to junk it up with a bunch of broken beach chairs and fishing poles. If you're left-brained, imagine it's a filing cabinet and the icons on your Desktop are the tabs on your file folders. Either way, the idea is to clean it up, make it nice, and configure it so that you can find what you want, when you want it.

Add or Remove Default Icons

You can remove many of the default icons on your Desktop to make it look tidy and make your computer start up a little faster when you first boot up. Of course, you can add icons that you need but are not there.

To add or remove default icons, follow these steps:

1. Right-click an empty area of the Desktop and choose Properties.
2. In the Display Properties dialog box, choose the Desktop tab.
3. Choose Customize Desktop to open the Desktop Items dialog box, which is shown in Figure 6-12.
4. In the Desktop Items dialog box, check or uncheck My Documents, My Computer, My Network Places, and Internet Explorer. (Notice you can also change the icons for these if you desire.)
5. Click OK in the Desktop Items dialog box and again in the Display Properties dialog box to apply the changes.

The Recycle Bin

You might have noticed that the Recycle Bin wasn't available for deletion when you were customizing the Desktop. Removing the Recycle Bin requires that you obtain a third-party application, and they are plentiful! If you've already obtained TweakUI from **www.Microsoft.com/windowsxp/pro/downloads/powertoys.asp**, you already have the capability. Just open TweakUI, click Desktop, and uncheck Recycle Bin. You'll want to remove the Recycle Bin only if you're trying to create an "icon-less" Desktop. Generally, the Recycle Bin is a necessary icon for the Desktop and we recommend you keep it.

Figure 6-12

Add or remove default Desktop icons in the Desktop Items dialog box.

Create Folders and Program Shortcuts

Having items on the Desktop that you use often can also help you work faster and smarter. You can add folders to the Desktop by either creating shortcuts to existing folders or creating new ones. You can add program shortcuts just as easily.

To create a shortcut to an existing folder that contains documents you access often, simply follow these steps:

1. Browse to the folder using Windows Explorer.

2. Right-click, point to Send To, and click Desktop (Create Shortcut). A shortcut will be placed on the Desktop.

Do this to create a new folder on the Desktop:

1. Right-click an empty area of the Desktop.

2. Point to New, and click Folder.

3. Name the folder, and then drag and drop files in there or add them there as they are created.

To create a shortcut to a program on your Desktop, locate it on the All Programs menu, right-click the icon, and drag it to the Desktop. Select Copy Here when prompted. You'll need to choose Copy Here so that the program will remain available from the Start menu for both you and others who have accounts on your computer. (If you can't find what you want on the All Programs menu, look for it using Windows Explorer.) A shortcut will automatically be created on the Desktop.

Identify the Gunk

Your Desktop probably has icons on it for the Recycle Bin, maybe Internet Explorer or My Computer, and most likely, My Documents. In the last few sections we've focused on adding icons you need. But you probably have a lot of junk you don't need on the Desktop, too. You'll want to decide what you want to get rid of, and later we'll show you how to get rid of it. To start this process, take an inventory of all of the application icons that you currently have and divide this list into the following groups:

√ Applications you can't live without (the ones you use quite regularly)

√ Applications you never use anymore or rarely use

√ Applications you don't even recognize

If you still have too many applications in the first group, you'll need to go through it again and narrow it down to just your top applications. The applications listed in your second group can likely be taken off your Desktop entirely (we'll show you how this is done shortly). For the third group, you should take a little time and review all of the applications you have here and reduce the list down to just the applications you actually need.

Removing Folders and Shortcuts

Removing shortcuts from the Desktop is as easy as right-clicking and choosing Delete. They just go away; no harm done. You can tell an item is a shortcut if it has a little arrow beside it, as shown in Figure 6-13.

You can also right-click and delete default folders like My Documents, My Network Places, My Computer, and Internet Explorer. Even though they aren't technically shortcuts, they'll be safely removed and their contents won't be deleted and moved to the Recycle Bin. However, if you want to remove a folder that *you created* on the Desktop and the folder is *not a shortcut* to another folder, you have to be more careful. If you delete a folder you've created on the Desktop, its contents will be deleted as well. Figure 6-14 shows the warning box you'll see when you try to delete a folder that is not a shortcut to another folder.

Figure 6-13
Removing a shortcut is safe; if
you don't see an arrow,
though, be careful!

Figure 6-14
Be careful when deleting folders you've created that are not shortcuts; their contents will be deleted.

TIP: Folders that are shortcuts to others have a small arrow on them.

Therefore, if you have created a folder on the Desktop and added data to it and
you later decide that you don't want it on the Desktop anymore, your best bet
is to drag and drop the file to another area. You can drag it to the My Documents folder, to somewhere in Windows Explorer, to a separate hard disk, or
even to a network drive. Dragging and dropping moves the file from the Desktop without deleting its contents.

Run the Desktop Cleanup Wizard

Once the Desktop is nice and neat and everything is organized just the way
you want it, configure the Desktop Cleanup Wizard to run every 60 days so
that you can avoid some of the major pitfalls in keeping your Desktop clean.
The Desktop Cleanup Wizard scans the shortcuts on your desktop and determines if they've been used in the past 60 days or if they haven't. If they haven't,
you'll be prompted to let Windows safely remove them.

To run the Desktop Cleanup Wizard and to configure it to run automatically every 60 days, follow these steps:

1. Right-click an empty area of the Desktop (by now that should be easy), and click Properties.
2. Click the Desktop tab and click Customize Desktop.
3. Verify that Run Desktop Cleanup Wizard Every 60 Days is checked.
4. To run the wizard now, click Clean Desktop Now.

Choose Non-System-Intensive Screensavers

If you've chosen a wacky screensaver, one that is complex, one that requires complex calculations, or one you've downloaded from a Web site that can't be trusted to create efficient program code, you might be seeing the effects of running a system-intensive or poorly designed screensaver. When a screensaver is used, the computer must offer up system resources to run it. If you're having problems with system performance, including slow response coming out of a screensaver, a screensaver that hangs or freezes up, or one that locks up the computer, you should switch to a non-system-intensive or a default Windows XP screensaver. Of course, the best option is to select None. This way, absolutely no system resources are used!

Even some of the Windows XP screensavers require a lot of system resources, though. Although one of our computers worked just fine when using the Windows XP Aquarium screensaver, when we upgraded, purchasing new fish and configuring seven of them to swim around on the office Desktop (that had 128 MB of RAM), it was just too much for it. It would hang up and sometimes even lock up the computer. These are common problems.

If you're having screensaver problems, select a screensaver that's not so complex, like the Windows XP screensaver or the Starfield screensaver:

1. Right-click an empty area of the Desktop, and then click Properties.
2. From the Screensaver tab, select a new screensaver.
3. Click OK.

About Themes

If you're concerned about performance, choose one of the default Windows XP themes, like Windows XP or Windows Classic. Other themes may use more resources with their fancy sounds and other amenities. However, if you're in it for the simple pleasure of having a nice background, screensaver, mouse pointer, colors, and interface, and if you have plenty of resources, by all means, browse for and choose a theme!

Here's how to explore additional themes and install them:

1. Right-click an empty area of the Desktop and click Properties.

2. From the Themes tab, use the drop-down list to see the available themes. If you've purchased and installed Microsoft Plus! or other software, you might have some already. If you only have the default themes, click More Themes Online, and click OK.

3. Browse through the information.

TIP: *We'll suggest you stay away from themes unless you have a screaming computer with resources that you don't need. Even our best computer gets sluggish when we apply one!*

Explore Folder Options

The Folder Options icon in the Control Panel offers many ways to enhance your computer's performance, enhance productivity, and enhance how you view windows and folders in Windows XP. To view the available folder options, open the Control Panel and open Folder Options, or right-click the Start menu, choose Explore, click Tools, and click Folder Options. You can also open this dialog box from inside the Control Panel, using the Folder Options icon. The Folder Options dialog box will appear, as shown in Figure 6-15.

You can enhance the performance of your computer by making some changes here:

√ If you have a specific file type that you'd always like to open in a specific program, you can configure file associations using the File Types tab. For example, if you want all of your JPEG files to open in Photoshop instead of Paint or the Windows Picture And Fax Viewer, you can make that change easily. Just click the File Types tab, locate the file type, click Change, and pick a program from the list. See Figure 6-16.

√ If you are running Windows XP on a laptop, if you spend most of your time computing in a non-networked environment, or if you only access one or two specific folders on a network, you can disable the Automatic Search For Network Printers And Folders. While this feature doesn't take up too many system resources, it does continuously scan for changes to shared resources on a network. If you don't need this, disable it from the View menu. It's the first option.

√ Windows creates and caches folder thumbnails in a cache file so that it can reuse them instead of creating new thumbnails each time you open the folder. You'll want Windows to create new folder thumbnails, so verify in the View tab that Do Not Cache Thumbnails is not checked.

Figure 6-15
Configure folder options for better performance.

Figure 6-16
Use Folder Options to change a file's program association.

√ If you are tired of Windows showing you pop-up descriptions for folder and Desktop items, from the View tab, deselect Show Pop-Up Descriptions For Folder And Desktop Items.

√ To change the default double-clicking with the mouse to single-clicking for opening files, from the General tab, make the desired changes.

√ Offline files are files that you copy from a shared folder on a network so that you can work on them while not connected. Upon reconnection, the files are synchronized. Offline files take up a lot of hard disk space, and if you aren't going to need them, don't enable them from the Offline Files tab. Check that tab to verify that this is unchecked.

√ From the View tab, verify that Launch Folder Windows In A Separate Process is not checked. Checking this will cause each program to open in a separate memory space and will slow down your computer's performance.

You should look through the items available to see if there's anything else you'd like to change. We choose to turn off Simple File Sharing, Show Control Panel In My Computer, and Show Hidden Files And Folders. You might decide after researching these options that you feel the same.

TIP: Click the question mark in the top-right corner of the Folder Options dialog box and then click anywhere in the box to get more information about a particular option.

Summing Up

Cleaning up and tweaking the Start menu, Desktop, and Taskbar might seem like simple cosmetic enhancements at first, but they aren't. Making programs readily accessible, having what you need on the Start menu, and using Quick Launch helps *Windows* work faster, and the result of that is that *you* work faster. Cleaning up the System Tray, limiting what programs start automatically when Windows starts, and using non-system-intensive screensavers and themes dramatically increases performance as well. Finally, configuring folder options can also increase performance in a variety of ways, including disabling functions that aren't necessary.

Preventing Spam Gunk

Degunking Checklist:

√ Develop a strategy of having three different e-mail accounts—
primary, backup, and disposable—to minimize spam.

√ Choose a primary e-mail address that is *not* vulnerable to
dictionary attacks.

√ Choose your e-mail client carefully—some clients are "gunk
magnets."

√ Don't post your primary e-mail address on the Web, nor
allow others to do so.

√ Obfuscate (obscure) your primary e-mail address when
posting to Usenet newsgroups.

√ *Never* try to "unsubscribe" from spammer mailings. (It's
really "subscribing" to *more* spam.)

√ Use a "disposable" e-mail address for communicating with
online vendors and discussion boards.

√ Choose, use, and update a separate spam filtering product
to reduce spam.

√ Learn about mail proxies and POPFile.

E-mail is the glue that holds your personal and business computing efforts together. But careless use of e-mail will attract gunk. Unfortunately, only a little carelessness will attract an almost *unimaginable* amount of gunk, in the form of spam. Spam is one of those phenomena where prevention is the very best cure. In this chapter, we'll show you how to degunk your PC by preventing spam from entering your inbox in the first place.

You probably are aware that spam is unwanted commercial e-mail, unless you've been living in a refrigerator box for the past several years. It is generally sent from companies that you have never had dealings with and want no part of. Much or even most spam is fraudulent—get-rich quick schemes, "pump and dump" stock scams, phony penis- and breast-enlargement pills, controlled drugs without a prescription, and so on. Most people agree that when they want to buy online, they will go looking for products. They do *not* want products to come looking for them in the form of spam.

As you'll learn in this chapter, you can do many things to minimize spam. Most of the suggestions are preventive, and only a modest amount of vigilance and housekeeping is required on an ongoing basis. Of course, if you let spam get out of control, you'll have a massive mess to clean up. In Chapter 8, e-mail housecleaning will be covered in more detail, where you'll learn how to clean up and organize your legitimate mail, as well as deal with spam that gets through your defenses. (Alas, some always will.)

Choose the Best E-Mail Addresses

Spam prevention begins with your e-mail address. Smart and serious e-mail users have more than one address to minimize their encounters with spam. There are three general categories of e-mail address that you should set up:

√   Primary e-mail address

√   Backup e-mail address

√   Disposable e-mail addresses

Your primary e-mail address is the one on your business card. You give it to your friends and business associates. It's the address that you want the world to use. It's also the one where you'll be fighting most of your spam battles. Your backup e-mail address should be a second e-mail account obtained from a separate e-mail hosting company that is not tied to your primary address. If the company hosting your primary address is down for some reason, you can then use your backup e-mail address until your primary address comes back online.

Your disposable e-mail addresses are those that you use knowing that you can cancel them at any point and lose nothing. Disposable e-mail addresses are often obtained from free Webmail sites. You generally shouldn't share them with friends and business associates. You use them for online commerce and other circumstances where you don't trust a person or (more likely) a company or Web site not to misuse the address—which mostly means, sell it to spammers. If anyone misuses a disposable address, you simply cancel the address and obtain a new, different one for further use.

Set Up Your Primary E-Mail Address

Your primary e-mail address should be accessible from anywhere. Here are some guidelines you should follow for setting up your primary address:

√ *Your primary address should not be the e-mail address that you obtain when signing up for a broadband Internet connection at home.* Many broadband providers do not allow you access to your e-mail account when you connect to the Internet at a wireless Wi-Fi hotspot or from a dial-up connection.

√ *If you connect via a dial-up network like AOL, that address is suitable as a primary address.* AOL and other similar networks like MSN have many dial-up "points of presence" around the country, and you can get in from any of them.

√ *The best primary e-mail address to have is one associated with a Web hosting account.* Most Web hosting firms offer some number of e-mail addresses (5 to 10 and often as many as 50) with a hosting account for your personal or business Web site. Multiple e-mail accounts are good, in case you have to abandon a primary account for spam reasons (more on this later). You'll find that there are virtues of setting up a primary address in this manner:

   √ You can access the account from anywhere you can connect to the Net. This is *extremely* important if you travel a lot.

   √ The e-mail address will be associated with the name of your domain, so it's easier for people to remember. It will also look "official" and professional. As an example, if your name is Andy Stanton and you own the domain **stantonservices.com**, your e-mail could be **astanton@stantonservices.com** and your web site could be **www.stantonservices.com**.

Set Up Your Backup and Disposable E-Mail Addresses

The address you obtain from your broadband provider makes a good backup address, as does an address from one of the free Webmail sites. Disposable addresses are also best obtained from a Webmail site. Here are a few guidelines to follow:

√   Make your backup e-mail account either your broadband ISP e-mail address or an account with one of the national e-mail providers like AOL. In a pinch, an address from a free Webmail account will do.

√   Obtain one or more disposable e-mail accounts from one of the free Webmail services. (More on using disposable e-mail addresses shortly.)

Avoid Spammer Dictionary Attacks

Many people who register their own personal or business names create an associated e-mail address by using their first name and the domain name. A consultant like our mythical Andy Stanton might register the domain stantonservices.com and create an e-mail account **andy@stantonservices.com**. You'd have to forgive poor Andy for not suspecting how much spam gunk such an address would attract. The problem lies with something called a *dictionary attack*.

Spammers pay nothing per message to send out spam. With broadband access, they can send literally millions of messages per day, making possible a peculiar way to gather e-mail addresses as spam targets. Spammers (using custom mailer utilities intended for spamming) choose a domain, like stantonservices.com, and start cranking out e-mail to addresses in a sequence that might look like this:

Abe@stantonservices.com

Abby@stantonservices.com

Al@stantonservices.com

Alan@stantonservices.com

Albert@stantonservices.com

Andrew@stantonservices.com

Andy@stantonservices.com

Ann@stantonservices.com

Anna@stantonservices.com

These names come from a dictionary of names and common words compiled by spammers from online dictionaries and e-mail addresses that they find on the Web. They use automatic mailer software, which generates small test messages. Many of these test messages have no body text at all. The mailer software keeps track of bounces—messages that come back because an e-mail address does not exist—and purges the address of any bounced message from the list of addresses mailed to. If a generated address receives a message that doesn't bounce, that address is considered "live," and spam will soon begin to be sent to it—*even if the address has never actually been used!*

This is legal, and costs nothing per address. Every day, spammers send literally billions of such test messages looking for new addresses. Avoiding dictionary attacks is simple, if not foolproof, by following these guidelines:

√ *Choose your e-mail address carefully by choosing a name or word that is not in any dictionary.* For example, don't use **andy@stantonservices.com**; instead, use something not easily guessed by a program. This could be your first initial and last name, like **astanton@stantonservices.com**, or something you make up yourself, like **rugster@stantonservices.com**, where "rugster" is a word you make up from whole cloth.

√ Don't use ordinary words that are in the dictionary (even peculiar ones like "hellion" or "symbiont") or words and names from popular culture, like "Gandalf" or "muggle."

√ *String words together, or make up new ones.* A well-known artist hit upon a magnificent e-mail address, which is **slavetohercat@stantonservices.com**. (The domain has been changed to protect her privacy.) She will never be hit in a dictionary attack, that's for sure.

√ *Don't use random strings of letters, like **jkwts@stantonservices.com**.* This looks like a "from" address generated by spammer utilities, and there are now filters that look for random-looking "from" addresses and treat them as spam.

√ *Don't use a middle initial.* It used to be effective to add a middle initial after a common first name, in an address like **AndyR@stantonservices.com**. In recent years, spammers have been cycling through first names and middle initials as well. If you have an unusual first name, it might be effective, but nothing beats a totally made-up word or phrase!

Choose Your E-Mail Client Carefully

You might be surprised to learn that the e-mail client you use makes a tremendous difference in how much gunk your e-mail system collects. This applies to both spam (the subject of this chapter) and e-mail gunk of other kinds, as will be explored in Chapter 8. There are hundreds of e-mail clients out there, many of them free, but a few of them costing much money. In this section, we'll discuss what to look for in a gunk-resistant e-mail client.

Be Careful with Outlook

Because of certain features in both Microsoft Outlook and Outlook Express, clever spammers have developed unique techniques for gunking up these clients with spam. Both these clients fail several crucial gunk tests, none of which are essential to their operation. (This subject will be explored again in Chapter 8, with respect to things other than spam.) The problem with both Outlooks concerning spam is fairly simple: Both are vulnerable to "spam beacons" executed with HTML images. (Some people call them "Web bugs" or "image beacons.") This is another scurvy spammer trick, one even more clever than the dictionary attack mechanism described earlier.

You can protect yourself better with Outlook or Outlook Express by using a third-party spam filtering package that integrates tightly with them. Neither package provides sufficient spam filtering capabilities, and Outlook Express stores what spam filtering word lists it supports in the Registry, which contributes massively to Registry gunk (more on that in Chapter 8).

Newer versions of Outlook have the ability to disable the downloading of "external content"; that is, images and documents that come from remote servers. This feature should defeat spam beacons, but there are several other reasons not to use it, which will be covered in Chapter 8. If you're considering adopting Outlook or Outlook Express, turn to Chapter 8 now and read the appropriate sections. Spam beacons are not the only issue at play here!

Watch Out for Spam Beacons

Understanding spam beacons requires understanding how spammers work. Spammers gather e-mail addresses however they can, via dictionary attacks and Web spiders, or simply by buying existing lists of addresses. They send out messages indiscriminately to millions of addresses. They sometimes remove addresses that bounce messages (more on this later). However, whenever they can verify that an address is good, they copy that address to a special list of verified addresses that they can then sell at a premium price to other spammers.

You do *not* want to verify your address to a spammer. Needless to say, replying to a spam message is one way to verify that your address is good. (You don't actually *buy* things offered in spam messages, do you?) A spam beacon can verify your address to the spammer if you simply open the message—or even preview it in the Outlook preview pane!

Here's how spam beacons work: Nearly all spam these days is formatted as HTML, which allows the embedding of images in text. A spam beacon consists of an image embedded in an HTML e-mail message. This image (which can be part of the message's art or advertising pitch, or even a single white pixel lurking in a corner of the message as a tiny "invisible" image) has a name that is uniquely coded to your e-mail address. The image's name doesn't have to *contain* your e-mail address, but it may contain a long string of numbers or characters that is linked, in the spammer's database, to your e-mail address.

When you open or preview a spam message, any images in the message's HTML are requested and downloaded from the spammer's image server. The server's log records which images are downloaded, and then the spammer database program builds a list of e-mail addresses from which the beacon image was downloaded. *Shazam!* The spammer knows that the message arrived at your inbox intact and was opened for display.

The key to avoiding spam beacons is to avoid downloading images embedded in HTML-formatted messages. One way to do this is never to open a spam message. Some messages, however, are carefully crafted so that you can't easily tell whether it's spam or not. Deceptive message subject headers like "In response to your recent message" may prompt you to open yet another stupid pitch for penis pills. After a while, most of us can smell spam a mile away, but those of us who get lot of mail from people we've never met (contact people at businesses are a good example) get messages that must actually be opened. It's also easy to open spam messages by accident, and it only takes one spam beacon hit to get your e-mail address on yet another list of "preferred" addresses.

The central spam problem with Outlook Express and versions of Outlook prior to Outlook 2003 is that there is no good way with either program to inspect the text of a message without also downloading the message's images. The versions of Outlook and Outlook Express in question both use Internet Explorer to display the message body. There is a way to disable image downloads in Explorer, but if you do, you can't use Internet Explorer to surf the Web and see images on Web pages. Worse, if you receive a message containing images that you *do* want to see (and there are lots of legitimate e-mail newsletters that contain images), there is no way to selectively turn image downloading off for individual messages.

Because the preview pane is simply an IE window, previewing a message in the preview pane is no different from opening it in a separate window. The images come down from the spammer's server, and the spammer has your number.

Use Alternative E-Mail Clients

When you go shopping for gunk-resistant e-mail clients, your top priority should be to look for features that circumvent spam beacons. There are two ways that e-mail clients finesse spam beacons:

√   Very simple e-mail clients don't render HTML tags at all and simply display whatever text is in the message. Because images are downloaded by the HTML <IMG> tag, this defeats spam beacons completely—but it also prevents you from seeing images in mail that you request or otherwise want to read. The client PCPine is free and perhaps the best example in this class, though it is *not* for beginners.

√ More sophisticated clients provide features for you to turn image downloads on and off *on a per-message basis.* They have a button allowing you to toggle image downloading on and off. Typically, you turn image downloading off and only turn it on if you receive a message containing images that you want to see. Highlight that message, and toggle images on. *Don't forget to toggle images off again before you move the message highlight bar to another message!*

The following e-mail clients from the second category include ways to defeat spam beacons. There are certainly others, and you should look closely before installing any client!

√ Poco Mail 2.6 and later allows you to "sanitize" a message by preventing image downloading on a per-message basis or alternatively (with V3.0) stripping out HTML tags entirely before display. (Earlier versions lack this feature.) The cost is $35. Visit **www.pocomail.com**.

√ Mozilla Thunderbird V1.0 allows the disabling of image downloads from the Options window, but it does not provide image disabling on a per-message basis as Poco does. Thunderbird is free and looks a great deal like Outlook Express, for which it is an excellent replacement. Visit **www.mozilla.org/ products/thunderbird/**.

√ Pegasus mail V4.1 calls spam beacons "Web bugs," but it's the same villain. Pegasus allows you to prevent image downloading, though not in as flexible a manner as you can with Poco. Pegasus is an excellent program and has the advantage of being free. Visit **www.pmail.com**.

√ Eudora V6 allows you to disable downloading of images from e-mail messages. The product is generally good, but at $50 it is significantly more expensive than PocoMail without being significantly more capable. Visit **www.eudora.com**.

Use Your E-Mail Address Carefully

If you're not careful about what you do with your primary e-mail address, nothing else matters. Once spammers lay hands on your primary e-mail address, they will send you spam forever. Verifying to spammers that your e-mail address is "live" and working (as explained in the previous section) definitely makes things worse, but as best as we in the industry can tell, addresses never "time-out," and experiments have shown that spam will be sent for years to an address picked up by spammers only once.

The following sections explain what *not* to do with your e-mail address, and why. None of this is any guarantee against ever getting spam in your inbox. Use an address long enough and spam happens. In general, you can't tell how a spammer gets your address, so trying to figure it out after it happens is pointless.

Never "Unsubscribe" from a Spammer Mailing List

Ever find it funny that a spam message rarely gives any crisp information concerning who and where the spammer is, but almost always includes a link to "unsubscribe"? That's because unsubscribing from a spammer's mailing list is *always* a hoax and a lie. The whole purpose of that unsubscribe link is to verify that your e-mail address is "live" and functional and that whoever it belongs to pays enough attention to their e-mail to attempt to get off of a spammer's list. That tags you not only as a live address but as a good prospect, one that the spammer can sell to other spammers for a good deal of money.

Never Post (or Let Others Post) Your E-Mail Address on the Web

Getting new addresses to spam is one of a spammer's highest priorities, and they go to great technological lengths to snag them. In the late 1990s, spammers took a hint from Web search engines and created "Web crawlers," or "spiders," that simply pulled down Web page after Web page, 24/7, and searched for that telltale @ symbol. If your e-mail address (which contains one of those @ symbols) happened to be in one of those Web pages, you were hosed, er, spammed.

The lesson is plain: Do *not* post your e-mail address in "naked" form on your Web page. The spamspiders are still out there, crawling day and night. Furthermore, make it clear to your friends and other contacts that they cannot post your e-mail address on the Web. This is a problem for people who are publicly known for some reason and people who serve on nonprofit boards and other things for which Web contacts are useful.

TIP: If you create a Web page for or serve as an officer or other significant figure in an organization with a Web page, use a disposable address for your entry in the "contacts" section of that Web page.

The only unbreakable (so far, at least) workaround for the spamspiders is to render your e-mail address in a graphic image and post the graphic image on the Web. The spamspiders are searching for text, so if there is no text associated with the image, there's nothing for them to grab. The downside to this is that people cannot simply click on the image and bring up an e-mail edit window, but that may be the price you have to pay.

Many people have written and used clever JavaScript functions that "obfuscate" (obscure) an e-mail address in the JavaScript source code, which then assembles it "on the fly" into a cleartext (readable) e-mail address when someone clicks on the link. This may reduce the number of spamspider hits, but it has two disadvantages:

√ No such system is unbreakable, and there are spammers who brag about their efforts to break JavaScript obfuscation code. Web spiders have been written that parse and execute JavaScript code copied from Web pages, and if the code can turn an obfuscated address into cleartext, the spider can, too. Because systems like this are an affront to spammers' intelligence, they are willing to expend enormous effort to break them—and once broken, they're broken forever.

√ The number is uncertain, but somewhere between 10 percent and 15 percent of all Web browsers disable JavaScript completely, and people using those browsers will not be able to click on your JavaScript obfuscated address link anyway.

Obfuscate Your E-Mail Address on Newsgroups and Discussion Boards

Just as there are spamspiders that crawl the Web searching for e-mail addresses to spam, there are spiders that download and scan Usenet newsgroups and Web discussion board postings for e-mail addresses. Postings to newsgroups and discussion boards often require the entry of an e-mail address of some kind. Some people who post anonymously simply make up a phony address, but if you want people to be able to reach you apart from the newsgroup or discussion board, obfuscating an address is necessary.

The idea is to create an address that is "broken" in a way that a spider cannot fix but that any reasonably intelligent human being can. For example, here are a couple of obfuscated forms of Andy Stanton's e-mail address, **rugster@stantonservices.com**:

rugster@stantonNOSPAMservices.com

rugster@stantonPULLTHISservices.com

As given, these addresses will bounce, unless you delete the "NOSPAM" or "PULLTHIS" text.

This system worked well for many years, but spammers (to whom such mechanisms are a terrible affront) have created ever more sophisticated spiders. These days, spiders are regularly searching for blocks of uppercase letters within an address that is otherwise completely in lowercase and stripping out anything in uppercase.

The current solution (current for how long, we're not sure) is to mix cases in an obfuscation, like this:

rugster@stantonPuLLThISservices.com

It takes a little more thought to remove the obfuscation, but most people (especially those used to the conventions of newsgroups and discussion boards) will catch on quickly.

By the way, it's now unwise to use the word "spam" in an obfuscation, whether in upper- or lowercase. Some have tried to spell it backwards, but "MAPS" has other meanings and can be confusing to newcomers.

One final note about discussion groups: Many people have reported that signing up for a Yahoo! Groups account opened the gates to huge quantities of spam, even though Yahoo! insists it does not sell lists of e-mail addresses to spammers. This has happened to many people in our immediate acquaintance, so we strongly recommend *against* creating a Yahoo Groups account.

Use Disposable E-Mail Addresses for E-Commerce

The largest and best-known e-commerce retailers like Amazon.com can probably be trusted not to sell your e-mail address to spammers. (They have too much to lose if it ever came out, for way too small a financial gain.) Unfortunately, midsize and especially smaller retailers are another matter. When creating an account with online retailers, always use a disposable e-mail address. These are e-mail addresses obtained from one of the many free e-mail services that are everywhere on the Web. They cost nothing, and when an address inevitably becomes a spam magnet, it can be discarded and another one obtained.

Nearly all e-mail clients of any consequence can support multiple e-mail accounts, with one e-mail address per account. Here are the steps to follow:

1. Set up a separate account for each address you use.
2. When you click the check mail button, the client will read them all and deposit all the mail from any of the several accounts in your inbox.

3. Consider creating a filter that will deposit all the mail sent to a disposable address (say, one devoted to use with a single e-commerce retailer) into a specific mail folder. Creating filters can be an advanced topic, and it's always very specific to a particular mail client. Whatever mail client you use, read your documentation and give it a try. Filtering can be very useful, even though it takes some practice to get it right.

If you limit the use of a disposable address to a single vendor, you'll be able to tell quickly if that vendor is selling your address to spammers, especially if you direct all mail sent to that address to a single folder. If the vendor does sell your address, write an angry letter to the people in charge there, indicating that you'll never buy anything from them again. It's the only way we'll ever break them of that habit!

Services That Manage Disposable E-Mail Addresses

There are online sites that offer paid services for creating and managing disposable e-mail addresses:

www.emailias.com

www.spamex.com

www.spamgourmet.com

All these sites work pretty much the same way, by allowing you to create what amounts to a self-destructing e-mail alias for your primary e-mail address. These aliases can then be sent to e-commerce retailers, and after a predetermined amount of time, or a predetermined number of messages sent back to the address, the address self-destructs.

These services are not hideously expensive ($9 to $20 per year, typically), but some of them allow you to make the mistake of replying to a message with your real e-mail address in the From field, which completely negates any benefit to using the services. Because there are so many free e-mail services out there, we don't recommend the use of online disposable e-mail services. Just get an account with BoxFrog or one of the multitude of others and use the address until spam kills it. It's as simple as that.

Use a Separate Spam Filtering Utility

As hard as you may try to avoid being spam bait, there's really no getting around it: Sooner or later they'll find you and the spam will begin arriving. The only way to deal with spam once it actually happens is to use some sort of spam filtering technology. Spam filtering is done when a program of some kind (whether your e-mail client or a separate spam filtering utility) inspects an incoming e-mail message and decides whether it's legitimate or spam. How it makes this decision is crucial, but how that decision is made may also be highly technical and difficult to describe.

In this section, we'll explain how spam filtering works and suggest how to use it to divide your spam from your "ham" (your legitimate e-mail).

A Short Spam Filtering Glossary

The best way to start is to define a few terms from the jargon associated with spam filtering. Most spam filtering products use more than one means of making the spam/ham decision, and you'll have to understand what they are to make them work.

Bayesian filtering. This is a fascinating technology that allows a spam filter to "learn" how to spot spam by using statistical analysis of message length and the distribution of words present in a message. Basically, you pass a certain number (at least 100) messages through a Bayesian filter and somehow indicate to the filter (generally by clicking a button) whether each message is spam or legitimate e-mail. The filter analyzes what words tend to be in spam versus real e-mail and then uses that analysis to "guess" whether a message is spam or not. If you're persistent about training a Bayesian filter, the filter gets better with each message it analyzes, and after a week or so its "guesses" will be accurate to better than 90 percent, and probably closer to 95 percent. Later in this section, we'll explain how to use POPFile, a completely free Bayesian spam filter that works very well.

Blacklist. A blacklist is a list of e-mail addresses or Internet domains from which all mail is to be considered spam and discarded. No further analysis is done. If a message's sender or the sender's domain is on the blacklist, it's spam. Some e-mail clients call this a *blocked senders list* or *banned senders list.*

False negative. When a spam message is mistakenly identified as a legitimate message, this is a false negative. A false negative will show up in your inbox with all your legitimate e-mail and you will have to delete it manually. It is very difficult to eliminate false negatives entirely, and if you try, you may increase the rate of false positives (see the next entry), which are *much* worse.

False positive. When a legitimate e-mail message is tagged as spam (and, worse, discarded with the rest of the trash), it's called a false positive. These are the bane of spam filters, and your main job will be to tweak your spam filter technology so that your false positive rate goes to zero. Doing so may increase your false negatives, but those are easier to deal with.

Magnet. This is a term used primarily by POPFile, but other filtering technologies are beginning to adopt it. A magnet is a user-defined term or address that "pulls" a message toward a spam classification or a non-spam classification. In POPFile, for example, if you create a magnet based on seeing your boss's e-mail address in the From field, that magnet will "pull" all messages from your boss into your inbox as real e-mail. On the flip side, you can define a magnet based on the word "Viagra" that will "pull" any messages with "Viagra" in the subject line to the trash folder, or to wherever else you banish spam. More on this later, in the description of POPFile.

Mail proxy. Nearly all e-mail clients allow some sort of spam filtering. However, many of the best spam filtering products are not e-mail clients at all but *mail proxies,* or programs that insert themselves between your e-mail client and the POP server from which your e-mail is delivered. All your e-mail passes through the mail proxy, which then filters for spam and either deletes it or marks it so that your e-mail client can delete it after you inspect it. POPFile, Norton AntiSpam, and McAfee SpamKiller are all mail proxies.

Whitelist. Many e-mail clients allow you to create a whitelist, which is a list of e-mail addresses or Internet domains from which you will always accept e-mail as legitimate. Your whitelist would thus contain the e-mail addresses of people and organizations that you trust—such as your spouse, friends, children, and coworkers—or newsletters or e-mail lists that you subscribe to. (A whitelist is the reverse of a blacklist.) Many spam filtering products allow you to import your Windows address book as a ready-made whitelist, under the reasonable assumption that your address book does *not* contain the addresses of spammers! (But because some spammers take advantage of this by forging the sender address as your address, do *not* put your own e-mail address in your whitelist!)

Filtering within Your E-Mail Client Is Not Enough

Virtually all e-mail clients have some ability to filter e-mail based on words found in the various message header fields or the message body. Some e-mail clients make this filtering easier to use than others. Perhaps the best in terms of filtering is PocoMail, especially in adding senders or whole domains to the blacklist. In PocoMail, you can right-click a message in the summary window and, from the context menu, choose to ban either the sender (for example,

kgrtn@spammer.com) or the whole domain (spammer.com.) This is *much* easier than in Outlook or Outlook Express, where several levels of dialog boxes must be traversed to ban a sender or domain.

If you get only a little spam, PocoMail or something like it may be all you need. However, simple sender or key word filters like those found in e-mail clients are becoming less and less effective as spammers become ever more clever at providing fewer "hooks" for a keyword filter to grab. Most modern spam has become exceedingly vague, using short, common words as much as possible. The worst spam (offering porn and drugs) is almost always sent using forged headers, which is something few e-mail clients can detect on their own.

Combating spam effectively, especially if you get more than 20 spam messages per day, really requires a separate spam filtering utility. There are many, and although most are commercial products, several free products exist. If you're shopping for a commercial product, be sure that the following is true:

√   *It supports your e-mail client and/or your e-mail service.* Some spam filtering products do not support MAPI e-mail systems, for example, or will work only with a short list of popular e-mail clients, typically Outlook, Outlook Express, and Eudora. Most spam filtering utilities do *not* work with Webmail accounts.

√   *You understand the costs and installation limitations.* Some products require an annual subscription fee. Many now require "activation," meaning that the software "phones home" for permission to run and cannot be installed on more than one computer in your home.

How Mail Proxies Work

Nearly all stand-alone spam filtering utilities are mail proxies. Unless you have some experience in the server world, the term "mail proxy" is probably new to you. In the simplest possible terms, a mail proxy is a software utility that you insert between your mail client and your mail server to process your e-mail before it is delivered to your inbox.

Mail proxies can be used for various purposes, but nearly all are used to filter spam. This filtering can be done in several ways, and many filtering utilities use several different methods to separate spam from legitimate e-mail, including whitelists, blacklists, keyword and key phrase filters, and Bayesian statistical analysis. Typically, a mail proxy will look at a message in the light of its various filtering technologies and then decide whether it's spam or legitimate. The mail proxy will then mark the message somehow, often by inserting a short tag at the beginning of the subject line, and then send it down to the e-mail client.

The e-mail client still has a part in the filtering task: It looks at the markers added by the mail proxy and routes anything marked as spam to its trash folder and anything marked as legitimate e-mail to its inbox.

This process is shown in Figure 7-1. The mail server is somewhere off on the Internet, typically owned and operated by your Internet service provider (ISP). The mail proxy and e-mail client are both programs that run on your PC, which is represented by the shaded box. When your e-mail client sends out its request for new mail, this request (which usually goes directly to the server) passes through the mail proxy. The mail proxy passes on the request for new e-mail to the server, which delivers new e-mail to the proxy. The proxy inspects and marks the new e-mail and then passes it on down to the e-mail client.

Figure 7-1
E-mail downloaded through a mail proxy.

In a sense, the mail proxy has two different "faces." From the perspective of the e-mail client, the proxy looks like an e-mail server. The proxy accepts requests for new mail and sends mail back to the client. From the perspective of the e-mail server, the proxy looks like an e-mail client. The proxy sends the server a username and password and accepts the mail that the server sends back. This allows both the client and the server to operate pretty much as they always did, when they only spoke to one another, without the mail proxy in between.

A mail proxy must be configured with your e-mail account information because it acts as an e-mail client "by proxy" when communicating with your e-mail server. How this is done varies by product, so follow the installer wizard or other documentation for the product that you choose. In the next section, we'll explain how to configure POPFile, one of the best spam filter products that you'll find anywhere.

POPFile: Excellent...and Free!

One of the most popular spam filtering utilities out there is also one of the most effective, as well as among the cheapest: Free! For these reasons, we'll explain POPFile in detail in this section. POPFile is a trainable Bayesian filter built into a mail proxy, and in our tests, it has managed to eliminate as much as 99 percent of incoming spam. (Most people report POPFile success rates of between 96 and 98 percent.) You have to be diligent about training it and keeping it trained over time, but if you do, the results are nothing short of magical.

POPFile is free and open source, and it may be downloaded from this URL:

http://popfile.sourceforge.net

POPFile is downloaded as a zip file containing a single setup.exe file. Once you download and unzip it, run setup.exe. It installs just as any Windows application installs, using a wizard that asks you questions until it knows enough to complete and configure the installed program. You can safely accept all the install wizard's default values until you get to the Buckets screen.

POPFile and Its Buckets

Most of the way through the POPFile install, you'll be shown a dialog box that asks you to choose the buckets that you'll need when using POPFile. A bucket is simply POPFile's name for a category into which e-mail may be classified. By default, POPFile creates four buckets on install: Inbox, Spam, Personal, and Work. Unless you intend to do more with POPFile than simply separate spam from ham, you only need the Inbox and Spam buckets. To eliminate the other two, check Remove for them before clicking Continue, as shown in Figure 7-2.

With the Inbox and Spam buckets defined, POPFile's install can go to completion, after which it will begin working. A yellow octopus icon will appear in the System Tray.

Configuring Your E-Mail Client to Use POPFile

The only real subtlety in configuring POPFile for simple spam filtering actually lies in setting up the mail server addresses in your e-mail client. POPFile itself requires almost no configuration at all. It doesn't need to know your mail server's address. It gets that from your e-mail client.

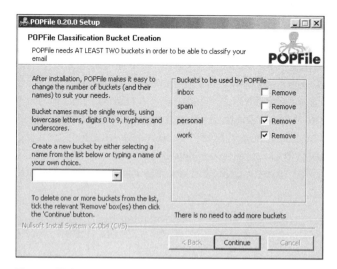

Figure 7-2
Removing unnecessary POPFile buckets.

What you need to do is find the place in your e-mail client where addresses for mail servers are displayed and edited and change them in the following fashion:

1. Change the address of the POP e-mail server that delivers your e-mail to 127.0.0.1. That is the IP address on which POPFile "listens" for commands and from which it delivers mail. From the perspective of your e-mail client, POPFile is your POP mail server.

2. This is the tricky one: Change the value in the username field to the real name of your POP mail server followed by a colon and the username you use to log into that server. For example, if the name of Andy Stanton's POP server is **mail.stantonservices.com** and his username is **astanton**, the value he would need to enter here is **mail.stantonservices.com:astanton**. (Bold is used for clarity only.)

What happens here is that, when Andy Stanton clicks the button directing his e-mail client to check mail, his e-mail client will send the string **mail.stantonservices.com:astanton** to POPFile at the IP address 127.0.0.1. POPFile separates the mail server name and the username and uses those two separate strings to log into the remote POP server. Once the connection has been established, the e-mail client sends its password to POPFile, and POPFile simply passes it along to the remote POP server. After that, the conversation between the mail client and the mail server continues normally until the connection opens for the downloading of new mail from the POP server.

Using and Training POPFile

POPFile is unobtrusive and runs silently in the background. You'll know it's working if you see a little yellow octopus icon in your Windows System Tray. (It's not a very good icon, and at very high screen resolutions, it may look like a nondescript yellow splotch.) You don't have to tell POPFile to download mail. You tell your e-mail client to download mail and the client requests mail from POPFile. POPFile then requests mail from your remote POP mail server and examines the mail as it passes through on the way to your e-mail client. Unless you configure it otherwise, it will add a little prefix to the subject header of each message: [spam] or [inbox]. This allows your e-mail client to filter messages to either the trash (for spam) or to your inbox.

That's all you have to do! The real work in using POPFile lies in training it. After you bring e-mail down to your e-mail client, you must double-click the octopus icon in the System Tray to bring up POPFile's management window, which will appear in your default Web browser. Click on the History link in the upper-left corner and you'll see a screen like the one shown in Figure 7-3.

Figure 7-3
The POPFile History screen.

The History screen contains one line for each message that has passed through POPFile. A message will remain in the History screen until you delete it. You can delete messages from the underlying History database one message at a time, an entire screen of messages at a time, or all messages (however many there might be) at once.

Note that each message has a classification; in Figure 7-3, all three messages shown are classified as spam. If all messages are classified correctly, nothing further needs to be done and you can delete the messages from the History screen. If any messages are misclassified, you can train POPFile to do better by changing the classification shown. This is done by selecting a new classification from the drop-down list to the right of the classification link. This pull-down list will contain all buckets defined within POPFile, and in most cases, it will consist of only Spam and Inbox. Change the classification of any messages that you consider misclassified, and then click the Reclassify button. POPFile will change the classification of those messages and redisplay the History screen with the new classifications displayed.

TIP: *If you forget to click the Reclassify button after changing a message's classification, the training will not "take." Also, once you delete a message line from the History screen, you can no longer go back and reclassify it. Make sure you're certain of message classifications before you delete messages from History!*

POPFile does its best to come to a reliable decision on which bucket a message belongs in. However, when the decision proves difficult to make according to its statistical model, POPFile may punt and call a message "unclassified." It is then up to you to train POPFile to put the unclassified message in the correct bucket. Each time you do this, POPFile's model becomes a little sharper and POPFile will make future decisions more accurately.

The more messages that pass through POPFile, the more "certain" it becomes of its classification decisions. When you first install POPFile, it will "know" nothing and will call all messages "unclassified." Over the first few days, you will probably be changing a lot of message classifications. You'll be reasonably busy training for probably the first couple of weeks, but after a month POPFile should be accurate well over 90 percent of the time, and probably higher than that. (One of the consolations of getting a hundred or more spams a day is that POPFile will learn *very* quickly to distinguish between spam and ham.) Achieving accuracy well over 90 percent depends on savvy use of POPFile's magnets, as explained in the following section.

Creating POPFile Magnets

After POPFile has been at work for awhile on your system, it may begin to seem that it's uncanny how well it picks out real mail from spam. There are some circumstances under which it stumbles, however, and the most important of those concerns mail that you may actually want but that looks like spam to POPFile.

Often the difference between spam and an e-mail newsletter is nothing more than your own choice: A company may send you a newsletter, and you may find it useful or interesting, even if it's peppered with sales pitches. However, if it resembles other newsletters that companies or spammers send you that you *don't* want, POPFile may have trouble telling the difference.

The solution is to define a POPFile *magnet* to "pull" a spammy-looking but useful newsletter to the inbox bucket. Even if a message would otherwise be tagged by POPFile as spam, a magnet can be defined to override POPFile's classification and tag the message "[inbox]" instead.

Magnets are also useful when you must have e-mail conversations about topics that spammers love, like mortgages and prescription drugs. Mention the sleeping pill Ambien in an e-mail message, and if the recipient gets the usual flood of drug spam, your message may end up in the recipient's spam bin.

Be careful not to use magnets the wrong way. Don't just define a magnet for every person in your address book. The problem with messages pulled one way or the other by magnets is that magnets override POPFile's normal decisions, and let message pass through POPFile unexamined. *Messages pulled by magnets don't teach POPFile anything.* If you use magnets on all your legitimate correspondents, POPFile won't learn to recognize messages from them. It'll pull those messages to your inbox, but it may also begin to make mistakes and pull spam to your inbox or other legitimate messages not covered by magnets to your spam bin.

TIP: *If among your regular e-mail correspondents is someone who sends you forwarded attachments, works in an industry whose terminology (like drugs or mortgages) is favored by spammers, or talks about great deals over at the Mall, that person may end up in your spam bucket more than other people. Create a magnet to your inbox with that person's e-mail address, and (like it or not) their messages will never be identified as spam.*

Creating a magnet is done from the Magnets screen, shown in Figure 7-4. There is some helpful explanation right on the Magnets screen, but the process is really very simple: You specify the type of magnet, which in POPFile's context indicates which e-mail message field to look in. You can choose the From field, the To field, and the Subject field. The value is the word, phrase, e-mail address, or domain to look for in that field. A partial match is still a match; in other words, the e-mail address **tjkqv@spammer.com** will match "spammer.com." "RC Model" matches both "RC Model Boats" and "RC Model Aircraft" Finally, you specify the bucket into which a matching message will always go. POPFile can be used to classify legitimate e-mail into any number of buckets, but most users simply specify two buckets: Spam and the

---

Create New Magnet

These types of magnets are available:

- **From address or name:** For example: john@company.com to match a specific address,
  company.com to match everyone who sends from company.com,
  John Doe to match a specific person, John to match all Johns
- **To/Cc address or name:** Like a From: magnet but for the To:/Cc: address in a message
- **Subject words:** For example: hello to match all messages with hello in the subject

Magnet type:

Subject ▾

Values:

[RC Model News]

Always goes to bucket:

inbox ▾   Create

Figure 7-4
Creating a POPFile magnet.

legitimate mail bucket, called Inbox. You can define separate folders (and magnets) for email newsletters, but there are gunk hazards in doing so. See Chapter 8.

When you have all three fields filled out, simply click the Create button to create the magnet.

Now, what magnets should you create? Here are some guidelines:

√   Create an inbox magnet for each e-commerce company with whom you do repeat business. E-mail from online retailers is easily mistaken for spam—after all, a lot of spam is from online retailers whom you've never heard of. If you buy books from Amazon.com, create a magnet for Amazon.com. If you use eBay, create a magnet for eBay, and so on.

√   Create an inbox magnet for each e-mail newsletter or list server to which you subscribe. Spammers often call their messages newsletters, so it's easy to mistake a real newsletter for a fake one.

√   On an ongoing basis, create an appropriate magnet for senders or subjects that POPFile tends to misclassify. POPFile can seem mysterious at times, so when you discern any pattern in what it's getting wrong, try to figure out a magnet to pull similar messages in the proper direction.

Avoid Triggering Other People's Spam Filters

While keeping spam out of your own inbox is probably much on your mind these days, keeping the messages that you send out of *other* people's spam filters is something you should also be thinking about. Here are a few tips to help you keep your mail from "looking like" spam:

√ *Avoid putting certain words in the subject header.* These include "free," "insurance," "mortgage," "penis," "enlargement," "refinance" and the names of many popular drugs, including Viagra, Xanaxx, Vicodin, Ambien, Hydrocodone, Lortabs, Valium, Levitra, and so on. Watch the spam that comes into your own inbox and avoid the distinctive words used in their subject headers. If you work in a field that uses certain spam-favored terms like "mortgage," "refinance," or "meds," try to keep them out of your subject line, if possible.

√ *Avoid using certain words in the body of your message.* The big offender here is "unsubscribe," which many people filter out as a sure-fire spam tell-tale. Don't write things that sound like a sales pitch if you can avoid it. Phrases like "limited time," "great deals," and so on will trigger a lot of spam filters, as will any verbiage that comes from the gutter or can be mistaken for gutter talk by a spam filter. (The sad poster child here is "summa cum laude.")

√ *Avoid including images in your e-mail.* Many people have become so desperate to filter spam (much of which uses images) that they filter on the HTML <IMG> tag and consign any message containing an <IMG> tag to the trash folder. If you have a need to send an image to someone, it might make more sense to direct them to a file on your FTP site (if you have one). You could also tell them in a separate e-mail that you're sending an image so that they can watch their spam folder.

√ *Send your e-mail as plain text rather than HTML.* Spam is most often sent as text formatted with HTML because many spammer tricks depend on HTML tags and comments. If you send plain text rather than HTML, many Bayesian filters will be more inclined to consider your note as legitimate.

√ *Make sure your PC's system clock is correct.* This is an odd one, but for reasons unclear (and spammers *always* have reasons!), much spam is sent with incorrect dates and times in the "time sent" field. We have heard reports of spam being sent that is two or three years old—and more than a few that are from several years in the future! (It is as easy to forge dates in the Sent field as anything else in e-mail headers.) Some major e-mail systems have begun to tag such misdated mail as spam. So if your PC thinks it's running in the year 2000, your e-mail will be sent with a 2000 date on it—and other people's mail servers may call it spam.

Summing Up

This chapter is about preventing spam from getting into your inbox. Spam is by far your worst e-mail problem. If you get enough e-mail, the sheer quantity of spam can be a source of gunk all by itself, especially as the years roll by. A modest amount of work can drastically reduce the amount of spam you receive. Learn how to avoid attracting spam to begin with, but also study filtering technology to automatically nuke the inevitable spam that does arrive. Your best spam solution is probably the free POPFile Bayesian spam filtering utility. It requires a little study, but nothing else in the spam-fighting world comes even close!

Cleaning Up E-Mail Gunk

Degunking Checklist:

√ Learn how to keep your current e-mail from going "under the fold" in your inbox.

√ Create a system of folders for classifying e-mail you want to keep.

√ Isolate time-delimited e-mails in folders that can be deleted or archived to CD after they're no longer relevant.

√ Don't retain e-mails with large binary attachments. Save the attachments elsewhere and delete them from your e-mail folders.

√ Inspect your attachments folder (if you have one) and delete binary files that have been saved elsewhere.

√ Check your outbox and drafts folders to make sure gunk isn't accumulating there.

√ Check to see if copies of your mailbase from previous e-mail clients are still on your hard drive.

√ Consider using a "file shredder" utility so that sensitive personal or financial data cannot be recovered after deletion.

Most households have something (usually in the kitchen) affectionately called a "junk drawer." It's the drawer where stuff gathers that doesn't fall into any of the other major stuff categories. If it's not pots, pans, silverware, or kitchen gadgets, well…throw it in the junk drawer.

The junk drawer is the place originally intended to hold just a few things: scissors, a ruler, and maybe a little box of rubber bands. Over the years, however, people end up tossing in wine corks with clever designs, 17 promotional beer openers gathered at home-and-garden shows, coupons, poker chips that Mom found under the refrigerator, Dad's spare sunglasses, old toothbrushes used to scrub grout, loose screws that fell out of something, and on and on and on. Eventually you have to dig hard just to find the scissors—assuming they're still in there somewhere.

Without realizing it, most people have allowed their e-mail inboxes to become e-mail junk drawers. Messages accumulate for many reasons, but they *do* accumulate, and before you know it you have hundreds—even thousands!—of messages sitting around. The oldest are forgotten, and it doesn't take long for any single message to pass "under the fold" (that is, scroll off the bottom of the display) and quickly slip your mind, perhaps for good.

The public has had access to the Internet for more than 10 years now. E-mail is no longer a new technology, and people who have used it heavily over the years can gather a great deal of e-mail that isn't spam. This "wanted" e-mail becomes gunk when it is simply forgotten or can no longer be located within the mass of other messages. In this chapter, we'll talk about how to keep your e-mail from congealing into endless megabytes of gunk. We're not dealing with spam here; for that, see Chapter 7. This is about the organization and housekeeping of your *mailbase*; that is, the body of "real" messages that actually matter to you.

Keep, Hold, or Pitch?

As with spam, the best way to eliminate "real" e-mail gunk is to prevent it from piling up in the first place. This requires that you think hard about each message as it comes in. In general, any e-mail message falls into one of three categories:

√   Mail with lasting value, which should be retained indefinitely.

√   Mail associated with a current project or otherwise limited by a calendar date that needs to be held for a period of time and then either archived or deleted.

√   Mail that can be dealt with right now and then deleted immediately.

These three categories of mail require action that you could characterize as "keep," "hold," or "pitch." Each time you look at a message entering your inbox, those three words should be kept in mind.

The 100-Message Rule

Most people who depend on e-mail try to adhere to a 100-message rule for their inboxes. Keep an eye on the number of messages your inbox contains, and when it tops 100, budget some time *right now* to get it down to about 50—or fewer. When you have more than 100 messages in your inbox, chances are that the oldest will be forgotten and just sit there gathering dust, making searches more difficult and time consuming.

If you're *really* disciplined, try to adhere to a one-screen rule. In other words, keep no more messages in your inbox than will display on a single screen. If you're busy and communicate a lot over e-mail, this will be extremely hard. Don't feel like a failure if you can't manage it. It's an ideal to strive for, not a requirement!

Is Autosorting a Good Idea?

Most e-mail clients have built-in general-purpose filtering machinery. With a little cleverness, you can create a filter to move incoming mail out of your inbox automatically, assuming you have someplace else to put it. (We'll cover creating a folder hierarchy for your e-mail in the next major section.) Most people think of e-mail filters in connection with spam, but in truth, filters have other uses.

For example, many people belong to e-mail mailing lists (often informally called Cleaning Up E-Mail Gunk *listservs*), which are party-line forums conducted over e-mail and associated with a given topic. For example, a listserv might be devoted to people who fly radio-controlled model airplanes as a hobby. Many of these lists have a lot of members who generate a great deal of e-mail, and these messages can gunk up your inbox very quickly. A filter can be created to look for some characteristic element in e-mail coming from that listserv and automatically move messages that satisfy the filter to a folder created specifically for that list traffic.

Many mailing lists add a tag to the beginning of the subject line of messages sent out from the listserv. For example, the tag [RC-Airmodels] might be added to the beginning of the subject line of mail sent from a radio-controlled model listserv. You can set up a filter to look for "[RC-Airmodels]" and move all messages bearing that tag to a folder you create for them.

This may sound useful, but it's a two-edged sword. Out of sight, out of mind. It's true—but "out of sight, forever in your mailbase" can be just as true. If you don't diligently classify and cull mail from listservs as it comes in, you run the risk of having *huge* quantities of mail piling up in a folder somewhere. Some of that may be worth keeping, but a lot may be irrelevant chatter, and if you use autosorting to put off the necessary decision making until later, you may be faced with having to read and judge hundreds of messages in one sitting, which would make anyone cross-eyed and after awhile may drive you to simply nuke everything in a fury of frustration.

It's Psychology, not Technology!

Deciding what messages to keep and what to pitch is really a matter of psychology rather than technology. You have to make those decisions sometime, and although technology can make some of those decisions easier, it can't make all of them for you. It's very easy to convince yourself that almost any message needs to be saved forever. Who knows whether it'll become useful in the future? Well, nobody—and that's what judgment is all about.

If you're really nervous about nuking messages, you can always consider the extra work of archiving them onto a CD so that they're not irretrievably lost. Almost certainly better is to develop the discipline of just letting them go. Time is precious these days—almost no one goes back and reads old e-mail "just for fun." Unless it has an objectively identifiable value for the future—financial or legal records, family history discussions, unique technical advice, or content that you can refer back to and use, things like that—steel yourself to just let it go. Here are some pointers to keep in mind when the fate of an e-mail message hangs in the balance:

√   *Is it relevant to legal or tax matters?* Most tax records need to be kept for seven years. E-mail invoices for business expenses, correspondence with your accountant, or anything you would need to either file a tax return or defend in an audit should be retained for at least those seven years.

√   *Does it really contain factual information?* Even if a message seems to be in a "keep" category, look closely. Does the message really contain factual information? Or does it simply say, "Got it! Looks good! Thanks!"

√   *Does the message stand alone?* Ask yourself if the message can be understood by itself or must it be read with other messages in a "thread" to be understood? Some e-mail clients can link separate messages into a thread, but many cannot, and you must fish out related messages by hand. If you have not retained earlier messages in the thread, an orphaned member of that thread may become cryptic, ambiguous, or simply useless. Dump the orphan,

even if you regret having dumped the rest of the thread. Wishing won't
bring it back. (Still, check your backups and archives to see if the others are
still out there somewhere!)

√   *Does it duplicate information you already have elsewhere?* If you subscribe to
several related e-mail lists, sometimes members will "cross-post" a message to
all of those several lists, and you may end up with three or four separate
copies of the very same message. This is a particular problem when you
create filters to autosort messages from e-mail lists into a separate folder,
where duplicates can be easily forgotten. Sometimes e-mail messages were
sent to you solely to convey a single Web link. You may already have that
link recorded in your Web browser bookmarks. If so, you can dump the
message without regret. Also, messages are sometimes sent with attachments,
and the messages themselves say little more than, "Here it is! Have fun!" If
you've saved the attachment file to an appropriate place, such messages
become just more gunk.

√   *Could you pitch the message after appropriate, simple action?* If a correspondent
sends you contact information, see if you've already copied it to your address
book. If so, the message is unnecessary. If not, copy the information to your
address book and delete the message.

√   *Has time and history rendered the message useless or misleading?* Messages, like
bad wine, can spoil. New information can render old information obsolete.
Old information can be found to be false. A message may say, "Your PR
contact at SurlySoft is Helena Handbasket, at 000-000-0000." Unfortunately,
you've learned that Helena has moved on to another firm, so if a message
makes your antennas twitch as no longer being true, do a quick check and
dump it. If someone has sent you a draft of a document and then later on
sends you the final copy, the draft may contain errors or omissions that can
trip you up if you mistake the draft for the final item. Nuke it!

Create a One-Screen Folder Hierarchy

The single biggest secret to keeping your mailbase manageable lies in creating
a suitable hierarchy for folders in which to store your messages. Most e-mail
clients come to you with just a few folders: Inbox, Outbox, Trash, and Drafts.
These four folders are the ones through which your daily mail passes. They are
not for storing mail over the long haul! For those "keep" and "hold" messages,
you need to create folders.

Nearly all e-mail clients allow you to create folders or mailboxes, which may
be displayed in a window to the left of the message panes themselves. Most
clients allow a folder *hierarchy*—that is, folders that contain subfolders—and

this makes organizing a very large mailbase much easier. It's not uncommon to find medical, legal, or technology professionals with *tens of thousands* of messages in their mailbases, and for people like that, a good many folders may be required to make sense of it all and allow individual messages to be found quickly when needed.

Keep Your Folder List to One Screen

The key to creating a folder hierarchy is to not have so many folders in the left margin that you forget you have them. The way to do that is to limit your folders to a single screen's worth. The rule of thumb is this: If you have to scroll a list of folders up and down, you have too many. If you feel you absolutely need more folders than will fit in a single screen, nest related folders together under a parent folder.

Deciding what folders to create (like deciding when to nuke a message) is more psychology than technology. Think hard about how you use e-mail, not so much in terms of who it comes from but rather what the messages are *about*. When at some point in the future you want to refer back to a message, you may recall who sent it, but primarily what you'll be looking for is the message's topic. Folders should thus be about topics and not people. Here are some examples of mail for which you could create folders:

√   Mail relating to your job

√   Mail relating to your church or civic groups (such as Lions, Chamber of Commerce, neighborhood association, PTA)

√   Mail relating to your hobbies and interests (such as programming, model railroading, kite flying, ham radio)

√   Mail relating to projects or research you're undertaking (such as research on a medical condition or for an article you're writing)

Just to give you an example, let's postulate a set of mail folders for our mythical Everyman, Andy Stanton, a computer consultant living down the street from the Andersons in Springfield:

In

Out   These four come standard with most e-mail clients.

Sent

Drafts

Boy Scouts   Mail about Andy Jr.'s Boy Scouts activities

Chamber of Commerce	Mail relating to Andy's C of C activities
Church	Mail about events and other things at St. James
Consulting Practice	A folder containing other folders; more on this a little later
Genealogy	Mail from relatives gathering family history data
Humor	For those funny messages Andy's brother sends out
Kitchen Remodel Project	Mail relating to Andy's remodel job on the kitchen
RC Airmodels	A hobby listserv Andy subscribes to

This is pretty straightforward and serves Andy well. It's a very nice folder list because it can be displayed on one single screen.

Keep Time-Delimited Mail in Separate Folders

Note in the list Andy's "Kitchen Remodel Project" folder. It contains mail from suppliers and from the contractor who is rebuilding the kitchen in Andy's house. The project is pretty intense, but it is definitely time delimited. After the project is done, the mail in the folder is no longer especially useful, and it certainly won't be referred to on a daily basis, as it was during the project's execution. Once his kitchen is completed, Andy can delete this folder or (more likely) archive the folder's messages to a CD and put it in a drawer somewhere. The folder itself can then be deleted from his folder hierarchy.

How you separately archive one folder among many depends completely on your e-mail client. With some clients (primarily the Outlooks), it's not easy; with others, it may be as simple as exporting a folder to a separate file. If your e-mail client gives you the option of exporting individual messages as separate EML files, this may be ideal because you can read the archived messages separately using a simple text editor like Windows Notepad if you ever need to refer back to them. If you archive a whole folder as a single file, you may have to reimport the folder into your e-mail client to read the archived messages again. Note that if you change e-mail clients after archiving a whole folder, your new client may not be able to read an archived folder exported from a different client. This is yet another reason to archive messages as individual EML message files and not whole folders. Virtually all e-mail clients can import EML files.

GunkBuster's Notebook: Managing Your Sent Items Folder

Every time you send a message to someone, a copy of it is saved in your Sent Items folder—and if you don't delete or move messages out of Sent Items, they remain there forever. People who have used e-mail for a number of years are often surprised to find that thousands of messages have accumulated in their Sent Items folder. Some management is called for.

Sent Items is useful as "short term memory" of messages that you've sent. Sometimes you recall that someone asked you to send a message to them for some reason and you can't recall if you actually did or not. Unsure? Look for messages to that person in Sent Items. This feature becomes less useful as time passes— e-mail conversations grow cold over a few months' time, and at some point messages in Sent Items might as well be trashed. This is *especially* true if they have attachments, as will be discussed a little later in this chapter.

A good rule of thumb is to remove messages from Sent Items after 90 days' time or less. "Removing" may mean deleting, but it may sometimes happen that a message that you sent someone is worth retaining as part of a larger conversation. For example, if you have a folder named Genealogy, you probably use it to store messages from relatives researching your family history with you on a collaborative basis. Information sent to them by you should probably be kept for future reference, and possible future sharing with other people whom you have not yet contacted. In cases like that, simply move the pertinent messages from Sent Items to Genealogy.

The important thing is simply to "look in on" Sent Items on a regular basis, or after any period of especially intense e-mail interchanges, especially if you've been sending messages with large attachments. Monthly is a good suggestion. Stick to it!

Use Nested Folders Carefully

Andy is a computer consultant, and he has a separate folder for all mail relating to his consulting practice. His consulting practice generates far more e-mail than all of his other interests and activities combined. Is one folder enough to manage it all?

No, it isn't. However, the single folder Consulting Practice doesn't tell the whole story. It contains a number of other folders that relate to his consulting practice:

Accounting	Mail from and to Andy's accountant
Clufre Realty	One of Andy's clients
Continuing Ed	Mail relating to night courses Andy takes

Dell Tech Support	Technical info about Andy's main PC
Gas Transport Inc.	One of Andy's clients
Harvest Moo Dairy	One of Andy's clients
Insurance	Mail relating to Andy's business insurance
Network Tech Support	Technical info about Andy's network
Sergeant Ron's Army Surplus	One of Andy's clients
Tax Matters	Mail concerning all tax issues

Andy actually has more folders within Consulting Practice than on his main screen. That's fine because Andy uses these folders on a daily basis and none of them is ever out of sight for very long. However, in general, it's not a good idea to put folders within folders unless you refer to the subfolders often. It's much too easy to forget a rarely used folder hiding under another rarely used folder in your hierarchy.

Even if you do create folders within folders, limit yourself to two folders deep. Go three deep or more and eventually you *will* forget about one or more of those deeply buried folders. Watch that little plus sign in front of a folder name. If you see a plus symbol, that means a child folder lies beneath the surface and should be visited now and then!

Don't Accumulate Attachments

E-mail attachments are separate files that "ride along" on an e-mail message. Attachments can be any sort of file, but often they are files that contain content other than text, like images or sound files. This means that they are often very large—sometimes megabytes in size—and if you accumulate enough of them, they can become a *huge* source of e-mail gunk.

An associate of ours tells the story of a clueless employee at his firm who was sent a humorous animation of an alien singing a disco song and decided to send it to every single person in the company. The animation was 4 megabytes in size, and when multiplied by the hundred-odd people in the company, it completely filled the company's already-strapped mail server. (This was some years ago, before 100 gigabyte hard drives were commonplace.)

How e-mail clients handle attachments varies. Attachments begin as separate files, but when mailed, they are encoded within the message, and then when received, they are again broken out into separate files. Most clients allow you to click a Save As link or button to store the attachment somewhere else on your hard drive. What you must remember is that even after you save an attachment somewhere, *it most likely still exists in your mailbase* until you delete the message it arrived with.

Worse yet, some older e-mail clients save attachments as separate files into a folder somewhere and the attachments remain in that folder even after you delete the message that originally carried the attachment. What you must do is look in your e-mail client's documentation to see where and how it stores attachments. There may be a separate folder (perhaps called Attach) where attachments live. Go to that folder and see what it contains—and be prepared to be surprised. You may be looking at 100 megabytes or more of files you don't need and may already have stored elsewhere.

If you have a folder with a lot of messages in it and you are looking for those messages containing attachments, see if your e-mail client has a column (most do) for an attachment icon (this is typically a paper clip). If so, make sure that column is displayed. You can also sort messages in a folder by size: The larger messages will almost certainly be carrying attachments.

Here are some guidelines for dealing with attachments:

√ Do not use your mailbase as a storehouse for attached files. When a message arrives with an attachment, *immediately* save the attachment to a separate location on your hard drive if it is to be retained. Otherwise, delete both the message and the attachment. If you want to retain the message but *not* the attachment, attempt to delete the attachment separately. (Some clients may not allow separate deletion of attachments and messages.)

√ Don't open an attachment unless you know what it is. If a message arrives with an attachment and you are not *absolutely* sure of what it is or who it came from, *don't open it to see what it is!* This is how viruses propagate. Be particularly wary of files with the extensions.exe, .com, .scr, and .pif. Remember that under Windows, opening an executable file runs it! This is idiotic, but it's a fact of life. "Opening" *should* mean "looking at" rather than "running," but we must deal with Windows as it is. *Always* keep an anti-virus utility running and up-to-date. Many anti-virus products insert a context menu item allowing the scan of a single highlighted file. If your anti-virus product has done this, you can right-click on an attachment file, select Scan For Viruses (or something close to that; see your anti-virus product documentation) and your anti-virus utility will scan the highlighted file. This is quick insurance. Get in the habit and you'll be at much less risk from viruses and worms!

√ Enable the full display of file extensions in Windows Explorer. Most Windows installations default to hiding the file extension, which is a *very* bad idea. Why? A Windows filename can legally have more than one period character in it. A virus can send a copy of itself with the name ParisHilton.jpg.exe. If your Windows installation is hiding file extensions, the filename of the virus will appear as ParisHilton.jpg. Double-click it in an attempt to view the "picture" and the virus has you by the hindquarters. To disable hiding of file extensions, bring up Windows Explorer and select Tools and then Folder Options. Click the View tab and uncheck the item marked Hide File Extensions For Known File Types. Then click OK.

√   Delete small files containing background graphics and other decorative items. Many e-mail clients send HTML backgrounds and decorative graphics as attachments, so you may see a multitude of very small files with obscure names in your attachments folder. If you don't recognize an attachment's name (especially a very small attachment), you probably don't need it and can safely delete it.

√   Watch out for attachments in your Sent folder! If you send messages with attachments to other people, most e-mail clients will save a copy of that message *and the attachments* in your Sent folder. If those attachments are large (say, an image or sound file), you may have a hundred or more megabytes of gunk cluttering up your mailbase in your Sent folder. This is almost certainly needless duplicate storage because you had to have a copy of each attachment file stored elsewhere to attach it to a message to begin with. The solution? Sort your Sent folder by message size and nuke every message containing an attachment.

GunkBuster's Notebook: Spring Cleaning on Your E-mail

If you send and receive any significant quantity of e-mail—and especially if you have a complicated folder hierarchy to store it in—you should budget one day a year for—"spring-cleaning" to make sure gunk isn't quietly accumulating in the far corners of your e-mail machinery. As with all e-mail management, it's less technology than psychology. The hardest part is simply deciding to do it and then following through.

Here's a simple checklist for your annual email spring-cleaning:

1. Schedule a full day for it. Egads...a day! Who's got those to spare? Well, if you let your mailbase get away from you and gunk up, you will spend a lot more time than that over the coming year straightening things out and looking for lost messages in the morass.

2. Before you do anything else, count the number of messages in your mailbox. No e-mail client that we know of will give you a single figure totaling your stored messages, but many (PocoMail first among them) will tell you how many messages are in each folder. Just take a pocket calculator, go down your list of folders, and add them up. Prepare to be surprised! (And if you're a good record keeper, try to keep a record of the size of your mailbase over time. If it's significantly bigger each time you check, you've got some serious degunking to do!)

3. Begin with your Sent Items folder. It keeps a copy of every single message you send, and few of those are worth keeping. Keep nothing in Sent Items that's more than 90 days old. Older messages should be either deleted or (if they're important enough to keep) moved to a folder where related messages (say, for tax matters, discussions on genealogy, and so on) are kept.

4. Next, go through your inbox and either delete or classify anything beyond your 100 most recent arrivals. Pay particular attention to that murky area "beyond the space beyond the fold," where messages have been lying fallow for a month or more. Force yourself to deal with anything unpleasant or difficult that's been awaiting action. If you're convinced you can't bring it down under 100 messages, you're fooling yourself. See if you need to add a folder or two for new interests or topics that have generated e-mail that doesn't quite fit anywhere else. But whatever you have to do, get it down to 100 messages or fewer!

5. This is the hard part. Pour yourself a cup of strong coffee, start at the top of your folder list, and see what you no longer need to keep in each folder. No longer interested in radio controlled models, sold your plane, and haven't flown since last April? Archive or delete the whole folder. Sometimes a message that looked like a keeper last year doesn't look quite as essential this year. Let it go. Sometimes messages that you thought were forever were really time limited. Be ruthless. It's the only way to stay ahead of your mailbase.

6. This is pure psychology, but it works: When you're done, count up the messages in your mailbase to see how many you've eliminated. Keep a record somewhere (a short text

file in your mailbase folder will do) indicating how large your mailbase is this time. It helps make it all seem worthwhile to know that you're actually staying ahead of things. You don't necessarily have to *shrink* your mailbase (unless it had gotten out of control to begin with), but you sure don't want it to grow like a fungus!

Miscellaneous E-Mail Housecleaning Pointers

Beyond what we've previously mentioned in this chapter, there are some odds and ends to think about in terms of e-mail gunk. These are minor compared to sifting and organizing your mail and managing attachments, but every little bit of degunking counts.

Watch Out for Abandoned Drafts

Most e-mail clients have a folder for messages that you begin writing but can't finish in one session. This is generally called the Drafts folder, but some clients may call it the Outbox. (The term "outbox" is more commonly used for mail that is completed and waiting for you to log on to the Internet so that it may be sent.) Some e-mail clients will automatically save a message that you're writing to the Drafts folder after you've worked on it for more than a certain amount of time—and if you forget to send it, it will remain in the Drafts folder until you explicitly send or delete it.

You may well have several incomplete and abandoned messages in your Drafts folder. Open Drafts and take a look at what's in there. There may be nothing at all—or it may contain a lot of *really* moldy leftovers! Delete all messages in this folder that are not active projects.

Delete Duplicate Copies of Your Mailbase

All the major e-mail clients have the capability to import an existing mailbase from the other major e-mail clients. (If you're moving to or from a more obscure e-mail client, you may have trouble bringing your mailbase over.) However, after it has been copied over to your new e-mail client, there is still a copy of your entire mailbase stored with the old e-mail client, and that copy of the mailbase will remain on your hard drive, *even if you uninstall the old e-mail client.* If your mailbase is substantial, that can mean a *lot* of wasted disk space.

Of course, keeping the copy of your old mailbase on hard disk for a couple of weeks while you become familiar with the new e-mail client is not a bad idea (in case you decide you really don't like the new client). But at some point, you should delete the old copy of the mailbase. Deleting it is easy using Windows Explorer—the mailbase is nothing more than one or more files in a directory. Delete the directory containing the mailbase files and the mailbase is gone. Sometimes, however, the tricky part is just—*finding* the mailbase on today's cavernous hard drives. Table 8.1 summarizes how to go about finding the mailbases for some of the major e-mail clients.

Table 8.1　How to Find Mailbases for Common E-Mail Clients

Client Name	Path to check	Search for
AOL Mail	Program Files\America Online\idb	main.idx, main.ind
Eudora	Program Files\Qualcomm\Eudora\	in.mbx
Pegasus Mail	PMAIL\MAIL	*.pmm or *.cnm
PocoMail	Program Files\PocoMail\Mail	in.mbx
Outlook		*.pst files
Outlook Express		inbox.dbx

Keep in mind that all modern e-mail clients allow you to specify where the mailbase is stored. If you don't specify a location, it will use a default path, which is listed in Table 8.1. If you (or someone who configured your PC) changed the default so that your mailbase is stored elsewhere, you may have to find it by searching for distinctive filenames or extensions.

Outlook and Outlook Express can be configured many different ways, and there is no single path to check for either program. Outlook Express mailbases may be found by searching for "inbox.dbx" (the name of the inbox) and Outlook mailbases may be found by searching for files with a .pst extension.

There is a very big warning to be heeded when you want to delete a mailbase for "big" Outlook. Outlook's PST files may contain your copy of the Windows Address Book! Delete a PST file and you may delete your entire address book. This is unfortunate, because PST files are often very large and they do not compress very easily, even after you delete some or all of the e-mail messages they contain.

The rule is this: If you use Outlook, your Windows Address Book will almost certainly be stored in a PST file. If you do not use Outlook, your Windows Address Book will be stored in a WAB file. Keep in mind that if you change from Outlook to some other e-mail client, your Windows Address Book will remain in the PST file you used while you used Outlook as your e-mail client.

Unfortunately, exporting mailbase and address book information out of Outlook to another e-mail client is extremely difficult.

Outlook Express E-Mail Gunk in the Windows Registry

Outlook Express has a habit of storing inappropriate things in the Windows Registry. The prime example is Outlook Express's blocked senders list, which is the list of addresses or domains whose mail should go directly to the Deleted Items folder. This list is stored in the Registry, and if you end up blocking hundreds of senders or domains (as most people who use e-mail a lot inevitably do), you will be gunking up the Windows Registry, big time.

If you use Outlook Express, blocked senders will be stored in the Registry. If you stop using Outlook Express and even uninstall it, the blocked senders entries will remain in the Registry until they are manually removed.

The only really safe way to remove these blocked sender entries from the Registry is to do it from within Outlook Express. You remove them using the same dialog box that you used to add them, and it's easy except for one thing: You cannot select more than one blocked sender at a time, and therefore you must remove them one at a time, selecting and deleting each one individually. If you have hundreds stored, this is a nuisance that may take some time.

Here's how it's done:

1. From within Outlook Express, select Tools, then Message Rules, and then Blocked Senders.
2. In the Blocked Senders dialog box that appears, you'll see that each blocked sender entry is a separate line.
3. Highlight the first entry and click the Remove button.
4. Repeat step 3 on subsequent entries until they are all gone.

If Outlook Express no longer functions correctly, or if it cannot see the list of blocked senders stored in the Registry, you have no choice but to edit the Registry directly to remove the entries. This is not tremendously difficult, but it's something that you do *not* want to get wrong! Damage the wrong items in the Registry and your Windows installation won't work correctly—and perhaps not at all. You should not attempt it without a solid understanding of what the Registry is and how it works.

It can be useful to examine the Registry to see if any blocked sender entries are stored there. We'll be explaining how you work with the Registry and use tools such as REGEDT32 in more detail in Chapter 13. For now, we'll show you how to quickly use REGEDT32 to locate blocked sender entries. Here are the steps to follow:

1. Run REGEDT32.exe.

2. Expand My Computer and highlight HKEY_CURRENT_USER.

3. Choose Find from the Edit menu and search for the string "Block Senders."

4. Expand Block Senders, and expand Mail beneath it.

5. Expand Criteria under Mail. You'll see a long list of Registry entries with hexadecimal numeric names like 001, 002, and so on. Each one represents a blocked sender. If you click on one of the entries, you will see it expanded in the right pane and the address or domain of the blocked sender will be visible.

RegEdit can also remove individual entries from the Registry, but unless you know *precisely* what you're doing, it's not a good idea to try.

Use a File Shredder after You Delete Messages Containing Personal or Financial Data

Most people send and receive e-mail messages containing personal or financial information that should not be available to all and sundry. If in the course of degunking your mailbase, you delete messages containing such sensitive information, understand that a clever enough person can recover that information, *even after it's deleted*. This is particularly important if you intend to sell or even junk your PC. Stories have circulated about people who deleted everything on their PC hard drives and put the machines out on the curb only to discover that identity thieves later recovered virtually everything that had previously existed on the hard drives.

The answer to this problem is to use what is called a "shredder" utility periodically. One of the best such utilities is Eraser, which is completely free and works very well. You can find Eraser at **www.heidi.ie/eraser/**.

Eraser has three general functions:

√   It erases files from the Windows Recycle Bin so that they cannot be recovered.

√   It erases individual files and folders so that they cannot be recovered.

√   It erases any data from the pool of unused space on your hard drive.

This last function is the important one when deleting messages from your mailbase. When you delete a message within your e-mail client, the disk space that the message originally occupied is returned to the hard drive's pool of free space.

The data is still present in that space; the only difference is that the space may now be used for writing other files and other e-mail messages. Precisely when a given block of free disk space is reused cannot be predicted, and your sensitive data may be lying around naked in the hard drive's free space pool for weeks or months before being used again.

When you give it the command, Eraser goes out and overwrites all the free space on your hard drive with random data patterns. Thus, anything previously stored in that free space is gone forever and beyond recovery.

When you install Eraser, it adds a small icon to the Windows System Tray. Double-clicking on this icon brings up the window shown in Figure 8-1.

Figure 8-1
Eraser's main window.

If there is no line in the task window like that shown in Figure 8-1, you will have to create one. Select File and then New Task. The dialog box shown in Figure 8-2 will appear. Select your main hard drive (or whatever drive your mailbase is stored on) from the drop-down list under the Unused Space On Drive radio button. Click OK and the task will be created.

You then run the task by highlighting the "Unused disk space" task and selecting Task and Run.

It's a good idea to run Eraser on the unused space on your hard drive regularly; once a week is probably often enough. Certainly if you intend to sell your

Figure 8-2

Eraser's Create Task dialog.

computer or give it to someone who should not see your personal data, delete everything that you don't want others to see and then run Eraser on the unused disk space.

Summing Up

The e-mail that you *want* to receive is no better than spam if it turns into gunk on your PC. Unlike spam, however, your own e-mail responds better to psychological than technological measures. You need to be ready to deal with e-mail *as it arrives*—and become an ace at deciding when to keep a message, when to hold it for a limited time, or when to deal with it (read it or reply) right now. As important as organizing e-mail into folders might be, no skill is more crucial than simply keeping the overall size of your mailbase down.

Ultimately, e-mail management is a lot like housecleaning: Devote a little daily effort to keep things under control, and then once a year be prepared to turn the place inside out and make it shine. Keep in mind that the more diligently you perform those daily chores, the less of an ordeal that annual "spring-cleaning" will turn out to be!

Installing Upgrades for Your System

Degunking Checklist:

√ Use Windows Update to get up-to-date and stay up-to-date.

√ Enhance performance and security with the latest high priority updates, software updates, and hardware updates.

√ Learn what updates you can do without.

√ Keep your computer safe and sound with the latest service packs.

√ Enhance the capabilities of your computer by upgrading from Windows XP Home to Windows XP Professional.

√ Enhance media output and performance by upgrading to Media Player 10 and Movie Maker 2.1.

√ Use instant messaging more efficiently (and have more fun) using MSN 7.0.

Y ou can get more out of your computer—including better performance, better security, and enhanced media capabilities—in a number of ways. You already know already that you can clean up the computer, do routine maintenance, stop unnecessary programs and services from running, and tweak XP to your heart's content. You also know that cleaning up your e-mail and spam is a good way to enhance performance, too. But it's just as important to maintain the security of your computer by staying up-to-date with Windows updates. The only real way to stay on top of the updates is by configuring Automatic Update, available in Control Panel, to obtain the updates automatically.

With Windows Update, you can enhance performance and security by downloading and installing high priority patches and software and hardware updates manually or automatically. Service packs are considered high priority, too, and it's extremely important to download and install them when they're available. Of course, not all updates apply to all computers or configurations, so in this chapter, you'll also learn how to distinguish between what you do need and what you don't. By understanding the difference, you can keep your computer as gunk free as possible.

In addition to *updates,* you can get *upgrades.* If you run Windows XP Home Edition, you can access XP's business-level features by upgrading from XP Home to XP Professional. No matter what edition of XP you run, though, you can enhance performance of some specific components by upgrading your software. You can also enhance performance for applications like Movie Maker and Windows Media Player by upgrading them to their newer versions. If you use Movie Maker or Media Player, these free upgrades are must-haves. (If you don't use these features at all, don't gunk up your computer by installing them!)

Use Windows Update to Stay Up-to-Date

Windows Update is the easiest and most efficient way to keep your computer safe and sound and up-to-date. Windows Update is Microsoft's way of making available all of the security patches, fixes, driver updates, software updates, and other important items that your computer needs to stay in good working order. It's extremely important that you either visit the Windows Update Web site regularly or configure XP to visit on its own, in the background.

Keeping your computer updated with high priority updates and software and hardware updates is crucial to maintaining a well-running, high-performance, and secure computing environment because without these patches and fixes, your computer is vulnerable to all of the newly found security holes to which hackers and attackers have an open door. These rogues can access your computer remotely (if they know how) and do damage in a number of ways. While some folks are a bit suspicious of the monitoring and downloading process, as you'll learn later, the information collected from your computer is not information that could personally identify you, your e-mail address, or your surfing habits (among other things).

Several types of updates are provided under the following categories: High Priority; Software, Optional; and Hardware, Optional. Figure 9-1 shows the Windows Update Web site and the updates available for one of our computers. This Web site is available at **http://update.Microsoft.com**, and we'll show you how to use it shortly. You'll notice that this system has been kept up-to-date; there is only one high priority update, four software updates, and one hardware update. The hardware update is for a modem we no longer use, so we'll choose not to install it. We'll take a look at the software updates and decide if those are needed before installing them, too. We will install the high priority update.

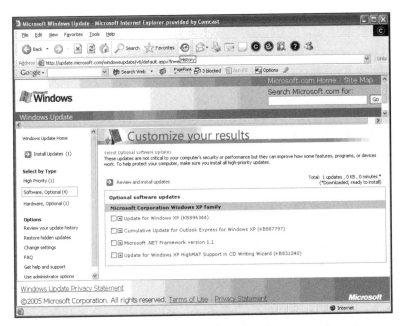

Figure 9-1
You can manually obtain updates from the Windows Update Web site.

In the following sections, you'll learn the various ways to get updates, why they are important, and how to decide if the updates are necessary or not. You'll learn how the updates enhance the security of your computer and why high priority updates must be installed if you expect your computer to continue to run smoothly and without problems. You'll also learn how to obtain Service

Pack 2 if you have a slow Internet connection and downloading it would take too long. Finally, you'll learn why high priority updates are so important and why they should be installed whenever they are offered.

TIP: *High priority updates are often created to resolve known issues with the operating system. These known issues generally have to do with security holes and vulnerabilities recently discovered. If left unpatched, these vulnerabilities will leave you open to hackers, viruses, worms, and other security threats. These, in turn, can seriously gunk up your computer.*

Get Updates Automatically or Manually

Although you could visit the Windows Update Web site weekly to check for new updates and install them manually, it's much easier to simply configure Windows XP to get them automatically (and in the background) while you're online. If you're online a lot, you should configure Windows Update to automatically check for updates and then notify you if and when updates are available. Then, you can see what updates there are and decide if you need them or not. If you need them, you can install them.

It seems logical that using the automatic settings to download updates would slow down your machine, especially if the updates are downloaded during the day and at the same time that you're trying to download a new screensaver! However, XP's Help And Support files state that the updates will be downloaded in the background and will not interfere with or slow down network activities such as Internet browsing. If you'd like, though (or if you believe you notice slower response time while Windows Update does its thing), you can easily instruct Windows to search for updates late at night (or some other time) when your computer isn't being used. This will let you get the maximum benefit of automatic updates, while at the same time avoid any (perceived or real) delays due to the system resources they require.

If you aren't online very much, having XP get the updates automatically won't work for you and you'll have to make it a point to go online once a week or so and check yourself. Staying updated is a fairly common problem for those who use laptops and travel a lot, those with slow Internet connections, or those who simply don't go online very much. Automatic updates might be disabled if you are in a corporate environment, too, and you might simply want to get the updates manually if you have an aversion to things being automatically downloaded to your computer. Whatever the case, staying updated is important, and there's a setting for you.

GunkBuster's Notebook: Yeah, But Is Windows Update Secure?

There's no reason you should be concerned about your PC's security and Windows Update. "Although Windows Update must scan your computer to provide you with the appropriate files, patches, and security updates, it does not collect your name, address, e-mail address, or any other form of personally identifiable information. The information collected is only used during the period of time that you are visiting the Web site, and it is not saved." (This is taken directly from the Windows Update Privacy Statement.)

If you are concerned about what is collected when your computer is scanned, the information it acquires is listed here:

√ Operating-system version number

√ Internet Explorer version number

√ Version numbers of other software

√ Plug and Play ID numbers of hardware devices

√ Region and language setting

√ Product ID and Product Key (As with other information collected, the Product ID and Product Key are not retained beyond the end of the update session, but if the Product ID is *not valid*, that information *is* retained.)

In addition, the site and transmissions are protected and well maintained, so there's no need to be worried about hackers, viruses, worms, or getting the wrong updates. You can imagine the uproar if the Windows Update site was not secure! So, if you're using a legal copy of Windows (which you should be), if you log on to the Internet frequently, and if you want to get your updates automatically, configuring automatic updates is definitely the way to go.

Get Updates Automatically

Our computers are configured to get updates automatically, and we think it's the best option. Here's how to set it up (or disable it):

1. Right-click the My Computer icon on the Desktop or the Start menu and choose Properties.

2. Click the Automatic Updates tab. This is shown in Figure 9-2.

Figure 9-2
It's generally best to configure Automatic Updates to
get updates manually.

3. Read through the four options. Figure 9-2 shows that we've checked
    Automatic (Recommended). With this setting enabled, Windows Update
    software is automatically downloaded and installed at a specific time each
    day or once a week, depending on your personalized setting).

4. If you do not want to have the updates automatically installed, choose from one
    of the other options. We'll suggest if another option is chosen, it is the second
    one, Download Updates For Me, But Let me Choose When To Install Them.

5. Click OK.

If you've taken our advice, Windows will now get the updates automatically,
and you'll be better protected and get better performance for it. When using
Automatic Updates, you'll be prompted that updates are ready with a pop-up
balloon and an icon of the yellow shield in the System Tray.

Get Updates Manually

If you want or need to get Windows updates manually, you don't have to disable Automatic Updates unless you just want to. Getting updates manually is
easy and you can do it anytime you'd like. To get the updates manually, follow
these steps:

1. Click Start, point to All Programs, and click Windows Update. You'll be connected to the Windows Update Web site appropriate for your country.

2. Once connected, wait for the scan of your computer to complete. The amount of time it takes to get the information depends on the speed of your connection to the Internet.

3. On the left side of the page, notice the categories: High Priority; Software, Optional;, and Hardware, Optional. You can click each link to see what is available.

4. Finally, read through the following sections to determine what updates you need, and then continue the process to select, download, and install the updates you want.

High Priority Updates and Service Packs

High priority updates are just that, high priority. You absolutely must download and install them if you want your computer to run efficiently—there's just no getting around it. If you find out after checking that you have 5 or 10 high priority updates, set some time aside, log on to the Internet, and get them manually, or stay logged on overnight and let Windows get them for you. We find that it's much more effective just to let XP do it automatically. You still get to decide what you want to install, and you still have complete control over what is installed and what isn't.

TIP: Install all high priority updates, even if you don't think they apply to you or your system.

Service packs are also considered high priority updates. If you find out you need a service pack (SP2 is out now) and you don't want to wait for it to download, you can obtain the service pack on disk. Visit **www.microsoft.com/ windowsxp/downloads/updates/sp2/cdorder/en_us/default.mspx** to place your order. Believe it or not, it's free, too, and you're not even charged for shipping. SP2 contains the other updates you're probably also missing. So if you have dial-up, a laptop, or are rarely online, this is a great option for you. You'll also have it just in case you switch computers or have to perform a reinstallation.

Software and Hardware Updates

Other updates that you should consider include software and hardware updates. These updates are updates and fixes for the operating system itself and can include fixes for bugs in the system, updates to service packs, and updates to components like Media Player or Movie Maker. Such updates may even include new items as they are available. At the time this book was written, there were updates for Movie

Maker and Media Player, and an update to SP2. There were also important security updates and a new Windows Malicious Software Removal Tool. (You might have noticed that there are Windows XP updates you might not need, like one for Microsoft .NET Framework Version 1.1 or an update for a modem you no longer use. Refer to the GunkBuster's Notebook "What Updates Are Really Necessary?" for more information on how to decide what to install.)

We always enjoy running across driver updates with Windows Update. Driver updates appear under the Hardware, Optional list and will make your computer and attached hardware run better. These can include updates for modems, printers, scanners, cameras, BIOS, and any other number of internal or external components. Seeing them on the Windows Update Web site means they're safe, too; so if you have an unsigned driver and are looking for a newer one, look here first! We suggest installing all hardware driver updates that are available for hardware you still use.

TIP: You can also increase performance by downloading and installing PowerToys. The best PowerToys we've discovered are detailed in Chapter 15.

Windows Malicious Software Removal Tool

Sometimes you'll run across some rather interesting and unexpected items from Windows Update. The Windows Malicious Software Removal Tool is one of them. Available in 2005, once downloaded, this application runs one time to check your computer for malicious software. This includes a check for well-known viruses and spyware such as Blaster, Sasser, and MyDoom. It tries to remove anything malicious it finds. A new version is available each month, providing a sort of anti-virus program that you can use to keep your computer clean (that is, if you're not on the Web very much!). Still, a third-party tool is best.

GunkBuster's Notebook: What Updates Are Really Necessary?

As you read the descriptions for some of the available Windows XP updates, you might wonder if all of the updates in this category are really necessary. They aren't, and you'd be right to wonder! You should always read what each Windows XP update contains before installing it. If you are getting the updates manually from the Windows Update Web site, the description of the update is included on the Web site. If you are getting an update automatically, click Details in the Automatic Updates dialog box to see what the update involves. Figure 9-3 shows an example of one such Windows XP update.

Review and install updates   Total: 0 updates , 0 KB , 0 minutes

Optional software updates

Microsoft Corporation Windows XP family

☐ ☐ Microsoft .NET Framework version 1.1
   Download size: 23.1 MB , 14 minutes
   The .NET Framework is a component of the Windows operating system. For developers, the .NET
   Framework makes it easy to rapidly create powerful software that maximizes performance, scalability,
   opportunities for integration, reliability, security, and the end-user experience, while minimizing the costs of
   deployment and management. After you install this item, you may have to restart your
   computer. Details...
   ☐ Don't show this update again

Figure 9-3

Don't download gunk you don't need.

This is one we decided not to install because it involves the .NET Framework, which is available for developers, and we are not .NET Framework developers.

You can make similar decisions. In our latest manual XP Update adventure, we found an update for Windows XP SP2. We think we'll install that one because it's an update for a service pack, which is a security update. However, we see no reason to install the .NET Framework update; it's for developers, and we're not developers. It also takes 14 minutes using a cable modem and will only gunk up our machine. If later on you install a .NET-based application and it fails to run, returning to Windows Update for the .NET update would be a good first step in troubleshooting.

If you need some help deciding what to install and what not to, take a few minutes to read the descriptions for each update. If the update is written specifically for developers (people who write software) and you aren't a developer, there's no need to install the update. If the update is for the Jet 4.0 database engine and you did not install and do not use it, there's no need for this update. Neither of these is defined as "High Priority" anyway, so we can choose not to install them without any repercussions.

If you read the description of the update and it looks like it applies to you or you'd like to be able to access the specific feature addressed, add and install it. A while back, we added and installed the Windows Error Reporting: Recommended Update. This enabled us to automatically view responses to Windows error reports. After an error occurred, we could immediately view the fix, workaround, or other information, which was quite helpful. We do not regret installing that update. If ever in doubt, install all high priority updates, and browse through the software and hardware updates, checking only what you recognize and think you need. Leave the rest alone.

Upgrade to Windows XP Professional

If you want to get more out of Windows XP and you're using Windows XP Home Edition, you might consider upgrading to Windows XP Professional. There's so much more you can do with Professional, and you'll find that your productivity increases right away. Windows XP has business-level features not available in the Home edition, including the following:

√ Remote Desktop: Connect to the office computer (also running Windows XP Professional) and work from home. You'll be able to access all of your data and applications, just as if you were sitting in front of the computer at the office.

√ Offline Files and Folders: Work on network shares while disconnected from the network server, and then synchronize the files when you go back online. You can work on an airplane, in a hotel, or at home.

√ Scalable Processor Support: Use dual processors for even faster performance. You can't use dual processors with XP Home.

√ File Encryption: Protect sensitive data with encrypted files.

√ Better Security: Use access controls to enhance security for files, applications, and resources.

√ Domains: Join a domain, configure group policies, and utilize roaming user profiles. These are all corporate-level perks.

√ Multilingual: Change the user interface language and get localized dialog boxes, menus, proofing tools, help files, and more. This feature is perfect for the multi-language household or small business.

Upgrading from Home to Professional isn't necessary if you don't need any of these extras. However, if you see one you like in the list and you'd like to try it, you'll have to shell out the $150 (U.S.) or so that it will likely cost you!

Upgrade the Media Applications

The versions of Windows Media Player and Windows Movie Maker that shipped with your copy of Windows XP are likely not the newest versions available. Windows Media Player 10 and Movie Maker 2.1 are now available, and the downloads are free! Both enhance their respective applications immensely, and you'll notice a major change right away in performance, ease of use, options, components, graphical interface, and features.

To see what versions you have, open both Windows Media Player and Windows Movie Maker, both available from the All Programs menu, and choose Help>About *<name of application>*.You can see what version you have from the information box that appears. Figure 9-4 shows an example. Here, Windows Media Player has been updated to Version 10, the latest available when this book was published. We'll cover degunking both applications in Chapter 11, "Degunking Windows Media."

Figure 9-4
Use the Help>About option to see what version of Media Player or Movie Maker you have.

TIP: If you don't have the latest versions, you can get them from the Windows Update Web site or by configuring Windows Update to retrieve updates automatically.

Upgrade to MSN Messenger 7.0

If you use Windows Messenger to text-message in real time with your friends and family, consider upgrading to MSN Messenger 7.0, which offers more features than the version of Windows Messenger that came with Windows XP. Although *adding* programs might seem to contradict our whole "degunking" strategy, increasing performance and enhancing ease of use is certainly a major part of making your computer work better.

With MSN Messenger 7.0 you get these improvements:

√ Integrate a Web cam and microphone easily and have audio and video conversations with others.

√ Use new emoticons, backgrounds, dynamic display pictures, winks and packs.

√ Play games with your buddies using the new Messenger launch site.

√ Save conversations.

√ Add mobile phones, publish phone numbers, and instant message between platforms.

√ Set alerts for stocks, sales, airfare, shopping, news headlines, weather, and more.

√ Share activities using applications like Photo Swap, The Conversationator, File Sharing, MSN Calendar Sharing, Xpress Greetings, Whiteboard, Remote Assistance, Application Sharing, and more. Figure 9-5 shows these activities.

Figure 9-5

New MSN 7.0 features are awesome.

If you're interested, visit **http://messenger.msn.com** for more details and for downloading. Once downloaded, MSN 7.0 acts as a separate program; it is not an upgrade to Windows Messenger. You'll want to tell Windows Messenger you don't want it to start automatically and tell MSN Messenger you want it to start automatically. (You can do that easily from the Tools menu.)

NOTE: *Don't confuse MSN Messenger 7.0 with MSN 8 or higher. MSN Messenger 7.0 is a free messaging program and is quite different from MSN, which is an online service that provides features such as parental controls and shared Internet surfing.*

Summing Up

Although degunking generally consists of getting rid of stuff, this chapter focused on improving your system by adding stuff. Windows Update was introduced as an important tool for enhancing security, performance, and overall protection. High priority updates and service packs should always be installed, driver updates are almost always desirable, and software and hardware updates may or may not be needed. Beyond the updates, you learned about upgrades. Windows Professional was introduced, and if you need the business-level features available from XP, you should consider this upgrade.

You also learned that for greatly enhanced performance and ease of use, you should upgrade to Windows Media Player 10 and Movie Maker 2.1 (if you use these features). MSN Messenger 7.0 offers new productivity tools and more options than Windows Messenger does. Each of these upgrades enhances your computer's performance by offering additional features and better media quality.

Surviving Service Pack 2

Degunking Checklist:

√ Verify that you have Service Pack 2 and get it if you don't.

√ Allow Active Content in Internet Explorer.

√ Learn how to use the new pop-up blocker and the Internet Explorer Information bar.

√ Enable live links, allow pictures, and allow attachments in Outlook Express e-mail.

√ Tweak firewall and virus protection settings in Security Center.

√ Get rid of warning messages from Windows Security Center.

√ Learn where and how to troubleshoot problems noticed after the Service Pack 2 installation.

√ Learn how to uninstall Service Pack 2.

I f you have Automatic Updates enabled, chances are good you already have Service Pack 2 for Windows XP. It likely downloaded and installed itself automatically, and we bet you didn't even take notice. However, while Service Pack 2 was being installed, it made some changes to your system to make it more secure. These changes were likely *quite* noticeable.

You may have learned you had Service Pack 2 (SP2) after seeing a few of these changes. Perhaps Outlook Express stopped giving you the option to open e-mail attachments and wouldn't show pictures embedded in e-mail messages, or you may have figured it out when you started getting annoying pop-ups about the status of your anti-virus software. Although SP2 is a necessary update to Windows XP, and enhances both the usability and security of your PC, it can certainly throw things out of whack.

In this chapter, we'll walk you through some of the more common complaints about SP2, such as the inability to view active content on Web pages or click Web links included in e-mails after SP2 is installed. We'll also show you how to get the most out of the new features, including Windows Firewall in the Security Center. We'll show you how to reset Outlook Express's security settings and how to troubleshoot any other problems you think were caused by SP2. Let's start with verifying you have SP2 installed and getting it if you don't. (Despite the problems, you should certainly have it!)

Make Sure You Have Service Pack 2 and Get It If You Don't

There are several ways to find out if you have Service Pack 2 installed, and the easiest is to open Control Panel and look for the Security Center applet. This is shown in Figure 10-1. If you have it, you have SP2 and you can skip to the next section. If you don't, right-click the My Computer icon on the Desktop, choose Properties, and click the General tab. If you don't see Service Pack 2 listed as shown in Figure 10-2, or if you have SP2 but no icon in Control Panel, continue with this section to get it (or repair it).

Ways to Get Service Pack 2

The easiest way to get SP2 is through Automatic Updates. Just make sure it's enabled as detailed in Chapter 9 and that you log on a few times a week for a few hours so updates can be obtained. With Automatic Updates enabled, the necessary files will be downloaded automatically and you'll be prompted by a pop-up balloon in the lower-right corner of your screen when it's time to

Figure 10-1

The Security Console is added to Control Panel when SP2 is installed.

Figure 10-2

System Properties show the operating system and all service packs.

install. You can also manually download SP2 from **www.microsoft.com/ windowsxp/sp2/default.mspx**.

Problems with these two options could arise if you aren't on the Internet very much or if you have an extremely slow connection. It may take way too long to download SP2, especially if you're on a pay-as-you-go service. If that's your situation, you should opt for getting the service pack mailed to you on a CD. It's free, and there isn't even a shipping or handling fee. To order a CD, go to **www.updatexp.com/xpsp2cd**. (You can also borrow one from a friend if you know someone who already has it.)

TIP: As with any installation, make sure your PC meets the minimum requirements and that you read and understand the included information. This includes getting rid of spyware, getting manufacturer updates, and backing up personal files. It is extremely important to heed any warnings, too, such as closing any open programs during installation.

Installing Service Pack 2

If you've downloaded the service pack files from the Internet via Automatic Updates, you'll be prompted by a balloon tip in the lower-right corner to install SP2. If you miss it, don't worry, there will be an icon in the Notification Area of the Taskbar, a yellow shield with an exclamation point inside it, which will remain there until you install SP2. You can click the icon to start the installation whenever you're ready. See Figure 10-3. You can continue to work at your PC while the updates are installed.

If you obtained the files via manual download, simply click Run when prompted or locate and click the executable file associated with it on your hard drive, as you would with any downloaded file. Finally, if you requested the CD, just pop it in the drive and follow the instructions.

Let Internet Explorer Explore Again

The reason that problems arise when you install SP2 is that some of the security settings are automatically changed back to their defaults in the process, causing some programs to not respond as you'd expect, like Outlook Express and Internet Explorer. Apparently, it's your job to figure out how to change them back because there are no instructions that clearly spell out how with SP2.

For Internet Explorer, this means that content Microsoft deems "potentially dangerous" will be blocked, including ActiveX installations, pop-ups, download processes, and active content. While this makes surfing the Internet safer

Figure 10-3
Notice the yellow shield in the Notification Area of the Taskbar and the dialog box to install the updates.

and more secure, it can cause problems when you need to see the content, such as a pop-up window that shows a close-up of an item you're shopping for or ActiveX controls that allow you to access features not available in standard HTML content. To view blocked content safely, you'll need to understand how the new Information Bar works and how to change security settings in Internet Explorer.

Allow Active Content and View Blocked Pop-Ups

Active content, including ActiveX controls, let you interact with Web pages instead of simply viewing them. For instance, with ActiveX content enabled, you can go to a Web site and play games, hear interactive sounds, view animated items, and work with interactive features. ActiveX controls are created and used by Web site designers and downloaded and executed by Web browsers. Unfortunately, because they are programs that execute, ActiveX controls can also be malicious and cause harm to your PC. ActiveX controls can delete files, steal your personal information, and wreak havoc on your PC.

Therefore, you have to decide what sites you're going to trust and what sites you aren't and make a decision about how you're going to deal with ActiveX content when it arises. While you can enable all ActiveX content in Internet Explorer's security settings, we don't think this is the best option. We believe you should leave the security settings for ActiveX content as is and use the Information Bar to enable ActiveX content only for sites you trust. You should also leave the pop-up blocker enabled, which is the default setting when SP2 is installed.

Figure 10-4 shows the Information Bar. Depending on what site you're visiting and what content was deemed potentially dangerous, the options you see in the Information Bar will vary. In this particular instance, a pop-up ad has been blocked. Clicking the Information bar in this instance offers four options:

√   Temporarily Allow Pop-ups: Allows pop-ups on the current Web page.

√   Always Allow Pop-ups From This Site: Allows pop-ups to always appear on the current site.

√   Settings: Offers choices to turn on or off pop-up blocker and show the Information Bar when pop-ups are blocked (checked by default) and an additional option called More Settings. More Settings allows you to manually input addresses of Web sites from which you want to allow pop-ups.

√   Information Bar Help: Opens the Help pages for the Information Bar.

| Pop-up blocked. To see this pop-up or additional options click here... | ✕ |

Figure 10-4

Sometimes the Information Bar tells you a pop-up has been blocked; you can click the Information Bar to see available options.

You won't see the Information Bar in Internet Explorer unless something has been blocked. There are seven messages the Information Bar can display. They each deal with either installing and using ActiveX controls or downloading files to your PC. When you see any message from the Information Bar, you should assess the risk at the site you're visiting, click the Information Bar, and make a choice from the options. Generally, options include downloading (or not downloading) a file, installing (or not installing) software, changing (or not changing) a security level for Internet Explorer, allowing (or not allowing) blocked content, showing (or not showing) restricted content, and viewing related topics about the information you're seeing.

Reconfigure Outlook Express

Service Pack 2 barrels onto the scene, changes a bunch of settings, and disappears, leaving nothing but a trail of frustration for Outlook Express users. It's like when your kid comes home from college for the weekend and "optimizes" your home theater system. It takes days just to figure out how to play a DVD again. SP2 is no different. You see, the folks at Microsoft figure that no one, and we mean no one, should *ever* open an attachment. If they didn't think that, they wouldn't have configured the SP2 security settings to disable this feature and confuse half the country. But they did, and we're here to help. And not only did they disable the option to open attachments, they disabled live links in e-mails and decided we shouldn't even see the pictures!

Now that's not all bad. There are reasons for such actions. Sure, attachments can contain viruses, embedded pictures and live links to unscrupulous Web sites, and active content in e-mails can be annoying as well as a privacy pest. Images can be dangerous because images in e-mails can be used to send information back to the sender, letting them know you saw their e-mail (generally spam). However, we're all going to need to open attachments, click links, and view active content at some time or another. In the following sections, we'll show you how to enable all of the things SP2 disabled.

TIP: *We're assuming you have anti-virus, anti-adware, and anti-spyware installed and keep it up-to-date. If you do not, you should leave the SP2 settings alone.*

Enable Attachments, Live Links, and Embedded Pictures

Everything you need to get Outlook Express working the way it used to is in OE's Options dialog box. Keep in mind, though, you still have to be careful. Opening attachments from people you don't know could allow a virus to propagate on your PC. Opening e-mail from spammers that includes pictures and other external content in HTML messages can allow spammers to know they reached a valid address and that you read their e-mail. You'll need to weigh these things against how important this content is. If you have a good spam-prevention plan in place and up-to-date anti-virus software, you should be good to go.

To reconfigure Outlook Express for functionality and usability, follow these steps:

1. Open Outlook Express and choose Tools>Options.

2. Select the Security tab.

3. To change the security settings, under Virus Protection, select Internet Zone (Less Secure, But More Functional).

4. Leave Warn Me When Other Applications Try To Send Mail As Me checked.

5. Uncheck Do Not Allow Attachments To Be Saved Or Opened That Could Potentially Be A Virus.

6. Under Download Images, uncheck Block Images And Other External Content In HTML E-Mail.

7. For most users, the last two options, Encrypt Contents And Attachments For All Outgoing Messages and Digitally Sign All Outgoing Messages, can be left unchecked.

8. Click OK.

Optimize the Security Center

There's not much do to at the Security Center (located in Control Panel). When SP2 is installed, it configures itself automatically. The firewall is enabled, automatic updates are configured to occur automatically, and the Security Center checks for any virus protection installed on your PC. When all is well, you never even know the Security Center is there. However, if something is amiss, such as a lack of virus protection software, you'll get pop-up balloons informing you of the situation.

You can also visit the Security Center and tweak the settings, and you can count on the Security Center to offer up notifications if something is suspect. Figure 10-5 shows what the Security Center should look like. Notice that all of the items are marked On.

Tweak Firewall Settings

A firewall is kind of like an alarm system you would install in your home. An alarm system is configured to make people authenticate themselves to get in, and it sets off an alarm if an intruder is present. Like a security system, a firewall allows only authenticated and appropriate data into your PC. Data that is harmful, including viruses and worms, are (most of the time) stopped at the door. These things cannot get past the firewall and onto your PC. That's the purpose of the firewall.

Because having a firewall is important to the security of your system, Windows Firewall should be left on unless you have some more sophisticated firewall in

Figure 10-5
Windows Security Center should look like this in most cases.

place. By sophisticated, we don't mean a router or a switch, though. We mean a third-party firewall you purchased that specifically states you should turn off Windows Firewall and that it will take over the firewall duties.

You can also configure Windows Firewall with more stringent settings than the defaults when you're connecting to a public network, such as in an airport or coffee shop. This is a good setting to configure when faced with such circumstances, to keep your PC safe from hackers who may be lurking in the shadows.

If you do decide to turn off or tweak the firewall, here's how:

1. Open Control Panel and open Security Center.

2. Under Manage Security Settings For, click Windows Firewall.

3. To create a higher security standard, select Don't Allow Exceptions in the Windows Firewall dialog box.

4. To turn off the firewall, select Off. See Figure 10-6. Note that this is not a recommended setting.

5. Click OK.

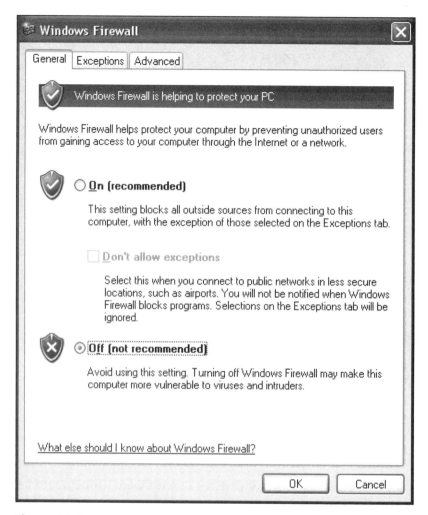

Figure 10-6
Turning off the firewall is not recommended.

As you can see in Figure 10-6, there are two other tabs. The Exceptions tab lets you state what, if any, exceptions should be made for programs and services available on your network and your PC. Some programs prefer an open connection to the Internet so these connections should not be blocked for these programs.

These programs and services can include "but are not limited to" the following:

√   File and Printer Sharing
√   Internet Explorer
√   MSN Messenger 7.0

√   Remote Assistance

√   Remote Desktop

√   UPnP Framework

√   Windows Messenger

Chances are, several of these are checked already. You can check or uncheck services and programs, or click Add Program to add a program to the list. This really isn't necessary, though; if you decide to use a program that is blocked by the firewall, you'll be prompted to unblock it.

The Advanced tab offers advanced features. We'll suggest you don't muck about in here for now. If you decide later you want to tackle these settings, make sure to read all of the Firewall Help files in the Help and Support Center.

Automatic Updates

We talked about Automatic Updates in Chapter 9. Automatic Updates helps you stay up-to-date with the latest security patches, upgrades, fixes, and device drivers and should be enabled. You can configure Automatic Updates settings from Control Panel>System, but you can also configure them in the Windows Security Center. To manage Automatic Updates from the Security Center, follow these steps:

1. Open Security Center from Control Panel.

2. Under Manage Security Settings For, select Automatic Updates.

3. Configure Automatic Updates as you deem appropriate, keeping in mind what is recommended. We chose Automatic (Recommended) and chose to update daily.

4. Click OK.

Configure Virus Protection

If you have anti-virus software, it's likely that the Security Center knows about it. If it doesn't know about it, or if you don't have any anti-virus software installed, you'll be prompted regularly to do something to secure your PC. You have two choices when prompted: you can either install anti-virus software or turn off the notifications. We suggest the former, of course, but you can always turn off the notification if Windows is nagging you unnecessarily:

1. Open Security Center from Control Panel.

2. Click the arrow next to Virus Protection and click Recommendations (see Figure 10-7).

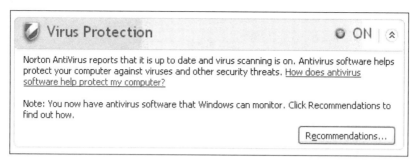

Figure 10-7
Recommendations is the key to turning off notifications about inadequate virus protection.

3. In the resulting Recommendations dialog box, uncheck I Have An Antivirus Program That I'll Monitor Myself.

4. Click OK to exit.

Get Rid of Unnecessary Messages

The only real downside to Security Center is the endless nagging and annoying notifications regarding things you've configured, know about, or don't want to do anything about. If you turn off Windows Firewall, you'll be prompted forever about it, even if you have a highly sophisticated firewall installed. If you have anti-virus software that Security Center doesn't recognize, you'll get pop-ups about that, too. If you're getting notifications from Security Center you don't want, you can disable notifications. Here's how:

1. Open Security Center from Control Panel.

2. In the left pane, under Resources, select Change The Way Security Center Alerts Me.

3. In the Alert Settings dialog box, check anything you don't want to be notified about. See Figure 10-8.

4. Click OK.

Find Solutions for Other SP2 Problems

Since SP2 was made available, problems have continued to arise that relate to it. This is true of virtually any software, but especially for something like a service pack that must work universally with all products, including all hardware and software. If you experience anything odd after installing the service pack, or if you believe a current problem is related to it, there are several places to look to find a solution.

Figure 10-8
Disable alerts to get rid of annoying pop-ups from Security Center.

There are two excellent Web sites you can use to search for information about problems you may have with SP2. You can access the Microsoft Knowledge Base at **www.support.microsoft.com** or the Windows XP Expert Zone at **www.microsoft.com/windowsxp/expertzone**. Searching the Microsoft Knowledge Base for "Service Pack 2" yields several helpful articles:

√   875364: Detailed installation walkthrough for Windows XP Service Pack 2

√   883775: Device drivers known to cause instability in Windows XP Service Pack 2

√   167665: Cannot browse secure Web sites with Service Pack 2

√   875356: How to configure the Windows Firewall feature in Windows XP Service Pack 2

√   883259: How to install and configure Bluetooth devices in Windows XP Service Pack 2

√   302971: "Stop 0x1E" or "Stop 0xc5" after you install Service Pack 2 and you use Logitech mouse drivers

The Expert Zone has the following articles:

√   Expert Zone Support WebCast: Wireless home networking and Windows XP Service Pack 2

√ Introduction to Windows XP Service Pack 2

√ Preventing lockups when upgrading to Windows XP Service Pack 2

√ Windows XP Service Pack 2 strengthens the defense against spyware

There are more where these came from. In fact, we'd venture a guess that any problem you could possibly have with Service Pack 2 is in these archives somewhere. Perform the searches and include a word that applies to the problem you're having and you'll likely find what you need quickly (for instance, "Service Pack 2 and Logitech Mouse").

Uninstall Service Pack 2 (If All Else Fails)

You can uninstall Service Pack 2 if you think you simply can't recover from the installation, but in most cases, this is unnecessary. The answer to any problem you are having is out there somewhere, and it's worth the effort to find it. We'd rather you spend a few minutes looking for a solution to why your mouse doesn't work properly than uninstall SP2 and leave your PC open to intruders and malicious software. However, if you must, there are several ways to remove Service Pack 2:

√ From the Control Panel: Locate Service Pack 2 and click Remove.

√ From Start>Run: Type
c:\windows\$NtServicePackUninstall$\spuninst\spuninst.exe, click OK, and then work through the removal wizard.

√ Use System Restore to restore your PC to a date prior to installing Service Pack 2.

Summary

In this chapter, you learned how to obtain Service Pack 2, what changes it makes to your PC during installation, and how to revert to prior settings if desired after installation is complete. Since Service Pack 2 also includes new Windows features, such as the Security Center, where the firewall, automatic updates, and virus protection can be configured, you learned how to tweak those to get the best performance for your needs. While it's important to have SP2, problems do arise, so you learned where and how to find answers to common questions regarding the changes, incompatibilities, and known problems with hardware and software.

Degunking Media

Degunking Checklist:

√ Get Media Player and Movie Maker updates.

√ Organize Media Player's playlists, and create your own auto playlists.

√ Remove duplicates and unwanted media from the Media Player Library.

√ Back up and restore licenses for music.

√ Organize source and project files so Movie Maker can always find them.

√ Delete unnecessary Movie Maker files.

√ Understand how large or small a movie should be to e-mail, save to CD, or save to DVD.

√ Get rid of unwanted media packs and other downloads, or get those downloads if you think you'll use them.

Windows XP comes with two media utilities, Windows Media Player and Windows Movie Maker. You use Windows Media Player to play music, videos, DVDs, and short e-mail video clips, and to play movies you create from your own personal video files. You also use the player to organize your media files, including DVDs, music, videos, and TV recordings.

Movie Maker is the second media utility. You use Movie Maker to make your own movies, specifically from video footage you've taken with your video camera and uploaded to your PC. Both applications become gunk magnets quickly if you use them often, though, but sit quietly and cause no gunk if you don't. If you use either of these utilities, continue reading this chapter. If you don't, you can skip this chapter and move on to other important degunking tasks.

NOTE: We'll assume that if you're reading this chapter, you've had experience using both Windows Media Player and Windows Movie Maker and that you are somewhat knowledgeable about their features and components.

Get Media Updates

When you purchase software, you can always expect an update sooner or later. Some applications require updates regularly, like anti-virus and anti-spyware software, while others only require updates a few times a year (or less). You should get these updates when they are offered for several reasons: they make the software more secure, repair known problems, and oftentimes, offer a new interface and/or new features. Such is the case with the latest updates for Media Player and Movie Maker.

To see if you have the latest version of Windows Media Player, open the application and choose Help>Check For Player Updates. (You may already have the latest version because your PC is new or you've already obtained the most recent updates via the Automatic Updates features.) If you see the message shown in Figure 11-1, you'll know that you are all set. If you don't see this message, you'll be prompted to install the updates.

TIP: Open Windows Media Player from Start>All Programs>Accessories>Entertainment> Windows Media Player.

Finding out if you have the latest version of Movie Maker isn't as simple. There's no Help>Check For Movie Maker Updates option available, so you have to go to Microsoft's Movie Maker home page to see if there is anything new. To do that, click Help>Windows Movie Maker On The Web, and once you are at the Web site, look for update notices. At the time this book was written, there was

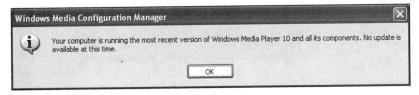

Figure 11-1
You should see this message when you check for player updates; if you don't,
follow the directions for downloading the most recent version.

a new version, Movie Maker 2.1. However, because it is a component of Service Pack 2, you likely already have it. If you have Service Pack 2, you have the latest version of Movie Maker (as it stands now).

TIP: Open Windows Movie Maker from Start>All Programs>Accessories>Entertainment> Windows Movie Maker.

Degunk Windows Media Player

It was quite difficult for us to decide what to introduce in this part of the chapter. Windows Media Player has a tendency to get really gunked up, very quickly, and in multiple areas of the application. We had to pick the most frustrating gunk in Media Player, and there was plenty to choose from. In the end, we decided to focus on getting rid of duplicate music files, managing mismanaged playlists, dealing with lost licenses for purchased media or a failure of purchased media to play, getting rid of duplicate links, and deleting unwanted media in the music library. These are all common and aggravating issues, and chances are, you need help with at least one or two of them. Let's start first with Media Player's playlists.

Control Your Playlists

Playlists are Media Player's way of giving you control of your music. You use playlists to organize music, play music, and create music montages, including creating lists of songs you want to burn to CDs. You can create playlists based on mood, genre, artist, rating, date played, date added, and more. Unfortunately, your playlists *lists* can become quite a mess. An example of this is shown in Figure 11-2.

As you can see in this figure, there are plenty of playlists. Many of them we didn't create, including most of the ones listed under Auto Playlists. While auto playlists are nice, having too many makes finding what you want difficult.

Figure 11-2

Playlists are a good idea, but your Library can quickly become overrun, making the playlist you want hard to find.

Additionally, some of the lists under My Playlists are outdated and we no longer listen to them. So the first step in degunking Windows Media Player involves cleaning up the interface by deleting unwanted playlists.

TIP: Auto playlists are created by Media Player (or by you) and are "live," meaning they change based on how often you play a song, the characteristics of the song, or how you've obtained, rated, or when you listen to a particular song. Auto playlist are updated each time you open Windows Media Player.

To delete a playlist under My Playlists or Auto Playlists:

1. Right click the playlist to delete.

2. Choose Delete from the options.

3. When prompted with the question "Are You Sure Your Want To Remove The ....Playlist From Your Library?," tell Windows Media Player what you want to do. You have two choices:

   i. Delete From Library Only

   ii. Delete From Library And My Computer

4. Click OK.

NOTE: When you delete playlists, you don't delete the songs in them from your library. You only delete the playlist itself, which contains only links to songs, not the actual music files.

Create Useful Auto Playlists

While we're on the subject of playlists, you should be taking advantage of Auto Playlists. Auto playlists are a good way to quickly create playlists that match criteria you set, and that change automatically based on your listening preferences. For instance, you can create an auto playlist that only plays songs you've listed to 100 or more times, and you could name this playlist My Favorite Tunes. Each time a new song reaches that threshold, it would be added automatically to the playlist. You can also create auto playlists based on a song's characteristics, including:

√ Bit rate

√ Date added to a library

√ Total count on weekdays

√ Total count on weekends

√ File size

√ Length

√ Mood

√ Title

You can even create custom criteria based on what a song does or does not contain. To create an auto playlist, follow these steps:

1. Open Windows Media Player.

2. Click the Library tab.

3. Right-click Auto Playlists and click New.

4. Name the new auto playlist descriptively. We'll create an auto playlist entitled My Favorite Songs.

5. Under Create An Auto Playlist That Includes The Following, click Click Here To Add Criteria. Select a criteria from the list. We'll choose Playcount: Total Overall.

6. In the Play Count - Total Overall choices, as shown in Figure 11-3, configure your criteria by clicking the choices. We'll choose Is Greater Than, and type in 100. (Notice you can continue to add criteria to your heart's content.)

7. Click OK.

Locate the new playlist under Auto Playlists (it should be highlighted already). Next, check out the songs in the list. Continue to edit and create new auto playlists to organize your library.

Figure 11-3
Configure criteria in the New Auto Playlist dialog box.

Finding Missing Media Files

As you work your way through your library, you'll often come across songs that won't play for one reason or another. Perhaps you only "rented" the songs from your music provider, and when you canceled the music subscription to that service, you no longer had licenses for them. Perhaps they've been deleted from your hard drive. Or, perhaps you mucked about in there and changed where your music files are stored, and now Media Player can't find them. Whatever the case, you're likely in a position where you need to determine what music files are really available, and then to spend some time deleting files you can't access (or don't want).

TIP: File names that have an orange exclamation point beside them are either missing or do not have valid licenses.

The first step to taking control of Media Player is to first search your hard drive for all of the media files on it. The missing files could still be on your PC, but may have been moved or copied to a folder the player doesn't recognize. Here are the steps to follow to tell Windows Media Player to search for all of the media files on your PC to see if you can resolve these issues:

1. Right-click the Library tab, point to Tools, and select Search For Media Files.

2. Configure search options to search through all drives on your PC.

3. Choose to search through New Files And All Existing Files In Library (Slow).

4. Leave checked Add Files Previously Deleted From Library and Add Volume Leveling Values For All Files (Slow). (We'll delete files you don't want in the next section.) See Figure 11-4.

Figure 11-4
Make sure Windows Media Player knows where all of your media files are located.

5. Click Search. Figure 11-5 shows that Media Player has found and added lots of new files.

After this search is complete, you should notice new entries to your library. As you can see in Figure 11-6, the library looks pretty clean, except for some duplicate files here and there.

Figure 11-5
The search results will show the number of files being added to your media library.

Figure 11-6
Windows Media Player can search for missing files and add them to the library.

Deleting Media Files You Don't Want

Once Windows Media Player knows where all of your files are, you can continue degunking by deleting items you don't want. Deleting music tracks is kind of like deleting playlists, except when you choose to delete a music track from both the media library, and your PC. The music tracks are gone for good.

If you choose to delete the file only from the library, you can still retrieve it from your hard drive if you decide you want it later. You have to be careful though; if you are deleting a song from your library because you don't like it and never listen to it, don't leave it on your hard drive to take up space and gunk up your My Music folder. Just get rid of it.

To delete any music track:

1. Locate the track in the Library.

2. Right-click the track and choose Delete.

3. In the Windows Media Player dialog box, choose to either delete the file from the Library only, or to delete it from both the Library and the Computer.

4. Click OK.

You can delete complete albums in the same manner.

Remove Duplicate Links in the Music Library

Duplicate file names in the Media Player Library can be a real pain. Sometimes, it's just a glitch in the viewer, but other times, it's a problem with your settings or a problem with the player itself. It can also be that you have actual duplicates of your music, and if that's the case, you'll need to root out and delete the extra copies.

Figure 11-7 shows some serious gunk in the form of duplicate files. What is shown is a terribly gunked up All Music list. If you see duplicate file names in your Media Player Library like what is shown here, try the following to get rid of them:

American Pie [Complete Original Version]	Don McLean	Classics
American Pie [Complete Original Version]	Don McLean	Classics
And I Love You So	Don McLean	Classics
And I Love You So	Don McLean	Classics
Baby The Rain Must Fall	Glenn Yarbrough	Nipper's Gr
Back to the Black Sands	Pam Green	Dilemmas
BilliardWorldTheme		
BlueGem		
BOMB		
Both Sides Now	Judy Collins	Colors Of
The Boy in the Bubble	Paul Simon	Graceland
The Boy in the Bubble	Paul Simon	Graceland
BrickWorldTheme		
By Baby	The Pretenders	Get Close
California Dreamin'	The Mamas & The Papas	Entertainm
Catch The Wind	Donovan (Rock)	The Very E
Cavalry to the Rescue		
CheeseWorldTheme		
Chiara	Andrea Bocelli	Cieli Di Tos
Chill Factor	The Pretenders	Get Close
The City Of New Orleans	Arlo Guthrie	Hobo's Lull
The City Of New Orleans	Arlo Guthrie	Hobo's Lull

Figure 11-7

Duplicate file names (or files) are a common problem for Media Player users.

1. Click the Library tab, then click the Now Playing tab, and then click the Library tab again. Sometimes, this does the trick.

2. If that doesn't work, press F3 on your keyboard to open the Add To Library By Searching Computer dialog box.

3. Click Browse, and locate the folder that holds your music files and likely contains the duplicate entries.

4. Click Search.

5. To delete any other duplicate files, right-click the file and choose Delete.

If this doesn't solve your duplicate files problem, or if you still have lots of duplicate files, you will have to recreate your media library. In doing so, you may also rid Media Player of any other lingering problems you may have:

1. Close Windows Media Player.

2. Right-click Start and choose Explore.

3. Choose Tools>Folder Options, and the View tab.

4. Verify Show Hidden Files And Folders is selected. If it is not, select it.

5. Click OK.

6. Locate the database file on the computer. It is located in the C:\Documents and Settings\<user name>\Local Settings\Application Data\Microsoft\ Media Player\CurrentDatabase_219.wmdb. (Databases for earlier versions of the player will have a different number after CurrentDatabase.)

7. Right-click the file and choose Rename.

8. Change the files extention from .wmdb to .bak.

9. Restart the player.

10. Wait while the library repopulates.

11. Right-click the Library tab, point to File, point to Add To Library, and choose By Searching Computer.

12. Choose All Drives in the Add To Library By Searching Computer when prompted and accept the remaining defaults.

13. Click Search.

14. The Library should now be free of duplicates, as shown in Figure 11-8.

Back Up, Restore, Manage, and Recover Lost Licenses

To play purchased music and music you've downloaded from legitimate sites on the Internet, you have to have a license for each track you want to play. (This is not generally true of CDs you own and copy to your PC.) The licenses

Figure 11-8
You can free Media Player of duplicates by recreating the media Library.

allow you to play the music on your PC, burn it to a CD, or copy it to a digital music player. If for some reason, Windows Media Player can't find a valid license, you'll get a message like the one shown in Figure 11-9.

Figure 11-9
You have to have a license to play music downloaded from legitimate Internet sites.

In Figure 11-9, the song "California Dreamin'" cannot be played. That's because, at one time, we were monthly subscribers to the service MusicNow, and we were only "renting" the songs we downloaded. As long as we paid our monthly dues, all of the songs we added would play. Since we're not monthly subscribers anymore, and since MusicNow has since changed their license policies anyway, we are prompted to either contact customer service if we purchased the song, or, delete it from our library. This kind of stuff is gunk, and the only way to get rid of it is to go through each song one by one, and manually delete the ones that don't have licenses. (That is, unless you can find a folder with all of those tracks in it.) Figure 11-10 shows Windows Media Player acquiring the license for a track. If it finds one, the song will play.

Figure 11-10
Windows Media Player acquires a license before it plays a song.

If you do have songs with valid licenses, you'll want to back up those licenses regularly and keep them in a safe place. If your PC crashes and you don't have proof you own the songs, you will have a terrible time recovering.

To back up your licenses:

1. Right-click the Library tab (you can actually right-click anywhere on the blue bar), point to Tools, and select Manage Licenses.
2. Note the location where the backup will be saved, or click Change to select a different location.
3. Click Back Up Now.
4. If prompted to replace a previous back up file, choose Yes.
5. Copy this backup to a flash drive, floppy disk, or network drive for safe keeping.
6. To restore the backups, repeat steps 1 and 2, and choose Restore from the options.

There are other things to watch for, such as what folder songs are downloaded to, how many times you are allowed to copy a song to other devices, and keeping an eye on titles of songs so you don't create duplicates, but we only have so much room in this chapter. Spend some time verifying that each song you have actually plays correctly, get licenses for the ones that don't play correctly and you want to keep, and go over your security and privacy settings. You'll be glad you took the time to perform these tasks.

Degunk Windows Movie Maker

As with Media Player, there are lots of ways to gunk up Movie Maker. Unlike Media Player, you generally do all the gunking up on your own! For the most part, the most common gunk comes from users not understanding the difference between source files, project files, and movie files, and deleting (or mismanaging) files that need to be kept. Along with deleting files that need to be kept, many people *never* delete *any* files they create with Movie Maker, and they end up saving folders full of unrecognizable files, unusable files, and unwanted files.

Right along with the gunk created by unorganized files and a lack of understanding of file types used in Movie Maker is the gunk created when a movie is created that's too large to be used for its intended purpose. You can't e-mail a 15 minute movie (it's just too large of a file), and you can't save a movie that's 120 minutes onto a single CD because a CD can't hold that much information. (Movie Maker won't let you break it up to store it on multiple CDs, either.) So in this part of the chapter, we'll tackle these issues. We'll start with distinguishing between source files, project files, and movie files, and what you do and do not need to keep.

Understand the Difference between Source Files, Project Files, and Movie Files

Source files are the raw footage you shoot with your video camera. Source files remain on the digital camera tape and almost never make it onto the computer. The reason is that once they are imported into Movie Maker and saved, they become a project file. You may still want to copy your source files on your PC, though, as a way to back up your tapes, or to save the original files for posterity. Whatever you do with your source files, avoid renaming, deleting, or moving them, otherwise you'll have problems when you're ready to complete your movie.

Project files are created from source files, and are Movie Maker projects in progress. You work with project files when you edit your source files, add music, add transitions, and create your movie. Project files always have a .MSWMM extension.

Movie files are completed movies. They are the final product. Unlike project files, they cannot be edited. Movie files are the files burned to a CD or DVD, and movie files open and play in Windows Media Player. Movie files can have various extensions, but Movie Maker creates Windows Media Video files which have the .wmv extension.

Organize Your Files and Delete Files You Don't Need

Because there are so many steps to creating a movie, including taking the actual video with a video camera, editing the ongoing project until it's perfect, and then creating a movie, you'll have lots and lots of files. Hopefully, you culled through some of these in Chapters 3 and 5. However, it can still be confusing. In Table 11-1, I'll outline when you should and should not delete specific file types.

Table 11-1   Manage Your Movie Maker Files

File Type	Keep Until...	Delete When....	Archive If...
Source File	You have created a completedmovie and are certain you will never need the original files again.	You've created a completed movie and have made backups of the movie.	You think you'll ever want the original files, or if you think someone else might.
Project File	You have created a completed movie you are positive you are happy with.	You are positive you will not create another movie from the file.	You think you'll want to edit the footage later and create another movie file.
Movie File	You no longer want to view the movie.	You no longer want to view the movie.	You need to free up space on your hard drive and/or you've archived the movie to a CD or DVD.

Deleting files was covered in Chapters 3 and 5. If you need more help, refer to those chapters.

Create Movies of Appropriate Length

Another common problem for Movie Maker users is creating the wrong size movie. You can't film your daughter's graduation, create a 90-minute feature film, and expect to e-mail it to your relatives. It's simply too large. The same is true of posting your movies to a Web site. If you want to create something that large, you'll have to burn it to a DVD and mail those DVDs out the snail mail route. (DVDs can hold 120 minutes of data.)

So what you have to focus on when creating a movie is how big the file you need to create can be. If you want to e-mail a part of your daughter's graduation for instance, consider importing the source files into Movie Maker, and deleting all but the part where your daughter receives her diploma, which took all of 35 seconds. Now that's something you could e-mail!

You can view the options for saving a movie in the Movie Settings page of the Save Movie wizard. There, you can peruse through the various choices, including the following (not a complete list):

√   High quality video (large)

√   High quality video (small)

√   Video for Pocket PC

√   Video for broadband

√   Video for dial-up access

√   High quality video (NTSC)

As you select each of these, the data stated for your movie size changes. As an example, one of our more lengthy movies, saved as Best Quality For Playback On My Computer, takes up 109.90 MB. Saved as a video for a Pocket PC, the size drops to only 12.77 MB. That's a huge difference. Figure 11-11 shows the Save Movie Wizard dialog box and the "Other Settings."

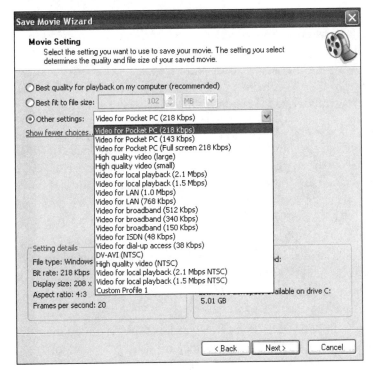

Figure 11-11
Make sure you view Other Settings and choose the one that is of the appropriate size.

To get to this screen and access these options:

1.   Open Movie Maker.

2.   Choose File>Open Project. Select a project.

3. Under Finish Movie, select Save To My Computer.

4. Name the movie file and select Next.

5. In the Movie Setting options, click Show More Choices.

6. Click each choice to see how different the file sizes can be, depending on how you choose to save.

7. Click Cancel.

GunkBuster's Notebook: Get (or Get Rid of) Media Packs, Transitions, Sounds, and Other Extras

If you've been using Windows Media Player and Movie Maker for a while, you've probably downloaded more than your share of media packs, transition packages, sounds, visualizations, and other "extras." Media Packs are fun because they offer free utilities, PowerToys, visualizations, skins, sound effects, and more, and they often follow a theme. The media pack for Windows Media Player is called the Windows Media Bonus Pack for Windows XP; the media pack for Movie Maker is called Windows Movie Maker Creativity Kit. You can get both from Microsoft. Just do a quick Google search and you'll see them.

Now, if you have these packs and don't use them, they're gunk and should be uninstalled. If you don't have these packs but think you'd like them, go ahead and download them and give them a shot. They may just make your media experience perfect! Either way, here are some more media packs and extras you may like; just make sure they don't become gunk! These are all free:

√ PowerToys for Windows Media Player for Windows XP: Contains a dozen new PowerToys for Windows Media Player including the Windows Media Player, Tray Control, the Playlist Import to Excel Utility, and the Media Library Metadata Update Wizard.

√ Windows Media Player for Windows XP Visualizations: Contains new visualizations including an MSN Photos Picture Viewer, Fireplace, and Trilogy.

√ Windows Media Player Skins: Contains new skins for the player including Stars and Stripes, Anime, and others.

√ Windows Movie Maker Creativity Kit: Contains sound effects, music loops, title videos, and images.

√ Plus! MP3 Audio Converter LE: Converts MP3 files to Windows Media Audio files and doubles the amount of music you can store on your PC.

TIP: Media packs can be uninstalled from Control Panel and Add or Remove Programs.

Summary

In this chapter, you learned how to degunk Windows Media Player and Windows Movie Maker. Windows Media Player gets gunked up with music that won't play, music that's disorganized, duplicate entries, and mismanaged licenses. Windows Movie Maker gets gunked up with too many useless files, and completed movies that are too big in size to be useful, such as when sending in an e-mail or burning to a CD or DVD. Finally, media packs are available if you want to enhance your media experience, but can become gunk quickly if forgotten about and left on your hard drive.

Optimizing Your Hard Drive and System Startup

Degunking Checklist:

√ Convert your file system to NTFS for better performance and security.

√ Resize hard drive partitions using third-party utilities to make more room for your applications.

√ Accelerate the boot process by cleaning up the Startup folder, tweaking the BIOS, and logging on automatically.

√ Use third-party utilities to enhance the boot-up process.

√ Use system utilities like Dr. Watson, Network Diagnostics, and others to find problems and optimize performance.

√ Get rid of unsigned files and drivers to speed up the boot process and your drive in general.

√ Configure System Properties to enhance system performance.

Your hard drive must be optimized for you to get the most out of your computer. We've done a little of that by deleting unnecessary files and programs, running Disk Cleanup, and running Disk Defragmenter. However, there are other things you can do to enhance your hard drive's performance. We call this "advanced degunking," and it includes using NTFS, configuring the startup options, using system diagnostic tools, and tweaking System Properties for enhancing system performance.

Use NTFS

Whether you are using Windows XP Home or Professional, NTFS (NT File System) is the recommended file system. If you aren't familiar with file systems, they are the basic machinery for managing your hard drives, and you have the option of choosing between three: NTFS, FAT (short for File Allocation Table), and FAT32, which is an extension of FAT for 32-bit computing. NTFS is the most powerful of the three because it offers enhanced security features, including file encryption and disk quotas. It also works much better with large disks than other file system configurations do. With NTFS, you can maintain control of the files and folders on your system and protect them from being viewed by other users on your computer. With FAT32, all users have access to all files on the hard drive, regardless of their account type. If you share a computer, NTFS is absolutely necessary.

It's easy to find out what file system you use and convert if necessary. Once you convert to NTFS, though, you can't convert back to FAT or FAT32 without reformatting the drive, so make sure you won't need to. The only reasons to keep a FAT or FAT32 file system is if you dual-boot with an earlier operating system like Windows 98 or Windows NT 4.0. Most earlier versions of Windows cannot access an NTFS partition. If you aren't dual-booting to an older version of Windows and are using Windows 2000 or XP, you're good to go with NTFS.

Converting to NTFS

You can find out if you have drives formatted with NTFS by using My Computer. Open My Computer, right-click the drive icon, and choose Properties. From the General tab you can see the file format of that drive, as shown in Figure 12-1.

Figure 12-1
A hard drive's Properties box shows the file format type.

If your disk drive is FAT or FAT32, it's in your best interest to convert to NTFS. Converting to NTFS is done from a command prompt:

1. Click Start, point to All Programs, point to Accessories, and click Command Prompt.

2. Type *convert* drive_letter: */fs:ntfs*. Press Enter. For example, to convert the C: drive, type the following:

   convert C: /fs:ntfs.

   If the drive is already formatted as NTFS, your screen will say "Drive C: is already NTFS."

3. Reboot as prompted.

Resize Your Partitions

You might have two or more partitions created on a single hard drive. Many times, C: contains the system files and D: contains data. The C: partition is usually quite small compared to the D: partition. If you've installed lots of applications, games, service packs, updates, and other necessary items on this partition, you might be running a little low on disk space on the C: drive.

If you want to enlarge the space given to the C: partition, you'll have to purchase a third-party utility like Partition Magic. Partition Magic and programs like it can be purchased online or at your local computer store. Once the program is installed, you'll have the option to drag using graphical partition windows to increase or decrease the size of the partitions. Having the freedom to resize partitions on the fly is quite powerful. By increasing the space for the system partition, you can increase performance.

TIP: *Heed all warnings about backing up data before resizing partitions with a third-party tool. Sometimes good intentions to resize partitions end up with unfortunate results.*

Gunkbuster's Notebook: Beware the 137 Gigabyte Barrier!

There was a time when a 100MB hard drive was considered immense, but hard drive technology has advanced hugely in the last five years. Today a 400 Gigabyte drive is relatively inexpensive, and 250 GB drives are commonplace. You need to be aware of a rather odd and little-known limitation called the 137 GB barrier. If you buy a hard drive with more than 120 GB capacity, some older software may malfunction, particularly software that manages disk partitions. Windows XP "knows" about the 137

GB barrier and will not give you any trouble. (Windows 2000 needs to be patched to use disk partitions larger than 137 GB, and Windows 98, well, forget it.)

If you have older versions of Partition Magic or other partitioning software like System Commander downstairs on the shelf somewhere, *do not use them with hard drives larger than 120 GB!* Installing an older partition manager on a very large drive may not only render your PC unbootable, but may also destroy the low-level formatting on the hard drive. Recovery is possible, but difficult and time-consuming.

The rule of thumb is this: Don't use a version of a partition manager utility that is older than the hard drive you install it on. If you buy a new drive with more than 120 GB (capacity jumps from there to 200; typically, there are no 137 GB drives) buy a new partition manager along with it, and dump any older versions. New partition managers work with older, smaller drives, so there is no need to keep that dangerous old stuff around.

Degunk the Startup Process

Does it seem like the time it takes for your Windows XP machine to boot up is longer than it used to be? It probably is. By the time your office suite, anti-virus program, music software, drivers, Internet connection firewall, and all of your programs load, you've booted a lot of software! You can speed up the boot process by cleaning up the Startup folder and deciding what starts automatically.

Clean Up the Startup Folder

The programs in the Startup folder start automatically when Windows starts. The more items you have in there, the longer the boot-up process will take. Figure 12-2 shows our Startup folder. You'll notice it's empty. We don't like to sit around and wait when our computers boot!

By default, many programs place themselves in the Startup folder and thus start automatically at boot-up. The sad thing is that you probably don't even need these programs. You can remove them from the boot-up process by using the Start Menu Properties dialog boxes or simply by right-clicking, which we'll do next. However, many programs that aren't listed in the Startup folder start automatically. We discussed those programs in Chapter 6 and used msconfig.exe at the Run line to open the System Configuration Utility to tell XP to not start them. Refer to Chapter 6 if you skipped that part.

Figure 12-2
If you don't want to wait around for unnecessary programs to start after Windows boots, empty the Startup folder.

If you have items in the Startup folder that you no longer want to start automatically, remove them by following these steps:

1. Click Start, point to All Programs, point to Startup, and take a look at the entries.

2. To delete an entry, right-click and choose Delete. This will not delete the program; it will only remove the shortcut from the Startup folder.

You can also add entries to the Startup folder. This may appeal to you if you open the same programs every time you boot your PC and you have to open them manually. For instance, if you always open Outlook Express, Photoshop CS, and Microsoft Office, you can put shortcuts to those items in the Startup folder. Since those programs can take a while to open and initiate, you can boot your PC in the morning, make coffee and pour yourself a cup, and upon your return, all of the programs you need will be open and ready to go. This is degunking finesse, because you don't have to open the programs you want manually and then wait around for them to initiate!

To add entries to the Startup folder, right-click the program icon and drag and drop it to the Startup folder. Choose Create Shortcut Here. When you drag and drop an EXE file, the program will start automatically. You can test it by moving Notepad there; on boot-up, Notepad will open automatically.

If you've deleted items from the Startup folder, you should notice a change immediately in how fast your PC boots. (This change will be much more noticeable on older, slower PCs.) As mentioned earlier, though, there are lots of applications that boot that aren't located in that folder. Next, we'll clean up the boot process even more.

Clean up Third-Party Programs

Many programs that are not in your Startup folder start automatically when you boot your PC. In Chapter 6, you learned how to locate those programs using Run>msconfig.exe. You can also take control in other ways, though, by watching your PC boot and keeping a close eye on what comes up.

When one of our computers boots, we have the following items start, none of which are in the Startup folder:

√ Norton AntiVirus

√ Pop Up Stopper Free Edition

√ Lavasoft's Ad-Watch SE

√ MSN Messenger and various third-party plug-ins

√ Spyware Blaster

In reality, though, this particular computer needs this level of protection (minus MSN Messenger), so it isn't really gunk. But that's not to say you aren't booting things you don't need. Watch carefully, and if you see something you don't want to boot each time Windows does, open the program, locate the option to change the program's boot behavior, and change it.

Clean Up the Boot Process

There are lots of other ways to clean up the boot process to make it faster. Some, like enabling Quick Boot in your BIOS, have their downsides, and we're not going to mention them here. There are specific tests your computer really needs to run, and we're all for letting the boot-up process take two or three more seconds rather than disabling important system checks. Our goal is to degunk our machines as much as possible, but we also want to do this safely. There are a few things you can do that might not hurt, like skipping the floppy drive search (a second or two), disabling boot delays, logging on automatically, and disabling unnecessary services.

Tell the BIOS to Skip the Floppy Drive Search

Chances are good that your computer spends a few seconds looking to the floppy disk drive for operating system files when it boots. This might not be necessary if you have a fairly new computer and can boot to a CD (if booting to the hard drive fails). To change this default setting, you'll have to enter the BIOS. Note that many new PCs do not come with a floppy drive, and thus, this step is unnecessary.

While entering the BIOS might seem like a simple task (just press the right key combination or the correct function key at the right time during boot-up), it isn't always that easy. Some computer manufacturers would rather you not mess around in there and don't make it that easy to find. We had one computer that didn't make it easy: We had to wait until the blinking dash appeared in the top-right corner of the splash screen, and then we had to hold down the F3 key (while touching a nose with a left index finger). If you did that at the wrong time, no BIOS!

If you don't know your key combination and it isn't listed at boot-up, try pressing F1, F2, F3, or similar keys at the splash screen. If that doesn't work, you might have to visit the Web site of your computer maker and search through their knowledge base. Once you can access your BIOS, walk through the pages using the arrow keys and change or disable the floppy drive search at boot-up.

TIP: *Before getting too involved in changing advanced features of your BIOS, back it up. There are several third-party utilities available for this purpose, including Bios1.35.1 from www.bioscentral.com.*

Don't Configure a Boot Delay

If you have a boot delay configured and you don't have a dual-boot system, you're just wasting time! Do this to find out if you have a boot delay:

1. Open Control Panel (click Performance And Maintenance if you're using the default theme), and then open System.
2. Click the Advanced tab.
3. Under Startup And Recovery, click Settings.
4. Change the Time To Display List Of Operating Systems field to 0 seconds. Click OK twice to close out the dialog boxes.

Log On Automatically

If you are the only user of your computer, and if the computer is in a safe physical environment (that is, in your house, where other people can't routinely get to it) you can configure Windows XP to log you on automatically, without using the Welcome screen and without using the standard Log On To Windows dialog box. Be warned, though, each time the computer boots up, your account will open automatically!

Here's how to configure automatic logon:

1. Click Start, and click Run.
2. Type *control userpasswords2*, and click OK.

3. Verify that the box called Users Must Enter A User Name And Password To Use This Computer is checked, and then select the account that you want to configure as the primary logon.

4. Next, remove the check mark from Users Must Enter A User Name And Password To Use This Computer and click OK. Confirm your password and click OK.

One of our computers is configured for automatic logon, but only one person uses it, and there are few guests. However, when guests do arrive, auto logon is disabled and the Guest account is enabled, just to be safe.

Use the System Configuration Utility to Speed Up the Boot Process

In Chapter 6, we used the System Configuration Utility to disable unwanted programs that start automatically and store themselves in the System Tray. (Typing *msconfig.exe* at the Run prompt opens the System Configuration Utility.) By disabling unwanted programs, you can make the boot process a bit faster. There are other options that can be configured using this utility to enhance your computer's performance.

Generally, the System Configuration Utility is used as a diagnostic tool to uncover and repair boot problems. It allows you to check and uncheck items like drivers, services, and startup programs, and to see which other items are the culprit for the particular problem you are having. In our case, though, we simply want to enhance the boot process, so we'll concentrate on that for now. The following list includes some of the useful degunking/souped-up tasks you can perform:

√   Remove unwanted boot paths: When your system boots, Windows will search specified directories (boot paths) to look for files that it might need. Over time, various boot paths might get set up that you no longer need. These unnecessary boot paths can be acquired when Windows is reinstalled or if a reinstallation fails or if you copy or delete partitions. The fewer places that Windows needs to search when it boots, the better.

√   Remove programs that aren't required at boot-up: These are located under the Startup tab. We talked about this in Chapter 6.

√   Remove services you no longer need: Services are located under the Services tab; there will be more on what services you can uncheck later in this section.

To perform one or more of these tasks, open the System Configuration Utility by typing *msconfig.exe* in the Run dialog box. Then verify, check, delete, and uncheck the following items as they pertain to your system and needs:

√ From the Boot.ini tab, click Check All Boot Paths. If you see a boot path that is no longer needed, you'll be prompted to remove it from the Boot.ini file.

√ From the General tab, Selective Startup should already be selected and Load Startup Items should be filled in with a square. If the General tab does not look like the one shown in Figure 12-3, select Selective Startup, click the Startup tab, and uncheck programs you know are not needed at boot-up. Refer to Chapter 6 for more help on this.

Figure 12-3
Make sure you have configured the System Configuration Utility to selectively start up.

√ Click the Services tab and sort the services by clicking Essential. Make sure that Hide All Microsoft Services is not checked. If a service is essential, you'll see the word "Yes" in the Essential column. You'll notice right off that many of the services *aren't* essential, including Fast User Switching Compatibility, Help And Support, Messenger, Smart Card, Task Scheduler, and items that came preinstalled on your computer, like a Media Music Server or programs you installed yourself. If you decide that you never use Help And Support, Task Scheduler, and smart cards to log on, you can uncheck these items. Don't uncheck anything that you don't recognize or can't find information about in the Help files, though. For instance, don't uncheck DNS Client, DHCP Client, or Internet Connection Firewall or your Internet adventures will be greatly affected.

√ From the Services tab, you can view the services in one of two ways. To view all services, leave Hide All Microsoft Services unchecked; to view only third-party services, check Hide All Microsoft Services. Many of these services are certainly not needed. Leave checked anything that has your anti-virus program's name listed in it, and don't uncheck anything you don't recognize, but certainly uncheck things you don't need. We unchecked several here, including VAIO Media Music Server (Application), VAIO Media Music Server (HTTP), and VAIO Media Music Server (UpnP). We know we don't need any of these things. Uncheck what you deem unnecessary (nothing essential) and reboot.

TIP: Keep in mind that you can always go back and recheck anything you've disabled.

GunkBuster's Notebook: Finding Performance Utilities on the Internet

You can find a lot of software utilities on the Internet that are either free or really inexpensive and can be used to improve the performance of your system. To see just how many there are, type *Freeware Shareware Windows XP Performance* into your favorite search engine. Our most recent search yielded over a million hits!

There are applications that claim to speed up the boot process, clean the Registry, "heal" the Registry, maintain peak performance automatically, optimize Windows, tune up Windows, edit partitions, and more. Be careful when you select, download, install, and/or purchase this software! Some of the code might not have been written by the most experienced programmers, some might contain spyware or adware, some might enable pop-ups or annoy you with a registration dialog for the rest of your life, or worse, they might even crash your computer. (We recently had an unpleasant experience with MSN Messenger Plus! 3. The only way to recover our hijacked search engine and get rid of pop-ups was to use a System Restore.)

Before downloading and installing anything, then, visit various sites and compare notes. You'll be able to find reviews on the latest freeware and shareware in a number of places, including reputable sites like **www.winfiles.com**, **www.pcworld.com**, and **http://download.com**. We found plenty about the MSN Messenger Plus! 3 download, including posts in several forums that said it was actually LOP, which is adware/spyware. Read the reviews first!

TIP: *The Google search "<product name> spyware" is a good thing to try if you suspect that a "free" utility has some strings attached. Replace <product name> with the name of the utility in question.*

View Errors with Dr. Watson

If you are having unknown problems with your computer that you don't believe are related to adware or spyware, and you think you might be having some internal issues, you can check Dr. Watson's log for details. If you see a lot of errors in there, you might consider looking for answers on the Web, doing a repair installation, or disabling incompatible software or drivers. Dr. Watson is a well-hidden feature of Windows XP, but it can be easily opened from the Run line. If you don't have any errors listed, you can be pretty sure that Windows XP is running well and has no internal errors.

Running Dr. Watson (Drwtsn32.exe)

Click Start, click Run, and type *Drwtsn32.exe* in the Run dialog box. Then click OK to start the program. You'll see a screen like the one shown in Figure 12-4. Notice that we're having problems with Outlook Express; it shuts down from time to time, usually when too many things are done at once, like sending an e-mail from a photo application or composing an e-mail while receiving e-mail simultaneously. This is probably just too much for our poor little 256 MB computer to handle!

You can view error logs by clicking the application error and clicking View. This information can be helpful when trying to solve a particular problem with a qualified tech support person. In fact, if you call tech support and say that Dr. Watson has determined that you're having problems with Outlook Express, you'll be one step ahead of the game!

Use Network Diagnostics

You can view problems with your network from Windows Help and Support Center. From the information provided, you can locate communication problems either on your network or when accessing the Web. The information provided can help you discover why you can't connect to the resource you need to connect to. Network Diagnostics checks connectivity for Outlook Express, Outlook Express newsreader, your Web Proxy if one exists, modems, network adapters, and network clients. To use this application, follow these steps:

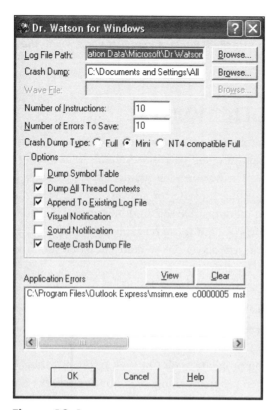

Figure 12-4

Dr. Watson can help you diagnose problems.

1. Click Start and then click Help And Support.

2. Under Pick A Task, select Use Tools To View Computer Information And Diagnose Problems. Pick a Task is located on the bottom right of the first Help and Support page.

3. In the Tools pane, select Network Diagnostics.

4. Click Scan Your System.

Get Rid of Unsigned Files and Drivers

Signed device drivers and files have been tested by Microsoft and are deemed safe and compatible. Those that are not signed might not be safe and might not be compatible. Unsigned device drivers and files associated with incompatible software is another area that can cause a computer to have a slow boot process, have a slow reaction time, or generally have unexpected performance errors (like a failure to come out of hibernation). This incompatibility can cause major problems, including unexpected shutdowns of applications, hardware that sometimes works and sometimes doesn't, hard-to-diagnose problems with the shutdown process (including the inability of the computer to shut down at all), and even blue screens and memory dumps.

You can see what unsigned files (including drivers) are installed on your system using the File Signature Verification utility, and you can do a little preventive maintenance by telling Windows you don't want to ever install unsigned drivers once these are uninstalled or updated.

Using File Signature Verification

Here are the steps to follow to scan for files and programs that do not have valid digital signatures:

1. At the Run line, type *Sigverif.exe* and click OK. You'll see the File Signature Verification dialog box shown in Figure 12-5.

Figure 12-5
In the File Signature Verification box, click Advanced to see whether drivers are signed or unsigned.

2. Click Advanced and notice that the box called Notify Me If Any System Files Are Not Signed is checked. Run the utility with this option.

3. Click OK and then click the Start button to have Windows look for files that do not have valid digital signatures.

4. Rerun the program with the second option, Look For Other Files That Are Not Digitally Signed, checked.

Once the scan is complete, you'll see a report similar to the one shown in Figure 12-6. Sort by file type to view programs that do not have valid signatures. But don't panic. Although these programs *can* cause system instability, that doesn't mean that they do. You don't have to go crazy here spending hours researching what each of these files do and what program they belong to. However, if after reading this section, you believe that you recently installed a new component with an unsigned driver and now you've noticed some system problems, consider searching for and installing a new driver for that device. In addition, if you have several unsigned printer files and you no longer own the printer, see what you can do about uninstalling that software (see Chapter 4). Use this tool as a basis to find out what is unsigned. Consider uninstalling third-party applications that aren't signed and/or reinstalling signed copies of system files.

Figure 12-6

The Signature Verification Results window shows files that are signed or not signed.

In this particular list, we can see that a file named lexgo.exe is not signed. After looking on the Internet, we found that this file was created by Lexmark, a printer manufacturer. We had a Lexmark printer years ago (in 2000), but we do not have one now. Our Internet search also yields hundreds of forum posts asking for help with this file and error messages received about it. We'll likely search now for Lexmark files and old Lexmark software and delete any Lexmark printers and their drivers.

You can find out what the many items in your results list are simply by typing them into a Web search engine, just as we did. For instance, typing in *ctregrun.exe* immediately brings up Creative Labs's registration reminder. This can obviously be deleted or uninstalled. Check out **www.greatis.com/appdata/ useless.htm** for a long list of useless files similar to this one.

TIP: If you've found software for hardware in this list, you may have also found a problem device. You can disable problem devices in Device Manager, although you might have to choose Show Hidden Devices from the View menu and then disable the device under the Non-Plug And Play Drivers list. You can also use Device Manager to update drivers; this will be introduced shortly.

Maintenance Sidebar: Set Driver Signing Properties

You can tell Windows to be more careful about installing unsigned drivers from the System Properties dialog box. Open Control Panel and Performance And Maintenance (if using the XP theme) and click on System. Click the Hardware tab and click Driver Signing. The Driver Signing Options dialog box is shown in Figure 12-7.

Figure 12-7
Make sure you aren't downloading unsigned drivers without first being prompted.

We prefer the Warn setting. With this selected and made the system default, we'll be prompted each time an unsigned driver is going to be installed and we'll have the option to install or not.

Updating Unsigned Drivers

If you find out that your printer, scanner, camera, or some other piece of hard-ware has an unsigned driver, you can search the Internet for a newer, signed one. Many times, these newer drivers can be found by running Windows Up-date. Windows Update is nice because the drivers are downloaded and installed automatically, so it should be the first place you look. Other times you'll have to visit the manufacturer's Web site.

If you find a newer driver from the manufacturer's Web site, you'll need to download it and save it to your computer. Then, you can use Device Manager to update the device driver easily. Here are the steps to follow:

1. Right-click My Computer and click Properties. You can also open System from Control Panel.

2. In the System Properties dialog box, click the Hardware tab and click Device Manager. If you notice any items with a red *X* or a yellow exclama-tion point, that particular piece of equipment has problems with either the driver or the hardware itself. Double-click on the item to see what the problem is. Figure 12-8 shows an example.

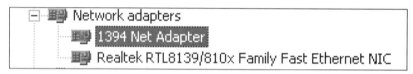

Figure 12-8

A red *X* indicates a serious problem.

3. Expand the hardware trees, and locate the item you want to update. Double-click it to open its Properties dialog box.

4. To update a driver, click the Driver tab, and click Update Driver. Browse to the location of the saved, updated driver and follow the prompts to install it.

TIP: If the new driver doesn't work as planned, use Device Driver Rollback. However, don't install a different driver before rolling back to the old one. Device Driver Rollback only remembers the last driver Installed, and no more further back in time than that.

In addition to installing a newer driver, you can disable a device from Device Manager. If you are positive a specific device is lousing up the system and causing performance problems, disable it for a while and see if the problem goes away.

Error Checking

Your hard disk won't run optimally if there are bad sectors on it. Sectors are where data is stored, and if any sectors are damaged and you try to write data to them, you're going to run into problems. To scan for bad sectors on the hard drive, use the error-checking tool in My Computer:

1. Close all running programs, and from the Start menu, click Open My Computer.

2. Right-click the disk you want to check for errors and click Properties.

3. Click the Tools menu, and under Error-Checking, click Check Now.

4. In the Check Disk dialog box, shown in Figure 12-9, check Automatically Fix File System Errors and Scan For And Attempt Recovery Of Bad Sectors. Click Start.

Figure 12-9
You should check the file system for errors occasionally or anytime you think problems exist.

5. You'll most likely be prompted to restart Windows and let the error checking run on reboot. Click Yes to reboot, and then click OK.

After the computer boots up, the CHKDSK utility will run. Wait while Windows finds and fixes the hard disk problems. This might take a while, and your computer will be unavailable during this process.

Staying Degunked

Keeping your computer degunked isn't easy. It takes patience and perseverance, and a dedication to maintaining a healthy computer. That being said, it's also hard to know how often to perform the tasks outlined in this chapter. Table 12-1 gives you a general idea of how often to perform the tasks here. Use this table to guide you through the process of staying degunking and organized.

Table 12-1   Schedule for Staying Degunked and Organized

Task	How Often to Perform	Tips for Remaining Degunked
Convert to NTFS and resize partitions if needed.	Once	After purchasing a new computer, immediately convert to NTFS and get rid of unnecessary partitions.
Clean up the Startup folder.	Once every two weeks	Verify there are no unwanted items in your Startup folder.
Monitor login options.	Once a week	Verify that it is still safe to log on automatically. If you are expecting guests, enable the Guest account.
Use msconfig at the Run line.	Once a month	Verify that only items you want to start automatically are actually doing so.
Update unsigned drivers.	Once a month	Enable Automatic Update so that new drivers are automatically installed.

Run error checking utilities such as Dr. Watson, Network Diagnostics, and the File Signature Verification to diagnose problems. When problems exist, remove unsigned drivers, resolve networking problems, and fix disks. Recheck monthly.

TIP: Some features can be automatically configured to run on a schedule using Scheduled Tasks from Control Panel. You'll learn more about that in Chapter 17.

Summing Up

The main idea behind optimizing the hard drive is to get XP to boot faster, to get it to run faster, and to enhance the general performance of the computer. Some things that can make the boot process faster include cleaning up the Startup folder, modifying the BIOS so the floppy disk isn't accessed for startup files, logging on automatically, and disabling any boot delay currently configured.

Once your computer is booted, its performance can be enhanced by using NTFS, being aware of system errors and fixing them, detecting errors caused by unsigned device drivers or incompatible hardware, and finding physical problems with the hard drive itself. By repairing existing problems and configuring XP to run efficiently, you can improve performance dramatically.

Cleaning and Tweaking the Registry

Degunking Checklist:

√   Learn what the Registry is, why it isn't scary, and why it is important for degunking your PC.

√   Learn how to use REGEDT32 to view the Registry.

√   Use the System Restore feature to back up and restore the Registry.

√   Back up sections of the Registry using REGEDT32.

√   Use the Registry Clean Pro utility to automatically scan and clean the Registry.

√   Use REGEDT32 to make tweaks to the Registry that can help you with your degunking chores.

Oh no, here comes the Registry! Just hearing the name of this creature might send shivers down your spine. But the Registry is like the man behind the curtain in the *Wizard of Oz*. Once you finally meet this much-feared Windows character, you'll find that it isn't that scary. Of course, the Registry plays a very critical role in Windows. It is also a critical component that needs to be cleaned periodically to keep your computer running in top form. The Registry can easily get gunked up because Windows applications often store data in it but don't always clean up after themselves as they should. As you learn about how to clean and degunk the Registry in this chapter, you should always keep in mind that safety is our top priority when making changes to it.

The Registry is one of those Windows features that everyone is constantly warning you about. Many Windows users (and even power users) are afraid of it because they don't fully understand what it does and how it works. But in order to really degunk your PC, there are things you must know about the Registry, including how it is used by Windows, how program information is stored in the Registry, how you can clean it both automatically and manually, and how you can tweak it to improve the performance of your PC.

As you'll learn in this chapter, there are two categories of activities you can perform on the Registry that are critical to helping you degunk your PC:

√   Cleaning the Registry and repairing Registry keys

√   Tweaking and optimizing the Registry

To help you understand how the Registry works, we'll also show you how to manually view and edit data that is stored in there.

CAUTION! *Before you make any changes to the Registry, you should make a backup copy of it. If you edit the Registry and make a major mistake, you risk rendering your system unusable. If you don't have a backup, your only recourse would be to reinstall Windows. Don't be foolish and learn this lesson the hard way! Take a moment now to skip ahead in this chapter to the section that shows you how to back up the Registry.*

Inside the Registry

Windows used to have simple configuration files (called INI files) that stored important configuration information the operating system needed to perform critical tasks, such as starting up and loading programs, keeping track of program preferences, and storing and loading system settings for the Desktop. If you have been using Windows for a while, you probably remember these pesky INI files.

When Windows NT was born, these configuration files disappeared and were replaced by the mighty Registry. The Registry is essentially a big relational database that stores information needed by Windows, such as operating system configuration data, application settings, hardware settings, networking settings, and much more. This information is stored in a hierarchical format, much like your Desktop file folder system.

As an example, let's say that you are using Microsoft Word to edit a file. During your editing session, you resize your main document window. When you quit Word, the document window size settings will be saved in the Registry so that next time you use Word, it will open just as it was when you last left it. And you thought Windows did stuff like this by magic!

Because so much information is stored in the Registry, the Registry can easily get gunked up over time. Many of the applications you use on a regular basis will write to the Registry, and Windows itself is always storing information there. Most applications write to the Registry properly, but some don't—and the registry is a favorite target of adware, spyware, viruses, and worms. This can leave you with a Registry that has incomplete data and extraneous data, which in turn makes your computer run more slowly.

What makes the Registry so critical and complex is that it touches just about everything that Windows does. To manage all of the tasks that take place with the Registry, Windows fortunately provides built-in tools that help to keep the Registry working properly. But as with any component of Windows, gunk will seep into the Registry, and it can cause a lot of problems, such as slow performance and system crashes.

To operate as efficiently as it can, the Registry data is stored in a binary format. This means that you can't simply read or change the data in the Registry without using a special tool. In this chapter, we'll use the powerful REGEDT32 program to show you how to manually view and change data in the Registry. Then, we'll use a third-party tool to clean the Registry.

A Quick Note about Windows Versions

As mentioned earlier, the Registry has been around for a while, and it has evolved just as Windows has grown up and improved. Because of this, you'll find that different tools and procedures are required to work with the various versions of Windows (NT, 98, ME, 2000, and XP). Since the primary focus of this book is on degunking computers running Windows XP, we'll focus on the tools and procedures required to view, clean, and tweak the Windows XP Registry. As we go along, however, we will point out some of the tools and procedures that will work with other versions of Windows. The following list includes some of the main issues for working with the different Registry versions:

√ REGCLEAN.EXE, the popular Registry cleaning tool developed by Microsoft, does not work with Windows XP. It was designed for earlier versions of Windows and is no longer supported by Microsoft.

√ Techniques for backing up and restoring the Registry differ significantly from version to version of Windows. For example, Windows 98 and ME provide a system tool called Registry Checker that you can use to back up the Registry; this tool is not available with Windows XP.

√ While searching the Web for tips and utilities to clean, repair, and restore the Registry, be sure to match up the information and software you find with your version of Windows. Often, information on the Web may refer to older versions of Windows. If you are running XP, be sure to obtain the very latest information and utilities.

REGEDT32 Is Your Gateway to the Registry

Windows XP actually includes two Registry editing tools, REGEDIT and REGEDT32. We'll be using REGEDT32 in this book because it is slightly safer than REGEDIT for viewing and making changes to the Registry. REGEDT32 is safer because it does not apply the changes that you make to the Registry immediately. To apply the changes that you make, you must first close REDEDT32. This gives you a sort of insurance policy. By comparison, REGEDIT applies your changes as soon as you make them.

Here's a tour of REGEDT32:

1. Choose Run from the Start menu and type in REGEDT32.EXE.

2. The window shown in Figure 13-1 should appear. The information that is first displayed might look unfamiliar to you. Each entry listed is called a top-level *key* or *hive*. (You can think of a hive as a broad category.) Notice that there are five hives listed. Each hive stores all of the values that represent individual system settings.

3. Double-click the hive or folder labeled HKEY_USERS. Then double-click the folder labeled .DEFAULT that appears. This should create the screen shown in Figure 13-2.

4. If you then double-click one of the subfolders that appear, such as Console or Environment, you will see a window pane that displays specific keys along with their settings. For example, Figure 13-3 shows the view displayed when the Console folder is selected. Notice that the window displays keys with labels like FaceName, FontFamily, and FontSize.

Figure 13-1
Viewing your top-level Registry data with the REGEDT32 tool.

Figure 13-2
Viewing the default user setup data.

Each stored Registry entry is essentially a setting with an assigned value. The value tells Windows how to treat a specific setting. For example, the value assigned to the FontSize setting would tell Windows which font size to use as the default setting for the console display.

Figure 13-3

Viewing Registry keys and values.

The trick to dealing properly with the Registry is to understand that all of the data is stored (as keys and values) in a hierarchical manner. At the top level of the Registry hierarchy are the hives, or folders, listed in Table 13-1.

Table 13-1   Top-Level Windows Registry Keys

Hive	Description
HKEY_CLASSES_ROOT	This hive stores information about all file extensions, descriptions, icons, associations, shortcuts, automation, class IDs, and more.
HKEY_CURRENT_USER	This hive serves as a link to the currently logged-in user's key stored in KKEY_USERS.
HKEY_LOCAL_MACHINE	This hive stores all software, hardware, network, security, and Windows system information. This is the area where most of the Registry keys and values are located.
HKEY_USERS	This hive stores all of the information about all users and their individual settings. The setting values include environment variables, color schemes, fonts, icons, Desktop configuration, Start menu items, network, and more. Each time a new user logs on, a new key is created based on a default key.
HKEY_CURRENT_CONFIG	This hive is actually a link that points to the currently selected hardware profile stored in HKEY_LOCAL_MACHINE.

Back Up and Restore the Registry

Take a moment to follow these instructions and make a backup copy of your Registry. Put your backup in a safe place, and always make sure you create a new backup before you start to make any editing changes to the Registry.

The tricky part about backing up and restoring the Registry is twofold:

√ Because Windows is always using the Registry and part of it is always open, it is difficult to back up the entire Registry.

√ Each version of Windows provides a different process and tools for backing up and restoring the Registry.

In this section, we'll focus on backing up and restoring the Registry for Windows XP.

Fortunately, Windows XP (and all versions of Windows) automatically creates a backup copy of the Registry each time Windows is started. But for smart and cautious degunkers like us, this isn't good enough. You should also keep an additional backup in a safe place—you never want to take chances when it comes to the Registry! There are essentially three different techniques you can use to back up the Registry:

√ Use the Windows XP Backup utility, as covered in Chapter 15. This utility provides an easy way to back up your entire system. The only caveat is that you need to be running Windows XP Professional to have access to this backup program. Windows XP Home does not include it.

√ Use Windows XP's System Restore feature to create a restore point, which will back up all of the system data, including the Registry. The benefit of this approach is that you can easily restore your full system back to a previous state that you specify. The System Restore feature is described in more detail in Chapter 16, but we'll show you how to use it to back up and restore the Registry here.

√ Back up and restore selected parts of the Registry using the REGEDT32 utility. Technically, this utility provides a feature to back up the entire Registry; however, we recommend you only use this utility to back up selected Registry keys. We make this recommendation because the Registry is always accessed by Windows, and although you can save the entire Registry manually to one large file using REGEDT32, you will not be able to fully restore it. The Registry has special security settings on certain keys that prevent you from restoring it manually.

CAUTION! *One common misconception about the Windows XP Registry is that you can back up the entire Registry by simply making a copy of the Registry files. Although this technique could be used for Windows 98, Windows XP accesses many sections of the Registry directly. This means that Registry files could be open at all times, and you won't be able to back them up fully because they are in use by one or more subsystems within Windows.*

Use System Restore to Back Up and Restore the Full Registry

Using System Restore to back up and restore the full Registry is the preferred option because it will safely back up the full Registry. We suggest that you run System Restore manually by following the steps shown below, immediately before you make changes to the Registry. You should also do this before you make major hardware and software changes to your system; System Restore backs up all Windows parameters and settings, not simply the Registry.

Follow these steps to use System Restore:

1. Click Start and point to Programs, then Accessories, then System Tools and then click System Restore. This will produce the screen shown in Figure 13-4.

2. Select the Create A Restore Point option and click Next.

Figure 13-4

Using the System Restore feature to set a restore point.

3. Type in a name for the restore point you are creating and then click the Create button. Use a descriptive name such as "Backup before changing Registry."

4. The restore point will be created using the current date and time. The nice thing with this feature is that all of your system settings (including the entire Registry) will be saved.

To later restore your system using a restore point that you've created, do this:

1. Click Start and point to Programs, then Accessories, then System Tools and then click System Restore. This will bring up the same screen shown in Figure 13-4.

2. Select the Restore My Computer To An Earlier Time option, then click Next.

3. Select the restore point that you have previously saved from the list presented (see Figure 13-5) and click Next.

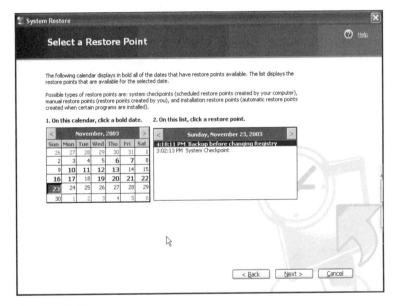

Figure 13-5

Selecting a previously saved restore point.

4. When the final screen is presented, click Next to start the process. Before you do this, be sure that all running programs have been closed and all of your data files have been saved. The System Restore feature will then shut down Windows and do its magic. After the restoration is complete, Windows will restart and return the settings that were in effect at the time you created the restore point. Keep in mind that System Restore may take a few minutes to restore your system.

When using the System Restore feature to create a restore point and then later restore your system, keep in mind that not only is the Registry data replaced, but all of your system-level information is restored as well. The restore process allows you to restore your computer without losing recently-added items, such as documents, Internet Favorites, e-mail messages, or your Internet History files. For more information on the benefits of the System Restore feature, and to learn additional techniques for how to use it, read Chapter 16.

Use REGEDT32 to Back Up and Restore Selected Parts of the Registry

If you need to back up a section of the Registry, such as a set of keys that you are planning to change, you can use the REGEDT32 tool. This tool provides a handy export and import capability so that you can back up only those parts of the Registry that you select.

To back up sections of the Registry, follow these steps:

1. Click Start and then Run and type in REGEDT32.EXE.

2. Locate the top-level set of keys that you wish to save. Remember that you can navigate through the Registry keys as if they were a set of folders. When you find the top-level key you want, click on it to highlight it.

3. Click My Computer to select it, and choose Export from the File menu.

4. Select the Selected Branch button in the Export Range section of the window, as shown in Figure 13-6.

5. Type in a name for the file and browse to a place to save it. In our example, we are saving the set of keys and their associated values that are assigned to the HKEY_CURRENT_USER section or hive.

6. Click Save to create the backup file.

To later restore the section of the Registry that you saved, follow these steps:

1. Click Start and then Run and then type in REGEDT32.EXE.

2. Locate the top-level set of keys that you wish to restore. When you find the top-level key you want, click on it to highlight it.

3. Click My Computer to select it, and choose import from the File menu.

4. Select the file that you created to store your backup data and click the Open button.

Clean the Registry

Because the Registry is like the central control system of your computer, whenever you install, uninstall, or reinstall software, changes will be made to Registry keys. Usually the programs you install and uninstall will do a good job of

Figure 13-6
Exporting a section of the Registry using REGEDT32.

setting themselves up and cleaning up after themselves; however, not all programs work with the Registry properly. Some applications simply don't remove all traces of themselves when you uninstall them. In addition, you might have programs that you simply deleted from your computer without running the proper uninstall procedures. (Now you know why you should not just delete a program by placing it in the trash. You actually need to run its associated uninstall program.) Finally, adware and spyware often leave unauthorized keys in the Registry that are not always removed with the spyware itself.

Over time, the Registry can get gunked up, and Registry gunk can cause problems such as these:

- Your computer may boot very slowly.
- Your programs may not launch properly.
- Your computer could crash unexpectedly.
- Your programs might have problems performing some operations, such as saving files to the proper directories, launching properly with the correct settings, and so on.

The more you do on your computer (if you install and remove lots of programs, for example), the more cluttered and bloated the Registry can become. In fact, if you followed the instructions in Chapter 4 and removed the extra programs that you don't need, it's likely that you've contributed to the clutter in the Registry. But help is on the way! By using a few carefully chosen products, we can clean up your Registry so it won't bog down your computer.

Use Registry Cleaning Software

Cleaning the Registry manually can an enormous task. As you learned earlier in this chapter, there are hundreds of keys to work with and potentially clean up. You could seriously damage the Registry if you are not extremely careful (or if you don't know what you're doing). A better way to clean the Registry is to use a third-party Windows Registry cleaning tool. There are many to choose from, which is both good news and bad news. Table 13-2 lists some of the commercial tools that are available.

Table 13-2   Software Tools that Can Be Used to Clean the Registry

Tool	Estimated Cost	Description
Norton SystemWorks	$70	Full-featured set of utilities that include a tool for cleaning the Registry.
Registry Clean Pro	$29.95	A safe utility that specializes in fixing errors and optimizing the performance of the Registry.
Registry Mechanic	$19.99	A program that allows you to safely clean and repair Windows Registry problems with a few simple mouse clicks.
Registry First Aid	$21.00	This tool is covered in Chapter 15.

In this chapter, we'll be using the Registry Clean Pro utility because it is easy to use, it provides a safe way to clean the Registry, and the company provides a free trial version that you can use for 30 days. Registry Clean Pro is safe because it never deletes a Registry key if this action could harm your computer. It also automatically creates a backup file before it removes any entries from the Registry. To clean the Registry, this utility scans all of your hard drives for the files and folders you have. It then scans the Registry to match up the files you have on your hard drives with the entries stored in the Registry. Its goal is to search out the Registry entries that are no longer valid and delete them. It can also produce a descriptive report that shows you the invalid Registry entries that Registry Clean Pro locates.

Here's how to clean the Registry with Registry Clean Pro:

1. Download and install the trial version of Registry Clean Pro from the company's Web site (www.registry-clean.com). You can also purchase the full version of the utility for $29.95 from the Web site. The trial version of the

software does a good job; however, there are a few sections of the Registry that it doesn't clean out, including the file extensions and COM/ActiveX sections.

2. Run the program, and the startup screen shown in Figure 13-7 appears.

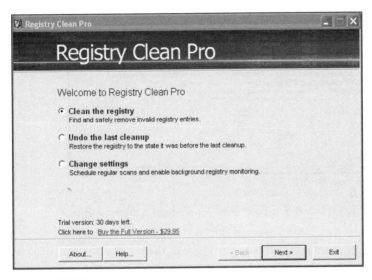

Figure 13-7
The startup screen for Registry Clean Pro.

3. Select the Clean the Registry option and click Next.

4. Select the Full Scan option and click Next. Registry Clean Pro will warn you to close all open applications that you have running. This is crucial because some programs may try to access the Registry during the scanning process.

5. Once you have closed all open applications, click Next to start the scan. Registry Clean Pro will then take a few minutes to scan your hard drives and the Registry. It will create a list of the invalid entries that it finds.

6. After Registry Clean Pro completes its scan, it will display a screen listing the total number of invalid entries that it locates. At this point, you can instruct the program to clean the Registry automatically or display the list of errors found. We suggest you first review the list of errors before you start the actual cleaning process.

7. Select the Display The List Of Errors option and click Next.

8. Registry Clean Pro will then display a screen showing the errors found. You can sort this view by description by selecting the Description option in the Show As drop-down box. Figure 13-8 shows an example of the descriptive

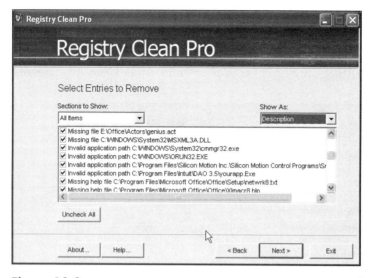

Figure 13-8
Viewing the errors found in a descriptive format from a Registry scan.

list. We recommend that you scan through the list of errors and make sure you don't see any you want to keep in the Registry. If you desire, you can unselect an entry.

9. After you have scanned the set of errors, click the Next button to return to the main scanning screen. Select the Clean The Registry option and click Next. Registry Clean Pro will then remove the invalid entries that it found.

TIP: *If you perform a Registry clean operation with Registry Clean Pro and you later decide you want to undo the cleaning operation, select the Undo The Last Cleanup option from the main screen and click Next. The Registry will then be fully restored to the state it was in before the last cleanup.*

The following sections of the Registry will be cleaned by Registry Clean Pro:

√   Startup

√   Shared DLLs

√   Fonts

√   Application info

√   Shared files

√   Help files

√   Most recently used list

√   File extensions

√   COM/ActiveX

Use Microsoft's RegClean to Clean the Registry in Windows 95/98/NT or Windows 2000

A few years back, Microsoft created a utility called RegClean.exe to help Windows 95/98/NT and Windows 2000 users clean the Registry. Unfortunately, this tool does not work with Windows XP. You might have guessed, RegClean is an older program and Microsoft no longer distributes it. It is, however, a free program and does a good job of performing a basic clean operation of Windows 95, 98, NT, and Windows 2000 registries.

Tweak the Registry

Now that you've learned the basics of how to use the Registry and how to clean it with an automated tool, let's look at some changes you can make to manually to improve the performance of your PC. The tweaks we'll make can also help you with some of your degunking chores. As we discussed earlier, it is very important that you back up the Registry before you make any changes to it. This is especially important if you make manual changes. The tweaks that we are introducing here are very simple ones and should not harm your Registry; however, you should always exercise caution and make sure your backups are current.

TIP: We also recommend that you make only **one** change to the Registry at a time. After you make the change, you should restart Windows and make sure that the change you made produces the effect you want. When it comes to tweaking the Registry, don't try to be too ambitious. Simple and slow is the best policy.

There are many different types of tweaks that you can perform to enhance the workings of your PC. For example, you can improve the appearance of your Desktop and display, make changes to the Start menu and Taskbar, improve how critical applications such as Windows Explorer operate, and much more. For this chapter, we'll focus on some simple tweaks that can help you with your degunking chores. If you want to learn more about how to safely tweak and optimize the Registry, a good site to explore is www.winguides.com/registry.

GunkBuster's Notebook: Editing Values in the Registry

As you start to change values in the Registry to perform different system tweaks, you'll quickly encounter the different types of data that are stored there. To make a Registry change, you'll need to understand the basics of data types. A data type essentially specifies the data format of the value stored for a setting. The following list includes some of the more common data types that are stored in the Registry:

√ REG_SZ—This data type is used to store text strings such as "Yes," "No," "filename," and so on.

√ REG_DWORD—This data type stores numerical data in hexadecimal or decimal format.

√ REG_BINARY—This data type stores binary data (0 or 1 values).

√ REG_EXPAND_SZ—This data type stores variables in string data format. The variables are replaced by applications.

√ REG_MULTI_SZ—This data type is used for lists or multiple values.

When you work with the Registry, you can easily determine the data type for a value that you want to view or change. Once you select a Registry key to view, as shown in Figure 13-9, you'll see three attributes displayed for each value in the viewing pane: Name, Type, and Data. The Name attribute provides the name of the value or setting that you can view and change. The Type attribute specifies the data type for the value. If you examine Figure 13-9, you'll notice that most of the data types for the values listed are REG_DWORD, which indicates they store a numeric value.

Figure 13-9

Viewing data types for Registry values.

Finally, the Data attribute shows the actual data value that is assigned to the setting.

To edit the data value for a setting, double-click the name of the setting. Figure 13-10 shows an example of the Edit Value dialog box that appears. In this example, we are editing the FaultTime setting. The value for this setting is entered in the Value Data field. Notice that it currently has a value of 0. Because this setting has a data type of double, you must enter a numeric value.

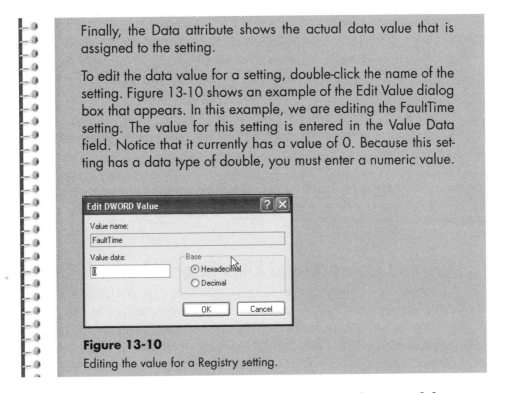

Figure 13-10
Editing the value for a Registry setting.

Turn My Documents into a Cascading Folder

If you've been following our advice earlier in this book to better organize your My Documents folder by creating subfolders within it, you probably have a number of folders stored within My Documents. Using the Registry, you can easily turn My Documents into a cascading folder, which will then allow you to easily access the subfolders. The best part is that you won't have to first open the My Documents folder to get to your subfolders. This might encourage you to keep your personal data better organized because you'll easily be able to get at the folders stored inside My Documents.

Here's how to make My Documents a cascading folder:

1. Choose Run from the Start menu and type in REGEDT32.EXE.

2. Locate and open the key HKEY_CURRENT_USER\Software\Microsoft\ Windows\CurrentVersion\Explorer\Advanced.

3. Within this key or folder, you will find values, or settings, that control different settings for Explorer. Locate the one named CascadeMyDocuments. (If this value is not available, you will need to create one, which we'll explain in step 5.)

4. If the CascadeMyDocuments value is present, double-click it. Change the value to Yes.

5. If the CascadeMyDocuments value is not present, right-click inside the window view pane where the values are listed and select New | String Value. A new string value will be created with a default name. You can then rename it CascadeMyDocuments and assign it the value Yes as shown in step 4.

6. Quit the Registry editor and restart Windows in order for this change to take effect.

TIP: *You can also set up your My Pictures folder as a cascading folder on the Desktop by following the preceding instructions, but this time, you add the string value "CascadeMyPictures" and assign it the value Yes.*

Display Compressed Files in an Alternate Color

If you receive numerous compressed files, such as zip files, you might have difficulty cleaning them up from your folders because they might blend in with all the other files. Once you uncompress a compressed file, you likely won't need to keep the compressed version of the file lying around. By eliminating unused compressed files, you can significantly reduce the gunk on your machine.

Fortunately, under Windows XP, you can use the Registry to tweak Windows Explorer so that compressed files and folders will be displayed in an alternate color. This tweak involves a two-step process. First you must "turn on" the alternate color feature, and then you need to assign a new color (if you don't want to use the default color of blue):

1. Choose Run from the Start menu and type in REGEDT32.EXE.

2. Locate and open the key HKEY_CURRENT_USER\Software\Microsoft_ Windows\CurrentVersion\Explorer.

3. Locate the value named ShowCompColor. This value is a DWORD value. (If this value is not available, you will need to create it.)

4. Set the value to 1 to enable the use of alternate colors. (The value 0 is used to apply default colors.) When this setting is turned on, the default color used will be blue.

5. If you want to use a color other than blue, create a new binary value named AltColor and set it to equal the hexadecimal RGB color value you want to use.

6. Quit the Registry editor and restart Windows in order for this change to take effect.

By highlighting compressed files, it will be easier to see which files you've uncompressed. If you regularly delete uncompressed files (after you've saved the components under their separate file names), you won't have a lot of gunk accumulating in this folder.

Display Hidden Files with Explorer

As you are using Windows Explorer to locate files to delete as part of the degunking process, you may need to view the hidden files. You can easily use the Registry to tweak Windows Explorer so that it always displays hidden files by default. Here are the steps to follow:

1. Choose Run from the Start menu and type in REGEDT32.EXE.
2. Locate and open the key HKEY_CURRENT_USER\Software\Microsoft_ Windows\CurrentVersion\Explorer/Advanced.
3. Locate the value named Hidden. This value is a DWORD value.
4. Set the value to 1 to enable the viewing of hidden files. (The value 2 is used to disable the viewing of hidden files.)
5. Quit the Registry editor and restart Windows in order for this change to take effect.

You can also view the hidden system-level operating system files with Windows Explorer by setting a different value in the Registry:

1. Locate and open the key HKEY_CURRENT_USER\Software\Microsoft_ Windows\CurrentVersion\Explorer/Advanced.
2. Set the value SuperHidden to 1 to show all hidden system files. (A value of 0 will hide system files.)

Once all of your personal files and folders (as well as system files) have been unhidden, you'll be able to see everything that is stored in your various folders. Hidden files can add more gunk to your hard drive because you won't know they are there and they will likely never be removed. Out-of-sight is not always the best policy when it comes to degunking.

Remove All Icons from Your Desktop

You can remove all icons from the Desktop if you desire. This is a good way to really clean off your Desktop. It involves another Registry tweak, so make sure you back up the system before you begin.

To clear the Desktop of icons, follow these steps:

1. Choose Run from the Start menu and type in REGEDT32.EXE.

2. Locate and open the key named HKEY_CURRENT_USER\Software_ Microsoft\Windows\CurrentVersion\Policies\Explorer.

3. Locate the NoDesktop value and double-click it. (If this value is not present, you will need to create it.)

4. Change the value to 1.

5. Quit the Registry editor and restart Windows in order for this change to take effect.

Summing Up

Cleaning your Registry can be an important part of the degunking process. And the best part is that you can use a safe third-party utility, such as Registry Clean Pro, to clean your Registry on a regular basis. But as you would before you make any changes to the Registry, make sure that you back it up first. With a clean Registry, Windows will function much more efficiently and you'll find that Windows and your various applications will load quicker. After you clean the Registry, you also might find that certain problems that you have been encountering with your computer go away. In addition to cleaning the Registry, you can perform a variety of Registry tweaks to help you improve the performance of your computer and the degunking process.

The Best Hardware for PC Degunking

Degunking Checklist:

√ Purchase and physically install extra RAM (memory) to enhance the performance of your computer.

√ Configure virtual memory settings to fully utilize the memory you have.

√ Add a backup device to perform reliable backups and store them off-site.

√ Add a second (or third) monitor to extend your Desktop and make room for all of your running applications.

√ Physically clean the computer.

√ Purchase a new computer (in case your PC becomes a lost cause) and transfer your files and settings.

√ Degunk a new PC.

Cs are about more than just software. You need enough (and the right) hardware to let the software work effectively, and you need to keep the hardware free of gunk. This chapter introduces you to the different types of hardware you can acquire to beef up your system, including RAM and additional monitors. You'll learn how to configure and take care of your existing hardware to get the best possible performance. You'll also learn how having the right hardware can help you with the degunking process. Adding RAM (physical memory) is the way to go if you want faster performance and can afford it; you'll notice a difference right away. Adding a second monitor can certainly enhance productivity, and installing a backup device can obviously enhance security (if you use it).

Beyond physical hardware, though, physically cleaning your machine is a good thing to do occasionally, too; dust and grime can cause problems. You can also tweak how the hard drive stores temporary data when RAM is full by configuring the virtual memory settings. If, however, after all of this, you determine that your computer is much too gunked up and you still can't get what you want out of it, you always have the option of purchasing a new one. If that's what you decide to do, you'll want to know all about the Files And Settings Transfer Wizard and how to degunk that brand-new PC before you use it.

Let's start with the most basic and fundamental way to enhance the performance of your computer—adding memory.

Add Memory

Adding memory is the easiest and fastest way to speed up and improve the response time of your computer. These days, purchasing an extra 128 or 256 MB of RAM won't break the bank. RAM stands for *random access memory*, and it's where XP stores data it needs or thinks it will need to complete a task like print a document, perform a calculation, or receive and open an e-mail. If your computer has 256 MB of RAM or less, you really need to upgrade to at least 512 MB. If you have 512 MB, you'll see a noticeable difference by upgrading to 1028 MB. If you're into performance, if you play games, or if you do a lot of multitasking between programs, you need to grab as much RAM as you can. My new Sony has three slots that can hold 512 MB each. You might discover you have the same options. Motherboards present in many new PCs can take up to 4 GB (4,000 MB) of RAM, and in many applications, especially those for manipulating graphics and video, that much RAM can make a *huge* difference.

RAM is an important component because it is used for the temporary storage of data and code that you need to perform a task like cropping or recoloring an image, multitasking between programs, and using commands like Copy and Paste. RAM is fast and can be accessed much more quickly than the hard drive. When RAM gets full, though, and there's no free space left for storing data temporarily, XP sends data over to the hard drive in an area called a *paging file*. Obviously, this happens a lot more often when you have smaller amounts of memory in a PC. Accessing data from the paging file on a hard drive takes much longer than accessing it from RAM on the motherboard, so if you are low on RAM, you're sure to experience slower response times.

Physical Installation

So, just how hard is it to purchase and install extra RAM? It isn't difficult at all! These days, you simply figure out what kind of RAM you have, walk into a computer store, and purchase it right off the rack. It used to be much more complicated than this, and you'd have to order directly from the manufacturer or, worse, take your computer to a shop. (Depending on your computer, you might still have to order directly from the manufacturer, but this is fading out quickly.)

The first step involved in adding more RAM is to take a few minutes and determine how much RAM your computer already has. You can do this in a number of different ways, including viewing the My Computer Properties dialog box or watching your computer boot up (if this information isn't hidden with a splash page). You can also use a neat little utility called System Information (msinfo32.exe), which can be used to access all kinds of information. Figure 14–1 shows the screen that this utility produces. Notice the trees on the left; each can be expanded to access other information. To view this information, click Start, click Run, and in the Run dialog box, type *msinfo32.exe*. Click OK.

Once you know how much RAM you have, you can decide if more would be better. In most cases, the answer is yes. There are many types of memory, though, so you'll have to make sure you get the right kind.

TIP: *Before running out to buy more memory, make sure your PC isn't already "maxed out." Many older PCs (especially those built prior to 2001) can only hold 512 MB of RAM—or sometimes less.*

Finding the Right Memory for Your Machine

There are many different kinds of computer memory: SIMMs, DIMMs, PC133, PC2100DDR, PC100, and lots more. You can't just go out and buy a memory stick; you have to know what kind you need to fit your PC. If you have the information booklet that came with your computer, you can find out what

Figure 14-1
System Information offers all kinds of information.

kind of memory you should get by reading the specs page. You can also take the booklet to the store with you and show it to the sales staff. If you purchased a computer from a major manufacturer like Gateway, Hewlett-Packard, Dell, IBM, or Compaq (just to name a few) and you can't find your information booklet, simply call tech support or visit the company's Web site. You'll find the information there.

TIP: We can't promise this will always work, but in general, typing www.<the company name>.com brings up the company's Web site. For instance, **www.gateway.com, www.dell.com, www.IBM.com,** and **www.hewlettpackard.com** all link to their respective Web sites. If you can't find the Web sites using this technique, simply search for it on the Web using any Web browser.

GunkBuster's Notebook: Using the Web to Decipher Your RAM

Many Web sites sell RAM (like www.crucial.com). These sites let you order the RAM you need directly from the Internet. Just enter into the Web form the type of RAM you want, pony up a credit card number, and wait for it to be delivered. There's no need to even go to the store!

If you aren't sure what kind of memory you need because you own a used computer or simply just don't know, many sites offer a look-up option, where you can type in your computer type and model, motherboard model, and other data to find out. Many sites offer a downloadable tool that will scan your computer and search out the required information. Crucial has a free downloadable tool called the Belarc Advisor. We ran it on our system and we were quite impressed. Even if you plan on purchasing your RAM in a store, you can use the automated tools that Web sites like Crucial make available to easily determine the RAM that you will need.

You can also download Belarc Advisor from the vendor's site: **www.belarc.com/free_download.html**

Installation Instructions

Once you have the new RAM in hand, you'll need to install it. Your RAM should come with installation instructions, but for the most part, installing RAM is as simple as turning off your computer, unplugging it, locating the slot on the motherboard, and popping in the RAM. Some RAM sticks pop straight in, and some slide in from an angle. Be careful when you install it, though; you don't want to "shock" the board or the RAM stick. Make sure you touch the chassis and that the computer is unplugged before performing any installations. Read the instructions carefully because different memory types install in different ways; however, installing RAM is generally quite simple.

TIP: It is extremely important to ground yourself properly before touching anything inside the computer case. It is our belief that purchasing a special grounding device is a must. Grounding bracelets only cost a couple of bucks and you can get them wherever RAM can be purchased.

Gunkbuster's Notebook: Replacing Existing RAM with Larger Modules

Suppose you look inside your PC and see that all of its RAM slots are already full. Don't despair! It's entirely possible that the PC was built with RAM slots that can hold newer and larger RAM modules. For example, a PC may have two slots, each holding one 128 MB module. If the slots are capable of taking 256 MB modules, you can double your RAM by simply replacing the two smaller modules with a pair of 256 MB units. Check your PC's documentation or vendor help site to see what the largest modules are that may be installed on your system. Then go shopping!

Removing existing modules is sometimes a little trickier than popping them in. Most DIMM and SIMM slots have two little levers, one at each end of the slot. When you push outward and downward on both levers simultaneously, the installed module will pop out. (Check your PC documentation to make sure that this is how it works. For most PCs, it is.) If the modules have been installed for a long time, they might be tougher to remove. Don't push so hard on the levers as to break them! (They're relatively fragile.) First, wiggle the modules sideways in their slots a little to loosen any ancient grime-gunk that may have lodged in the slot. Then pry one lever up just a little, and then the other lever, until the module has risen enough for the levers to easily pop it the rest of the way out.

Yes, it's extra money to buy all new modules, and there's no strong market for old memory modules, especially small ones. But short of buying a whole new PC, replacing RAM modules may be the only way to increase the amount of installed RAM.

Watch the Boot-Up Process

Once the RAM is installed, you can watch the boot-up process (if your computer doesn't have a splash screen that hides it). Here, you'll see the RAM being counted and tested prior to the computer starting up. You can also view the new RAM information from My Computer's Properties page or from System Information. You want to make sure your new RAM has been detected properly. If it hasn't, try installing it again, or contact the manufacturer where the memory was obtained for technical support.

Tweak Virtual Memory Settings

When RAM is full, XP sends temporary data and code to an area of the hard drive reserved for such events, and data and code are swapped back and forth between the RAM and this special area (the paging file) as needed. Because it takes longer to access data from the hard drive, you'll obviously want to have as much RAM as you can afford (assuming you are into increasing the performance of your computer)! However, no matter how much RAM you have, the data stored there will eventually be swapped, so you want to make sure that the settings configured for virtual memory are the best they can be.

Virtual memory is the imaginary memory area that makes the computer act like it has more memory (RAM) than it actually does. Virtual memory is implemented using a *paging file* (sometimes referred to as a *swap file*), which is generally located on the C: drive. You can set the size of this file manually if you'd like, or you can accept the defaults. There are two options to change: the initial file size and the maximum file size.

The initial file size box is the area where you provide the number of megabytes for the virtual-memory paging file on the selected drive, and it is where you set the initial (or beginning) size of the file. The maximum size box is the area where you provide the maximum number of megabytes that can be used for the file. The numbers configured here define the size of the paging file. If you want, you can leave your virtual memory settings to whatever Windows suggests, which is about one and a half times the amount of RAM on the system for the initial size of the file and about three times the amount of RAM for the maximum paging file size. However, there are a few tweaks you can make if you desire:

√   If you have less than 512 MB of RAM, leave the paging file as is, using the default settings.

√   If you have lots of RAM, say, a gigabyte or more, set the initial paging file to about half of the physical RAM and set the maximum size at three times the RAM.

√   If you don't have much free hard disk space, say a gigabyte or less, and upgrading is not feasible, set the initial paging file to 2 MB.

√   Keep in mind that an extremely large maximum paging file does not necessarily increase performance and may actually hinder it. You don't want to allot too much of the hard drive area to this file.

√   Even if you have a gigabyte or so of RAM, don't turn off the paging file. Some programs can crash if no virtual memory is available.

If you'd like to tweak the virtual memory settings, here's how you set a custom paging file in Windows XP:

1.   Right-click My Computer and click Properties.

2.   Click the Advanced tab, and under Performance, click Settings.

3.   In the Performance Options dialog box, click the Advanced tab.

4.   Under Virtual Memory, click Change.

5.   Configure the settings as you desire, and click Set. OK your way out of the dialog boxes. See Figure 14-2. If prompted, reboot your computer.

Figure 14-2
You can configure a system-managed paging file size
or configure your own settings.

A number of programs are available to help you boost the performance of your machine, including some that will automatically tweak the paging file. Walk into any computer store or search the Internet for *Windows XP performance enhancement software* and you'll find plenty!

TIP: On the Internet, check out www.acceleratedsoftware.net for some great acceleration tools.

Add a Backup Device

To protect yourself from disaster (a hard drive crash, a spilled cup of coffee, or a lighting strike, for instance), you'll want to back up your data regularly. While Chapter 17 is all about backing up your files, here we'd like to talk a little about selecting and adding a physical backup device.

External Hard Drive

Our favorite backup device is the external hard drive because we can connect it to a computer, do a backup, connect it to another computer, do another backup, and then unplug it and store it in a safe place until the next full backup is needed. It's important to be able to remove the backup device from the physical area where the computer is, in case of flood, fire, power surge, or other unexpected event. It doesn't do much good to have a backup of all of your important data on a device that can be destroyed by the same cup of coffee you spill on your computer! It's important that the backup can be stored in another area, another room, or even another building.

External hard drives can be purchased from almost any computer store and are generally plug and play. This means that you simply connect the power cord and connect the Universal Serial Bus (USB) or FireWire cable and the hard drive is automatically ready to go. Figure 14-3 shows an example of an installed backup device in My Computer. In this instance, the backup drive is currently connected to a server in a workgroup and can be accessed as a mapped network drive.

With this backup device available, you can either drag and drop folders such as My Documents and My Pictures or use Windows XP's Backup utility. You'll learn more about that later.

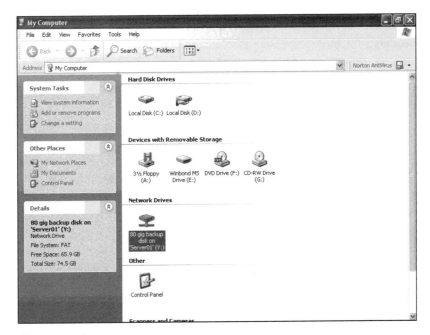

Figure 14-3
You can view installed backup devices in My Computer.

*TIP: If your PC does not have USB 2.0 ports, external USB backup drives will work **much more** slowly. If your PC has both USB 1.1 and the faster 2.0 ports, make sure that you know which is which (they are physically identical from outside the case) and plug the backup drive into **only** the USB 2.0 port.*

USB CD-R, CD-RW, DVD-R, DVD-RW

The Windows Backup utility can't write to CD or DVD drives that have the capability of being written to, but you can drag and drop files to the recordable CD device and burn CDs for the purpose of archiving. Archiving old data is necessary so that your hard drive isn't filled up with data you no longer access but want to keep. It's the same theory behind storing (but keeping) your old tax returns. Chances are good you won't need them, but you never know—and you don't have to have them perpetually gunking up the place.

*TIP: In acronyms such as CD-R, CD-RW, DVD-R, DVD-RW, **W** means the disc can be written to. **RW** means the disc is rewriteable, meaning it can be written to again and again.*

Installing a USB CD or DVD writer is generally done in the tower and can be quite complicated. If installing hardware inside the case exceeds your comfort level, you can either take your hardware to a computer shop or purchase an external rewriteable drive. External drives are generally plug and play, and although a bit more expensive than internal drives, they make great additions. Because they are portable, they can be used on any computer in the home or office (and even your laptop). Some people store them in their bank safe deposit boxes, and pull them out once a month for "off-site" backups!

Zip Drive

For everyday backups of your latest document, letter, picture, music download, or received files, you can use a Zip drive. Windows Backup Utility can save to a Zip drive, and you can drag and drop files. We have a 250 MB Zip drive that can be taken on trips along with a laptop. It's small and can be used to save virtually all the work completed while being away, including pictures. If you have a Zip drive, consider using it as a backup device to save each day's work in between regular full backups. Zip drives are also plug and play.

*TIP: Zip drives are becoming very outdated now. Most people are moving from ZIP technology to portable USB flash drives and carry them around on their key chains. USB flash drives are **much** more reliable than ZIP drives, especially the newer ZIP 250 and 750 models.*

Other Storage Options

Other options are available for backing up data, including tape drives and newer, portable USB drives that also double as MP3 players. Tape drives are rather expensive and unwieldy and are probably unnecessary for the average home user. However, the Creative Nomad, a small USB flash drive, fits in the palm of your hand or a pants pocket, can store 128 MB of data (that's like 88 floppy disks), and plugs directly into a USB port. It's plug and play, so it's easy to move data between non-networked computers, and it also is a fully functional MP3 player. As these devices evolve to store more data, they'll make excellent traveling backup devices. Flash drives are now becoming available that hold two GB or more of data, often for less than $100.

Figure 14-4 shows the Creative Nomad in My Computer, labeled MUVO. This device, as all other removable storage devices, will appear in My Computer where they can be accessed and configured.

Figure 14-4
USB flash drives appear in My Computer as external hard drives.

The most important advice we can give is make sure you actually *use* your backup device. Don't just put it on your desk to impress the neighbors. Develop a system whereby you back up your data on a regular basis. This is especially important as you become more diligent about removing files and programs as part of your degunking routine. Read Chapter 17 for more information on the Windows Backup Utility, including how to schedule backups to occur automatically.

Add a Second Monitor

If your monitor is all gunked up with running programs and you constantly have to toggle between them, consider adding another monitor. Adding a monitor can be beneficial when you use multiple programs and have to access multiple open windows, such as a day trader, programmer, or artist might need to do. Windows XP lets you add a monitor (if you have the required hardware) and then *extend* your desktop to it. That means you can add another monitor and open a couple of programs on one and a couple of programs on another, and drag items across the boundary between monitors as though both were a single device. This is a really neat feature that many users don't know about. It can quickly solve the problem of not having enough room on the screen to do what you want to do.

Adding a second monitor is easy if your computer is a newer model. Many newer computers come with display adapters that can already handle two monitors and are compatible with Windows XP. If you are one of the lucky ones, just turn off the computer, plug in the second monitor, and power it up. Then, turn on the computer. Finally, skip to the section "Configuring the Display Settings" later in this chapter to set it up.

Purchasing a New Display Adapter

If you have a computer that's a couple of years old (or older), you'll probably have only one display adapter. If that's the case, you'll need to purchase another display adapter and install it. Not all display adapters are alike, though, so make sure that the adapter you choose is fully compatible with Windows XP. If it isn't, although you'll probably be able to set up dual monitors, you won't be able to *extend your desktop* to the second one. (The second monitor will just show the same screen as the first.)

In addition to selecting an adapter that is compatible with Windows XP, you need to make sure you have a slot available on the motherboard that will accept it. There is more than one kind of video adapter slot. If you have the information booklet that came with your computer, a tech support line, or access to the company's Web site (if you purchased the computer from a large manufacturer), you might be able to find out if you have any open slots by calling or browsing their site. However, the easiest way to find out is to turn off the computer, unplug it, and open the case. Take a look at the motherboard, and see if there are any empty PCI (Peripheral Component Interconnect) or AGP (Accelerated Graphics Port) slots. You'll have to plug the new display adapter into it, so there has to be one available. PCI slots are long, thin areas that hold cards such as modems and network adapters. They are generally white. AGP slots are generally brown and are shorter than PCI slots. If you are unfamiliar with the inside of a computer, you should consider calling the manufacturer or tech support before going much further.

It doesn't really matter what monitor you use because almost any plug-and-play monitor will do. We have had a few issues with flat screens, though. If you're in doubt, visit Microsoft's Web site and check the hardware compatibility list. You can get lots of information from **www.Microsoft.com/windows/catalog**.

CAUTION: Just because you have an external port on your laptop doesn't mean you can get all of the perks of adding a second monitor. Many laptop display connections allow you to only show the desktop on another monitor; this is different from extending the desktop. If you run into this problem with your laptop, contact the manufacturer and ask for an adapter upgrade, if one exists. (They are rare.)

Physical Installation

After you've decided you have an available slot and purchased a new adapter, read the instructions for installing it. Installing a new display adapter generally consists of a few distinct steps:

1. Turn off the computer and unplug it.
2. Open the case and touch the chassis to ground yourself appropriately.
3. Remove the cover that corresponds to the open slot on the back on the computer case, usually held with a single screw.
4. Remove the display adapter from the protective packaging, being careful to touch only the edges.
5. Insert the new adapter into the PCI or AGP slot and use the screw you removed in step 3 to secure it.
6. Close the case, plug in the computer, and power it on.
7. Install any required software.
8. Turn off the computer, plug in the second monitor, and turn the computer back on. Configure the display settings as detailed in the next section.

TIP: If your computer has enough open slots, you can configure up to 10 monitors. (Your challenge then is getting them all on your desk!)

Configuring the Display Settings

Once the additional display card is configured and its monitor is working, you can configure the new monitor to show a duplicate of what is on the current monitor, or you can choose to extend the display to the second monitor. Extending the display is the best choice; with this configured, you can move applications over to the second monitor or view a large spreadsheet or image stretched over both.

Follow these steps to configure the display settings:

1. Right-click an empty area of the desktop and click Properties.
2. Select the Settings tab.
3. Click the monitor icon that represents the monitor you want to use in addition to your current monitor.
4. Select Extend My Windows Desktop Onto This Monitor, and click OK.

Now simply drag and drop (from the title bar of your open applications) any application or window you'd like to move to the new monitor and desktop. You're going to love this!

Physically Clean the Machine

We're not going to say that if you physically clean your machine you'll get better performance, but we will say that if you do, it'll likely last longer between repairs than if you never cleaned it. And a big part of the practice of degunking is to extend the life of your machine as much as possible! Maybe the mouse won't hang as often, or you can get a few extra keys to be less sticky, but for the most part, cleaning is a maintenance issue. There are parts of your computer that just collect stuff—your keyboard likely has crumbs in it, your mouse has lint around the ball, your monitor has grime, and the inside of your computer case is filled with dust. If you smoke, if you have cats or dogs, or if children have access to your computer, the problem certainly gets worse. You'll be surprised what you find while working through this section.

CAUTION: *Always turn off your PC and all components before cleaning them.*

Cleaning Keyboards, Mice, and Monitors

Your keyboards and mice will work a little better if you give them the once-over with a cleanser and remove particles hanging around in there. Monitors will look better if you do some dusting once in a while, and you might be able to use a light cleanser on them as well. If any instructions for cleaning came with your hardware, certainly follow them. For the most part, though, cleaning is a straightforward process.

Perhaps this is going to sound silly, but pick up your keyboard, turn it upside down, and give it a couple of good shakes. What fell out? A few eraser bits, a piece of bread, cat hair, a lost hamster, paper clips, and other odds and ends. This might seem like a primitive way to clean, but it works. Use compressed air to get out those stubborn pieces, or use a vacuum cleaner with attachments. (You can likely pick up a can of compressed air at your local hardware store.) Now, take a bit of liquid bleach cleanser on a clean, lint-free rag and gently wipe off the keys. Use Q-tips to get into the cracks if necessary, but be careful not to drip any cleaner anywhere. You want to get only enough on the rag to clean the stains; you don't want to immerse the keyboard in cleanser or let fluids dribble down between the keys onto the circuit board that holds them.

If you are cleaning a laptop keyboard, you might be able to pop up the keyboard and get under the keys to really clean the gunk out. If individual keys will pop off your keyboard (many do), you can use a small screwdriver to remove a key to get under where the grime really hides. If you use this technique, make sure you remove only one key at a time and replace it before you pop off another key. Otherwise, you could easily forget where your keys go and you'd end up with a real mess! Laptop keyboards really take a lot of "gunking" abuse because they are often used in environments that aren't always the cleanest, such as airports and hotel rooms.

If you have a generic, roller-ball mouse, flip it over, turn the backing plate in the direction its arrow indicates to get inside, and then take out the ball. Use a Q-tip and alcohol to carefully clean the ball and the rollers inside the mouse that the ball touches. You might have to reach in there to pull out the gunk that comes off. Make sure the ball and components are completely dry, and then replace the ball and clean the outside of the mouse with cleanser. (Consider replacing that worn-out mouse pad, too; it can have snags or uneven spots that cause the mouse to hang, and may shed fragments that can work their way inside the mouse or even into your keyboard.) Once you fully clean your mouse like this, you'll be amazed at how well it works.

TIP: The Q-tip and alcohol technique is a common one for cleaning the inside of a printer. Make sure your printer manufacturer agrees before proceeding, though. Oh, and don't forget to see what's hiding **under** that printer, too!

If you want to clean the outside of the computer case, do so carefully. A small rag with a little dish soap usually works, but you have to be very careful not to drip any cleanser into the case, the disk drives, printer ports, display ports, or USB ports. Getting these components wet can damage or destroy them. The same holds true of the back of the computer case where all of the external hardware plugs in. Don't go near that with anything wet at all. A good dusting with a dry cloth should do, and finish out all the cracks and crannies with clean, dry Q-tips.

TIP: Clean scanner beds with window cleaner and wipe until streak-free for better scans.

Finally, clean the monitor based on your manufacturer's instructions. If you have a regular plug-and-play monitor with a glass screen, you can usually clean the screen with a glass cleaner on a clean, lint-free rag. Turn it off first, unplug it, don't spray too much cleaner on the rag, and be sure to clean all of the streaks with a dry towel. If you have an LCD (or flat) screen, use a soft, dry cotton cloth. If that doesn't work, try adding a little rubbing alcohol on the cloth to remove the stubborn stains. As with cleaning your keyboard, don't let fluid run down the display face and into the body of the monitor.

TIP: CD-ROM drives can be cleaned with special CD-ROM cleaners you can purchase from a computer store. This generally involves inserting a disk with a small brush installed on the underside of it that will gently clean the lens.

Degunking Inside the Case

The inside of the computer case contains all of the working parts and should be cleaned at least twice a year to maintain optimal performance. Dust particles, animal hair, and cigarette smoke can get sucked into the computer via the air vents, and before you know it, these contaminants can corrode the circuitry and cause other problems.

Most experts agree that using compressed air is the best way to clean the inside of the computer case, although some prefer a vacuum. Either way, the procedure is basically the same. Here we'll detail the compressed air option:

1. Turn off the computer, unplug it, and carefully open the case. If the case opens on more than one side, open both sides.

2. Position the computer so that when you blow the compressed air into it, the dust will be removed from the case, not just blown around in it. You should also be able to vacuum up what is blown out, so don't blow all of that dust underneath your desk!

3. Hold the compressed air in the upright position and use the air quickly and in short bursts to remove the gunk.

If you're a smoker, have pets, or are in a dusty environment, repeat this procedure four times a year; nonsmokers, those without pets, and those in a clean environment should repeat this procedure twice a year.

Purchase a New Computer

Although I'll stress that this is a measure of last resort only, you might have reached the limits of what degunking can do for you if you have encountered the following situations:

√   You've removed all of the extra files and programs from your system but it still takes forever to start up and runs too slowly or you still have limited free hard disk space.

√   Your system crashes a lot, you can't figure out why, and you've already tried reinstalling the system with a clean install and updating all drivers. (This often indicates an intermittent connection somewhere on the motherboard.)

√   You find that you need to shut down your computer fairly often and restart it simply to make it run a little better, and calls to tech support don't yield results because the computer has been out of warranty for three years.

√   You've tried running newer releases of major software packages and they're unusably slow.

√   You've tried adding RAM and/or dual monitors but you don't have the slots.

√   You've considered adding a CD-RW but find you don't have an extra bay and it's not cost effective to add the drive.

√   Your hard drive is too small and not easily upgradeable. The 120 GB external hard drive you want to buy costs half as much as a new computer would.

√   Your computer just isn't repairable because you've spilled coffee on it, it's been dropped, or a power surge has damaged the motherboard.

WARNING! *Friends may suggest replacing or upgrading your current motherboard with a newer, faster one, but that is quite difficult and rarely a good idea. PCs from large vendors often use custom-designed motherboards for which no upgrade can be had, and it's sometimes very difficult to tell ahead of time whether a new motherboard will fit into your case and all the various wires will plug in correctly. If the tower is dead, buy a new one!*

So, what's a degunker to do? You might need to consider a new computer. If you are in this situation, we're not going to tell you what computer to buy, where to buy it, or what kinds of features it should have. What we are going to do is tell you about the pros and cons of transferring your data from your old computer to your new one and, if you decide to do that, exactly how it's done. Setting up a new computer always seems like a big headache and typically needs to be done when you simply don't have the time (like during the holidays or when you're working many hours of overtime). But there are some procedures that you can follow to ease the pain and save you time.

Transferring Data: Pros and Cons

When you get a new computer, you have a couple of choices. You can spend a day or so installing your applications, printers, scanners, cameras, disk drives, and drivers; another day copying your backed-up files, folders, and personal data; and a third day configuring your display settings, Internet connections, network settings, screensavers, Favorites, cookies, and security settings. Or you can spend a day with applications and hardware and use the Files And Settings Transfer Wizard to transfer your personal data and settings automatically.

The upside of the transfer wizard is of course the amount of effort required to set up your new computer. You get to keep your Internet settings, including Favorites and cookies; you get to keep your screensavers, desktop background, and other personal settings; and you get to keep your connections to the Internet and other networks without having to reconfigure them. This saves quite a bit of time. In addition, you can decide exactly what gets transferred. You don't have to transfer the My Pictures folder if you don't want to, and you have similar options with other folders and settings.

The downside to using the wizard is that you should ideally network the computers before you use it, which requires additional hardware like a hub or a null modem cable. If you already have a home network set up, this won't be a problem, but for newbies, this might seem like a lot of work. In addition, you won't get that "new computer" feel. You won't be able to start over, as it were, so if that's important to you, you'll want to consider configuring the new computer manually. We personally prefer to spend the time configuring the computer and transferring data the long way. Then we know exactly what's on it and where it's stored, and there are no possibilities of bringing on residual problems carried over from the previous malfunctioning computer. Besides, one of the best ways to decide if software, icons, and files are gunk or not is to move them piecemeal. (If the computer you are moving from is working well, though, and you simply want to create a clone or have purchased a faster, newer computer, the transfer wizard will be perfect.)

Using the Files And Settings Transfer Wizard

You can access the Files And Settings Transfer Wizard in the System Tools menu. It can be opened by clicking Start, pointing to All Programs, pointing to Accessories, pointing to System Tools, and clicking Files And Settings Transfer Wizard. The wizard opens and offers advice and techniques for connecting your computer and explains what you can transfer. Once you're connected, click

Next. The wizard is quite comprehensive in walking you through the process of transferring data. As shown in Figure 14-5, you can decide what exactly you want to transfer by adding or removing the appropriate folders and settings.

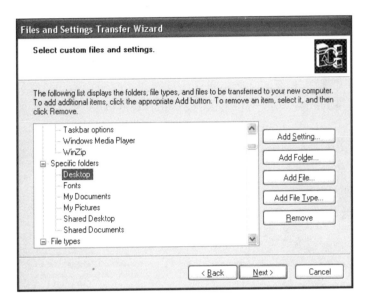

Figure 14-5
The Files And Settings Transfer Wizard helps you decide what to transfer and then helps you transfer it.

This wizard can be most helpful for those with the appropriate hardware and circumstances. If you are simply purchasing a new computer that will run faster and better than the one you have and you want to transfer your files and settings over, this is certainly the easiest way to go.

Degunk Your New PC

If you've purchased a new PC, you need to read this section. New PCs these days come with all sorts of gunk preinstalled, including free trials from Internet service providers, free trials of software, and installed software you don't want and don't need. You could have a couple of gigabytes of gunk on there you'll never use!

NOTE: This section is excerpted directly from another of our Degunking books, **Degunking Your PC**.

Here are some examples of what you can expect to find on a new PC from a major retailer or PC manufacturer; while reading through this list, try to decide if you'd use or appreciate this software or if you wouldn't:

√   A free trial of Microsoft Office or Norton AntiVirus.

√   A free trial for America Online and similar online service companies.

√   Unexpected Desktop pop -ups from the manufacturer, prompting you to upgrade your warranty, register, or visit its Web site.

√   Proprietary software from the manufacturer that you won't use, such as media music services, media installers, and "experience" software. 14-6 shows a search for "vaio" on a fairly new Sony Vaio PC.

Figure 14-6

Gunk, gunk, gunk, and more gunk. What *is* all of this stuff?

√   Third-party software you may not be interested in, including mapping software, encyclopedias, CD burning software, greeting card creation software, and image-editing software.

√   Bundled office software, including Microsoft Works, which you won't need if you already use Microsoft Office.

√   On PCs that are media centers, multiple DVD burning software applications.

√   Third-party software such as Quicken, Microsoft Money, Quick Time, MusicMatch, and Microsoft Picture It! (This type of third-party software will often time-out 30 to 60 days after you first use it.)

You need to get rid of what you won't need or won't be using right away. Don't let your brand -new PC become bogged down before you ever get the chance to gunk it up yourself! But how do you know what to keep, what you need, and what you can safely delete? It isn't that complicated, really. Let's start with the free trials.

Free Short-Term Trials

On almost any new PC, you can expect to find a free trial of something. It may be a free trial for AOL or another Internet service provider, which you can access from the Desktop, or it may be free trial software for an application, which you can access from the All Programs menu. Free trial versions of applications are "hookware," in that you can use them for a very limited time (sometimes only 30 days) and then must buy the full version. Don't get hooked! Figure 14-7 shows an example of an AOL shortcut icon on the Desktop. (You can tell it's a shortcut because of the arrow.) Of course, this is gunk, but how do you get rid of it? Can you? Should you? Will you mess up your new PC if you do? Those are all tough questions, and not too many people know the answers.

Figure 14-7
New PCs often come with gunk on the Desktop.

Free Trials on the Desktop

You may know that right-clicking any Desktop icon and choosing Delete will remove the icon from your Desktop, and you can do that to get rid of the gunk there, but what you may not know is that it will not remove the actual gunk from your PC. Right-clicking the AOL & Internet Free Trial! icon in Figure 14-7 and choosing Delete will delete the icon *only*. It *won't* delete the actual files from your PC. It's the files that take up hard drive space, not the icon. To delete the actual files, you need to look a little deeper.

The best way to delete files from a PC is from the Add Or Remove Programs applet in Control panel. The Add or Remove Programs window is shown in Figure 14-8. As you can see though, there's no AOL entry in there. If it were there, it would be located after Adobe Reader 7.0 and before Arts & Letters EXPRESS 7.0 Office. Tricky, tricky. In this case, you'll have to delete the files manually.

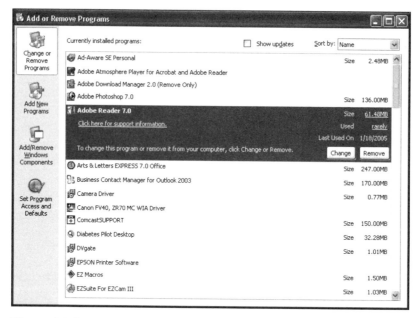

Figure 14-8

Sometimes there is no way to uninstall files using traditional methods, as unwanted programs are not available from the Add or Remove Programs applet in Control Panel.

TIP: Before manually deleting any files, you should create a restore point in System Restore. System Restore is available from Start, All Programs, Accessories, and System Tools.

Here's how to manually delete the files:

1. Right-click any shortcut on the Desktop that represent free trials of software you know you will not need.

2. From the resulting menu choices, select Properties.

3. From the Properties dialog box, choose Find Target.

4. Notice what is in the folder. In almost all cases, you can delete everything in there. If you're deleting Internet access choices, you may have several, as we do, including ATT, AOL, and EarthLink.

5. To delete any item, right-click it and choose Delete.

6. Close all windows and dialog boxes, and then right-click the unwanted Desktop icon and choose Delete to get rid of it.

7. Restart your PC and verify that there are no errors on boot-up. If there are, use System Restore to revert the PC to its prior state. If deleting entire folders caused errors, you'll have to look for an alternate way to delete the unwanted files, such as visiting the company's Web site, looking for an uninstall option in the folder that contains the program's files, or even considering leaving the files intact.

Free Trials in the All Programs Menu

If you see free trials in the All Programs menu, or if you open an application and it states that it is a free trial of the application, you'll have to decide if you want to pony up the extra money to get the full version or if you want to delete it from your PC altogether. Of course, we're here to delete stuff, so we'll assume that's what you want to do.

As with the Desktop, right-clicking any item in the All Programs menu and choosing Delete will only remove it from the list; it won't remove the gunk from your PC. The actual files will still be on there somewhere. And if you delete the application from the list now, you'll likely never notice it again and it will never get uninstalled.

Unlike deleting files by finding the target folder as we did in the previous section, it's better to get rid of applications using the Add Or Remove Programs applet in Control Panel. (Unfortunately, as we showed earlier in Figure 14-8, not all applications are listed there, and deleting entire folders is the only option.) Using the Add Or Remove Programs window, you can delete files safely, with virtually no chance of causing errors with your system. So first, let's use this applet to see what you have installed that you don't want, and then let's delete what you don't want:

1. Open Control Panel and the Add Or Remove Programs applet.

2. Scroll through the list and see if you can locate the trial software. It should be there. Also, look for software you know you'll never use, such as Quicken, Microsoft Picture It!, or Microsoft Money.

3. Each time you find an application you never intend to use, select it and choose Remove. Follow the prompts to remove the application.

4. In most instances, the process will occur automatically, although you may be asked to assist by responding that yes, you're sure you want to uninstall the program and by clicking Next a few times to complete the process.

WARNING! *If you're ever prompted, while uninstalling **anything**, to delete files that may be shared with other applications, always choose No To All. You do **not** want to delete shared files. Doing so could cause boot-up error messages or problems with other applications.*

We suggest, as noted before, that you create a System restore point prior to uninstalling programs or deleting files. That way, if something goes wrong, you can always revert back. We'll also suggest here that you reboot immediately after deleting programs and that when you're finished, you use Disk Cleanup and Disk Defragmenter to clean up the computer.

Software from the Manufacturer, Third-Party Software, Duplicate Software

The process for getting rid of software from the PC's manufacturer or from a third party is the same as getting rid of free trial applications. It's best done through the Add Or Remove Programs applet in Control Panel. This is especially true of software installed by the PC manufacturer.

To see what's installed on your PC, browse through the All Programs menu and look for your PC manufacturer's name. Figure 14-6 showed the search results for a Sony Vaio, and the same entries are also in the Add Or Remove Programs applet in Control Panel.

When it comes to uninstalling this kind of software, it's hard to know what you can and can't uninstall. It seems quite logical you'd need to leave intact anything the manufacturer installed. That's simply not true. The operating system contains the files needed to run the PC, and additional files added by the manufacturer are almost always unnecessary.

Here's a quick "for instance": Our Sony Vaio has lots of media applications (as you saw in Figure 14-6). A quick search on Google informs us that one of those applications is for turning our PC into a server so that networked computers can access media files. Whew! We're not going to do that, and thus, this software isn't necessary. Again, this is true for almost all manufactured PCs. You can safely delete these additional files once you know you do not want to use their respective applications. (Again, though, create a restore point, just to be on the safe side, and Google anything you're not sure about.)

Finally, some third-party software (and even free trial software) offers an Uninstall option right in the All Programs menu. If you can find that option, use it.

GunkBuster's Notebook: Duplicate Applications

Just because something came preinstalled on your new PC is no reason to keep or use it. Likewise, there's no reason not to uninstall applications you don't want to use or programs for which you have equivalents. Don't keep it just because you think you'"paid" for it; that's not a good enough reason.

Here's an example of duplication. We prefer Microsoft Office for writing, Microsoft Excel for creating spreadsheets, and Microsoft Access for our databases. Just because our new PCs come with Microsoft Works doesn't mean we need to change, and it doesn't mean we shouldn't uninstall the program. If we're not going to use it, it's just gunk.

You'll have to take inventory too. If you use Photoshop CS and you new PC came with Microsoft Picture It!, you may want to uninstall the latter. If your new PC came with Quicken but you use Quick Books, uninstall the former. Don't let someone else gunk up your brand -new PC.

Summing Up

In this chapter, you learned that enhancing your computer's performance with hardware and physical upgrades can really spark new life into it. You learned that adding memory is the easiest and fastest way to enhance a computer's performance and that an extra 128 MB or 256 MB of RAM can provide a surprising boost. Tweaking virtual memory settings and the paging file can help as well. Other hardware tweaks, like adding backup devices and second monitors and physically cleaning the machine, can also boost productivity and performance.

If performance is just about as good as it's going to get, if you have ongoing problems that can't be solved, if the computer blue-screens just as you're really getting the hang of that new video game, or if the computer has 128 MB of RAM and no slots to add extra memory, you might have to consider a new computer. If that's the case, keep in mind that there are tools available to help you make the transition.

PowerToys and Awesome Shareware

Degunking Checklist:

√ Learn what PowerToys offer and how they can help you with your degunking tasks.

√ Learn where to locate PowerToys, download them, and install them.

√ Use the TweakUI PowerToy to customize Windows settings.

√ Use the Virtual Desktop Manager PowerToy to organize your desktop.

√ Use Resize Imager to reduce the size of your graphics files.

√ Learn about today's other most popular PowerToys.

√ Locate WUGNET's (Windows Users Group Network) shareware picks. These shareware programs are deemed the highest quality in shareware for Windows.

√ Use shareware favorites including Registry First Aid, Pop-Up Stopper, FolderMatch, and System Mechanic to keep your PC running well.

√ Learn about Bloglines and RSS feeds and how these free technologies can help you keep in touch with your favorite news feeds and Web sites.

This chapter ends the advanced degunking section by describing some advanced power tools for your PC and some awesome shareware. The free power tools are aptly named *PowerToys*. PowerToys can be used to tweak your XP machine, including customizing keyboard keys, configuring a custom background for the Internet Explorer toolbar or the Explorer toolbar, and even using a shortcut to the Group Policy Editor for changing hundreds of additional settings.

The TweakUI PowerToy is an especially nice one to obtain because if offers the ability to change options that are difficult to find and configure or things that are hidden so deep in the Group Policy Editor you could likely never find them. Some of the tweaks are specific to TweakUI, though, options that aren't available In Windows XP at all. Here are a few examples of things you can do with TweakUI:

√ Define what order grouped items are listed (when button grouping is enabled).

√ Configure what the top left icon on the Desktop is.

√ Configure what can and can't be added to the Frequently Used Programs section of the Windows XP Start menu.

Having the ability to personalize your computer in this way can help you be more productive, locate things faster, and work more efficiently.

Other PowerToys are available that allow you to resize images with a single click and to toggle between programs more efficiently. There are lots of PowerToys to choose from, but in this chapter we'll mention only the ones we believe will help you enhance performance and/or work faster and smarter.

In addition to PowerToys, we'll introduce you to WUGNET, a users group that tests and picks the top shareware available on the Internet. Each week they feature a different shareware program. Most of the shareware programs are less than $30 U.S. and can be quite useful in enhancing the machine's performance. Many shareware programs help you look at the system configuration, Internet connection, and system resources and configure those items to work together and at peak performance by applying some tried-and-true tweaks. Some shareware programs perform the tweaks automatically, while others allow you to choose from recommended options. Either way, they almost always help you improve system performance, and if you can find one with good reviews and lots of downloads, you'll see what we mean. Because these programs can create performance boosts, they should be worth trying out.

Use PowerToys for Degunking

The PowerToys we'll talk about in this chapter are for Windows XP users. They're specially designed for XP machines and they're all free. Although there are numerous PowerToys, we'll only detail the ones we think will benefit you in everyday performance task enhancement.

Downloading and Installing

The PowerToys we'll introduce here will need to be downloaded and installed before you can use them. You'll download each of them from the same Web page: **http://www.microsoft.com/windowsxp/downloads/powertoys/ xppowertoys.mspx**. Once at the page, follow these steps to download and install any PowerToy:

1. Locate the PowerToy you want to obtain. Figure 15-1 shows the links to several PowerToys, including the Alt-Tab Replacement PowerToy and the TweakUI PowerToy.

Figure 15-1

Links to popular PowerToys are available at Microsoft's PowerToy Web page.

2. Click the link for the PowerToy you want and then click Save in the File Download box, shown in Figure 15-2. The Save As dialog box opens.

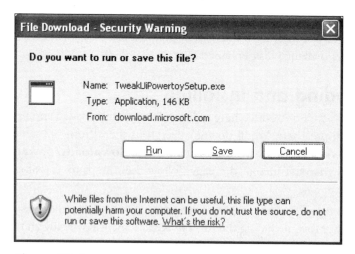

Figure 15-2
Choose Save when prompted, and then run the program once it's downloaded.

3. If you have a designated folder you use for saving file downloads, browse to it now. If you do not have a designated area for saving downloads from the Internet, in the Save As dialog box, click the My Documents folder. In the My Documents folder area, right-click an empty area, point to New, and click Folder. Name the folder Internet Downloads. (You'll only do this once, and from here on out, you'll save your downloads here.)

4. Select the folder where you want to save the file, and click Save.

5. As the download progresses, verify that Close This Dialog Box When Download Completes is not checked in the active download dialog box, as shown in Figure 15-3.

6. Close any open programs and click Run in the Download Complete dialog box.

7. Follow the directions in the wizard for installing the software, if prompted (some applications install without any help from you). Generally, the default settings are fine.

8. Locate the new program from the Start menu, All Programs list. Some PowerToys may appear in a folder called PowerToys For Windows XP, as shown in Figure 15-4.

Figure 15-3
Make sure Close This Dialog Box When Download Completes
is not checked, and once the application has downloaded,
click Run.

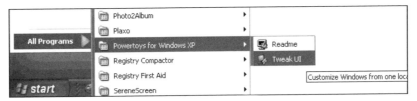

Figure 15-4
Some PowerToys appear in a separate PowerToys folder.

These steps can be used to download and install almost anything at all from the
Internet, even shareware. There might be additional screens, or perhaps an additional Web page to work through, but the process is the same. Locate and
choose what you want to download, save it to the hard drive, open the folder,
and install it.

---

*TIP: If you want to install a newer version of a PowerToy you already have, most of the
time you'll have to uninstall the old version first.*

Customize Windows Settings with TweakUI

TweakUI is a popular PowerToy, so we've chosen to introduce it first. It gives
you access to system settings that are not exposed in the Windows XP default
user interface, like mouse settings, Taskbar settings, Desktop settings, and Internet

Explorer settings. Figure 15-5 shows the interface, and we've expanded the Taskbar And Start Menu option. Here, it's easy to disable the balloon tips that pop up in the bottom-right corner of your screen reminding you to do everything from running the Desktop Cleanup Wizard to getting a .NET Passport.

Figure 15-5

Use TweakUI to get to the heart of Windows XP and change settings to suit your needs.

In addition to this marvelous tweak, there are hundreds of other things you can achieve with this software. While we can't possibly list all of them here, we can list our favorites:

√   About>Tips: View tips like "Press Win+L to unlock your workstation" and "Ctrl+Shift+Esc will launch Task Manager."

√   About>Policy: Run the Group Policy Editor, where hundreds of additional settings can be configured, including titles, bitmaps, and logos for IE's toolbar; password policies for users; local security policies such as requiring (or not) Ctrl+Alt+Delete on logon; whether or not to show the last username in the logon screen, and more.

√   General: Enable or disable menu and tooltip animation and fading.

√   Explorer: Configure what is shown on the Start menu, whether the document list should be cleared on exit, and whether to detect accidental double-clicks.

√   Explorer>Thumbnails: Set the image quality of thumbnails.

√   Explorer>Command Keys: Configure the keyboard's navigation keys and change what happens when a specific key is pressed.

√   Taskbar>Grouping: Configure in what order grouped applications are listed when grouping is used.

√   Taskbar>XP Start Menu: Configure what applications can or cannot appear in the Windows XP Start menu as frequently used programs.

√   Desktop: Remove all default icons from the Desktop or easily put them back.

√   Internet Explorer: Create a custom background for the Internet Explorer toolbar or the Explorer toolbar. This can include a picture or logo as well.

√   Logon>AutoLogon: Easily enable or disable automatic logon.

By using TweakUI to its fullest and by getting to know the Group Policy Editor, you can really personalize how XP works and looks. This is a must-have PowerToy.

After downloading and installing this PowerToy, work through the following tweaks to disable some of the more annoying aspects of Windows XP:

1.   Click Start, point to All Programs, point to PowerToys For Windows XP, and click TweakUI For Windows XP.

2.   Expand the About tree, and click Policy. In the Group Policy Editor pane, click Run Group Policy Editor.

3.   In the Group Policy window, expand User Configuration, Administrative Templates, and then Windows Components. Click Start Menu And Taskbar.

4.   In the right pane, take a look at the configuration options. Changes made here affect everyone who accesses this computer, even administrators. Consider configuring the following settings: Turn Off Personalize Menu, Turn Off Notification Area Cleanup, Remove Balloon Tips On Start Menu Items, and Remove Clock From The System Notification Area. (Okay, so perhaps the clock isn't annoying, but it's a cool option.)

5.   To enable or disable any setting, double-click and make the appropriate choice. Click OK and exit when complete.

Organize Your Desktop with Virtual Desktop Manager

Microsoft Virtual Desktop Manager (MSVDM) allows you to organize a busy and cluttered Desktop. If you work with many open programs, you can now manage them on four different Desktops. You can switch between the Desktops using buttons on the Taskbar or shortcut keys that you configure. If you always have Outlook Express open, put it on one Desktop. If you always have Internet Explorer open, put it on another Desktop. You can even configure different backgrounds on each Desktop!

Once it's downloaded, Desktop Manager is activated by right-clicking an empty area of the Taskbar, pointing to Toolbars, and clicking Desktop Manager. You'll see the numbers 1 through 4 on your Taskbar, and each represents an available Desktop configuration. You can see this in Figure 15-6.

Figure 15-6
The Virtual Desktop Manager offers icons for the four available Desktops in the Taskbar.

To configure the first Desktop, click the icon for number 1 and then open the program or programs you want to show on that Desktop. Then click the icon for number 2, and do the same. Once all four Desktops are configured, you can move between desktops by selecting the Desktop number from the Taskbar, using Alt+Tab, or selecting the Desktop you want when all four are showing. This provides a really neat way to unclutter your Desktop. Figure 15-7 shows four

Figure 15-7
Here, all four Desktops are configured.

Desktops configured, and they are all shown together. You can see all four Desktops at once by clicking the Preview button on the Taskbar, which is the icon to the left of the number 1. To select a Desktop, click it.

Here are some rules for working with the Virtual Desktop Manager:

√   To configure a Desktop, choose a Desktop number from the Taskbar and then open or start a program to use for it.

√   To create a Desktop background for a particular Desktop, right-click the Desktop number in the Taskbar (see Figure 15-6) and choose Configure Desktop Images. From the resulting dialog box, choose an image to use.

√   To configure a shortcut key for moving between Desktops, right-click a Desktop number in the Taskbar and choose Configure Shortcut Keys. Choose the key combination to get to the various Desktops you have configured.

√   To get help at any time, right-click any Desktop number in the Taskbar and click MSVDM Help.

√   To choose a Desktop when all four are showing, click on the one to use.

√   To show all four Desktops at once, click the icon to the left of the 1 in the Taskbar. It's called the Preview button.

√   To exit Virtual Desktop Manager, right-click the Taskbar, point to Toolbars, and uncheck Desktop Manager.

This software comes with complete help files and can be quite effective once you get the hang of it. It can be used to create a sort of quad-monitor effect, where programs can remain on a single Desktop until needed, thus not taking up space on the current one. It's well worth the download!

Resize Images with the Image Resizer

The two previously mentioned PowerToys offer lots of bells and whistles. The Image Resizer PowerToy, on the other hand, only does one thing, but it can really help you with your degunking work. It allows you to resize images with a single right-click to make them much smaller and reduce the space drain on your hard drive. It is also the perfect tool for resizing images to send to others via e-mail so that you don't gunk up other users' computers by sending out large files such as digital camera pictures.

Once it's downloaded and installed, simply browse to the picture to resize, right-click, and choose Resize Pictures. (If you don't see this option after downloading and installing the application, click Start, click Run, and in the Run dialog box, type *regsvr32 shimgvw.dll*.) In the Resize Pictures dialog box, choose the picture size you want and click OK. See Figure 15-8 for an example.

Figure 15-8

The Image Resizer PowerToy makes resizing images a snap.

Alt-Tab Replacement

The Alt-Tab Replacement PowerToy is a good one to have if you have lots and lots of open programs and you enjoy using Alt+Tab to toggle between them. With this PowerToy, you simply hold down the Alt key and click the Tab key to move between programs. Icons for the programs are shown in the Alt-Tab Replacement window, and you choose the program to open with the Tab key.

WUGNET's Shareware Picks

Shareware is software that you pay for and download from the Internet. There is a ton of shareware available. You can find many programs that can help you degunk your PC and improve the performance of Windows. Unfortunately, it's difficult to always know when a shareware program is a good one, short of purchasing and installing it or wading through various posted reviews. WUGNET, or Windows Users Group Network, has taken some of the guess-work out of choosing a shareware program. WUGNET offers its top shareware picks each week and states that they've been thoroughly tested in lots of environments and that they're priced appropriately. Although the list changes often, we always find lots of good shareware programs. For the most part, these programs are less than $30 U.S. To see what is available now, visit **www.Microsoft.com/windowsxp/downloads/wugnet.mspx**.

TIP: *If you find a program you'd like to purchase or try out, follow the directions given earlier in this chapter for downloading and installing programs. It's virtually the same process, except sometimes you have to pay!*

Keep Your Registry Clean with Registry First Aid

Gunked-up Registries can cause all sorts of problems, including blue screens, crashes, lockups, slow system response, and unexpected errors, as you learned in Chapter 13. Since it's nearly impossible to clean the Registry yourself, owning a Registry cleaning tool like Registry First Aid is almost a necessity. If working in the Registry scares you as much as it scares us, you're going to love this application. It scans the Registry for orphaned file and folder references, left-over files from deleted applications, obsolete Start menu items, invalid fonts, invalid paths, and more, and removes them from the Registry. If you haven't ever run a Registry cleaning program, this is an inexpensive way to try it out. In Chapter 13, we used Registry Clean Pro to clean the Registry. We'll now try a different Registry cleaning tool.

To download and install a trial copy of Registry First Aid, and to see what Registry First Aid can do for your system, follow these steps:

1. Visit **www.Microsoft.com/windowsxp/ downloads/wugnet.mspx,** and locate and click the link to download the free trial copy.

2. Click Open to run the program from its location, and when the download is complete, click Yes in the Setup dialog box to install the program.

3. Once it's installed, launch the application. (Steps 1, 2, and 3 are common steps for downloading and installing any program from the Internet.)

4. When the program starts, click Check The Registry For Errors and click Next.

5. In the page to select what to scan the Registry for, check all options. Click Start, read the information provided, and click OK.

6. When prompted, create a restore point using System Restore (it will open automatically).

Take a look at the incredible amount of invalid paths, obsolete Start menu items, invalid application paths, invalid Help files, invalid shared DLLs, autorun programs, unused software entries, and invalid fonts. Although the trial software won't fix all of these things for you, it does give you an idea as to why your computer runs slowly and hangs up. If you want to fix these things, you'll need to purchase the program.

NOTE: *With the trial version, you can only repair a few entries. For $28 U.S., we thought "What the heck?" and purchased the software. We were **extremely** impressed with the results, and our computers have never run better.*

Get Rid of Annoying Pop-Up Messages with Pop-Up Stopper Professional

Are you sick of those pop-up advertisements you get when you visit Web pages? This kind of gunk can really slow you down when you are trying to read your e-mail and get some important work done, and besides that, it's just plain annoying! There are lots of ways to get rid of them, some free and some not. We use the Pop-Up Stopper Free Edition, but Pop-Up Stopper Professional is also available. Pop-Up Stopper Free Edition is available from **www.panicware.com/ product_psfree.html**, and the Professional Edition is listed on WUGNET's shareware favorites list.

Pop-up stoppers like these block ads with any browser and with all Internet connections. They'll also give you immediate notification if any ad has been blocked. If you want to see the ad (or open the window), simply hold down the Ctrl key and click it again.

Pop-Up Stopper Free has several options for preferences that can be set. This dialog box is accessible by right-clicking the icon (a small white hand) in the System Tray and clicking Preferences. There are several things you can personalize:

√ Play a sound when a pop-up window is prevented.

√ Flash the System Tray icon when a pop-up window is prevented.

√ Display a pop-up bubble next to the system clock.

√ Change the mouse cursor briefly.

From the other tabs, you can also set these options:

√ Configure Pop-Up Stopper to start each time Windows starts (or not).

√ Purchase the full version.

√ Get updates.

Synchronize Your Folders with FolderMatch

When you make a backup of your data, you copy it and place the copy in a safe place like a separate hard drive, a Zip disk, or a CD. If you work on files at two different computers or physical locations (say, at work and on a laptop), you'll likely have two copies of some data as well. With two copies of the data, there's a good chance that the copies won't always be in sync and contain the same information. Files change often, as do contents of folders. Keeping your duplicate data organized and in sync can require quite a bit of time. To make this task easier, consider purchasing FolderMatch.

FolderMatch can automatically synchronize duplicate files and folders using your choice of comparison types. It's easy enough for the average user to understand, and powerful enough to please even the most sophisticated multitasker. It includes a full-featured duplicate file finder, which is also useful for locating unwanted duplicates of files. This feature can be especially useful when you are degunking your PC by removing all of the extra files. If you need to keep files and folders in sync, consider software such as this.

Keep Your Computer Running Smoothly with System Mechanic

System Mechanic is an incredible application containing 15 tools to keep your computer running smoothly. It can really help it run faster, cleaner, and error-free. It can even speed up your Internet connection. At the time this book was written, you could try out System Mechanic for free for 30 days, which is what we did, and if you like it, you can purchase it. That's quite a deal! (Visit **www.iolo.com** for more information.)

Here are some of the things the System Mechanic checks for and repairs:
√   Obsolete or duplicate files
√   Invalid Registry keys
√   Internet cookies and cache
√   Broken shortcuts
√   Duplicate files and drivers

In addition, this software allows you to do the following:
√   Customize Windows settings
√   Customize startup options
√   Optimize Windows configuration settings that affect your network and Internet connection speeds

Figure 15-9 shows the System Mechanic screen.

Bloglines and RSS Feeds

Bloglines is another free resource, available at **www.bloglines.com**. At Bloglines.com, you can create a personalized Web page that contains links to

Figure 15-9
System Mechanic is a good program for keeping a degunked computer in good working order.

your favorite RSS feeds. If you aren't familiar with RSS, it is another free resource, and it stands for Really Simple Syndication. RSS is a format for syndicating news and other content on Web sites, and subscribing to an RSS feed allows you to see only the newest additions to the Web site. With RSS, there's no need to wade through stuff you've already seen. For instance, if you often visit WUGNET (mentioned earlier in this chapter), you can use Bloglines to subscribe to WUGNET's RSS feed, and each day you can visit your personalized Bloglines Web page to see if that particular Web site has any new content. You can also subscribe to WUGNET's RSS feed directly from their Web site, and not involve Bloglines or any other resource at all. Once subscribed to a feed (in any manner), you don't actually have to go to the WUGNET Web site to find out if new content is added; Bloglines shows you immediately if there's any new content. If that's what you use, or the Web site informs you of it when you log on (such at at **www.wugnet.com**). Figure 15-10 shows how our Bloglines page is configured.

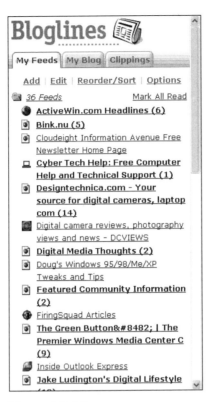

Figure 15-10

Bloglines can be personalized to keep track of your RSS feeds and let you know if any new content has been added to the Web sites you follow.

In Figure 15-10, you can see that we subscribe to several RSS feeds from various Web sites, including ActiveWin.com, Bink.nu, Digital Media Thoughts, Jake Ludington's Digital Lifestyle, and more. The numbers beside each bolded entry denotes how many new items have been added to the Web site since we last visited. As you can see, not all of our RSS feeds have new entries; thus, we have no need to visit those sites today. We will visit the ones that do show new entries. (After visiting the site, the Bloglines numbers return to zero.)

If you want to get started with RSS feeds and Bloglines, you'll need a quick tutorial:

1. Open two instances (windows) of Internet Explorer, and from one window visit your favorite Web site and look for the XML or RSS icon. Not all sites offer an RSS feed, but an increasing number do.

2. Once you locate an RSS or XML icon, click the icon and look for the RSS link on the resulting page. Figure 15-11 shows an example. Copy that link by dragging your mouse pointer over it, right-clicking, and choosing Copy.

Figure 15-11
Look for the RSS link in the code; it's usually the first link listed.

3. In the second window that contains Internet Explorer, go to **www.bloglines.com**. Click the Subscribe link and input the required information.

4. Right-click and paste the URL into the Blog or Feed URL window. Click Subscribe. You'll now see the new entry in your blog list.

Bloglines continues to make it easier and easier to subscribe to RSS feeds. Even if you can't find the proper link as required in step 2 here, you can type in the URL of the Web site you like and Bloglines will try to create an RSS feed for you. You can also use Feedfire, at **www.feedfire.com**, to create any feed, even from Web sites that don't have RSS already set up.

Microsoft's New Utilities

Finally, you'll want to keep an eye out for new utilities from Microsoft. We found one recently called the Microsoft USB Flash Drive Manager. This utility helps you back up and restore files you save to your USB flash drives. You can find this and other utilities at Microsoft's Windows XP Web page: **www.microsoft.com/Windowsxp**. Here is some other free software available from Microsoft:

√ Fun Packs - Fun Packs contain images, visualizations, music, photos, and templates that are based on holidays, seasons, and hobbies. We particularly liked the Winter Fun Pack 2004, complete with wallpaper that includes festive holiday images. (This becomes gunk if you don't use it.)

√ Updates - Windows Media Player 10, Movie Maker 2, Photo Story 3, DirectX 9.0c, MSN Messenger, and SP2 are all available. (Updates and upgrades are rarely ever gunk.)

√ TabletPC Utilities - Office XP Pack, Tablet PC Recognizer Pack, and more
let you do more with your TabletPC.

√ PowerToys - Mentioned earlier in this chapter.

√ Desktop Enhancements- Get themes and Media Player 10 skins, screen
savers and Desktop images, and more. (Gunk, gunk, gunk—be careful.)

TIP: *Revisit the PowerToys and add-ons monthly to see if you still need them or want them. Uninstall any items you no longer need.*

Summing Up

The purpose of this chapter was to help you degunk, secure, and personalize
your computer with PowerToys and shareware available on the Internet.
Shareware can enhance both the performance of the computer and how efficiently you work by using computer-powered tried-and-true tools for
degunking. PowerToys are free and can be quite useful, and Tweak UI is certainly a favorite for lots of folks. Shareware can also be quite effective in enhancing performance, from applications that synchronize duplicate files to those
that clean the Registry. Bloglines, in conjunction with RSS feeds, can help you
get the most out of your Web surfing and do more in less time.

Improving Security

Degunking Checklist:

√ Discover how secure your computer really is.

√ Protect your computer by purchasing and configuring anti-virus software.

√ Configure Internet options to protect, secure, and keep private information private.

√ Understand good and bad cookies and how to best configure Internet Explorer.

√ Create a Guest account and use it when company arrives.

√ Set local security policies that affect anyone who logs on to your computer.

√ Understand and set up a firewall to improve security.

S ecuring your PC is just as important as enhancing its performance, and that's what we're going to discuss in this chapter. It doesn't do any good to clean up, maintain, and organize your home or garage if you're going to leave the door unlocked for anyone and everyone to drop in without your permission. The same situation is true of your PC. Don't go to all of the trouble of getting it running efficiently, organizing all of its files, and performing scheduled maintenance when you've left a door open to hackers, viruses, worms, and adware or spyware programs, which in turn can really gunk up your machine.

How Secure Is Your PC?

Microsoft offers a free tool called the MBSA (Microsoft Baseline Security Analyzer) that will check your current security configuration and look for missing critical security updates, common security slip-ups, and other vulnerabilities. The program will then produce a report with instructions on how to repair the security issues it finds. You can decide after viewing the report if any items need attention. Using this tool is a great way to begin the securing process.

To run this free security check and view a report, make sure you are logged on as an administrator and connected to the Internet. Then follow these steps:

1. Click Start, and open Help And Support. In the Search window, type *MBSA*.

2. From the Suggested Topics options, choose Finding Out About Your Computer's Security Settings.

3. Read the article that appears in the right pane, and then click the link to access the MBSA page on the Microsoft Web site.

4. Read the article regarding the MBSA (Microsoft Baseline Security Analyzer).

5. Follow the links and download and install the application. You'll have to agree to let Microsoft see if you have a valid copy of Windows, and you'll have to install ActiveX controls if you haven't already. You'll be prompted to do these things. If prompted by your anti-virus software that a malicious script is present, choose to run the script after the program is installed. Make sure you download the version for your specific language; there will be several options.

6. In the installation box, choose Run. Work through the wizard to set up the program. Figure 16-1 shows a successful installation in progress.

7. Open the program from the Start>All Programs menu.

8. When prompted, choose the computer to scan (if several are listed), and select Start Scan. A sample report is shown in Figure 16-2.

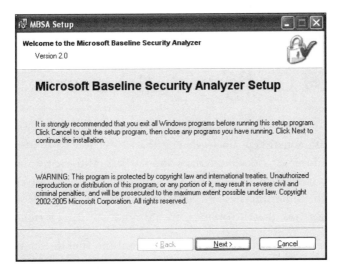

Figure 16-1

It may take a while to get here, but when you see this wizard, you're almost done.

Figure 16-2

A report of your security settings is produced after the application runs.

As you can see from the partial report shown in Figure 16-2, this computer has three serious issues. It's missing one Office security update, the Guest account is enabled, and there are too many administrators. With the report in hand, make the needed repairs, and then continue with this chapter.

Purchase and Configure Anti-Virus Software

Anti-virus software, when kept up-to-date, is the easiest way to protect your computer against Internet risks like viruses and hackers. Anti-virus software is fairly inexpensive, easy to install, and a snap to keep current. If you don't have it now, disconnect from the Internet and run out to the local computer store or stay online and visit your favorite online software vendor and get it right away!

Anti-virus software can protect against lots of different Internet threats, not just viruses and hackers. It can protect against unauthorized connections and privacy threats. It can repel unwanted cookies and Java applets and scan incoming and outgoing e-mail. Many of these products also include a personal firewall, which can provide even more protection. (We'll talk more about firewalls later in this chapter.) There are lots of anti-virus software manufacturers to choose from, including Symantec, Enteractive, and McAfee. Any of these can be trusted to do a good job at keeping your machine more secure.

Once installed, this software can be configured to suit your needs. Generally, the default settings are fine, but you might want to set the application to look for and download new security definitions every night (instead of the default, which is generally every week) if you want extra security. Also, you might not want to scan each outgoing e-mail for viruses. You can perform full system scans daily, weekly, or monthly and view reports of various activities. As a rule, consider the following configuration choices for your anti-virus software:

√ Set the anti-virus program to "auto-protect" and have it start each time you boot the computer. You should leave the application running in the background at all times.

√ Show the software icon in the System Tray so that it is easily accessible and alerts can be viewed easily.

√ Let your anti-virus program automatically repair any infected files it finds. Quarantine the file if the repair is not successful.

√ Perform a complete system scan at least once a week and perhaps daily (each night) for computers that hold sensitive data.

√ Enable script blocking so that malicious scripts (which can be viruses) are not run.

√ Scan incoming and outgoing e-mail for viruses.

√ Enable protection on any instant messaging systems you use.

√ Enable automatic and scheduled downloads of new virus definitions at least weekly. If you have a continuous connection to the Internet, configure definitions to be downloaded daily.

√ Enable protection from spyware and adware, if provided as an option.

√ When configuring e-mail protection, configure the application to automatically delete files that contain known viruses. (See Chapters 7 and 8 for more information on e-mail security.)

With all of these precautions in place, you should be pretty well protected against viruses, hackers, and general Internet threats. But you can do more. In the next section, we'll take security a step further by configuring Internet options.

TIP: *Anti-virus software doesn't protect against Internet pop-ups and is not the best solution for avoiding adware and spyware. You should also have third-party anti-spyware and anti-adware applications, especially if you have an always-on connection.*

Gunkbuster's Notebook: Don't Put New AV Software on Old PCs

There's a caution to keep in mind as you shop for anti-virus software: Products in that category are very "power hungry," in that they require a great deal of your PC's basic processing power. This is particularly true of the majors like Norton and MacAfee, which are constantly competing against one another by adding new features to their offerings. Both products have gotten so big and all-inclusive that they can overwhelm an older PC with a more modest processor speed and memory complement. Here's our rule of thumb: Do *not* install the major AV products on PCs more than three or (at most) four years old.

Sometimes you can find older versions of the majors sold used online, but be careful: Some vendors like Symantec do not support older versions after a few years. Even if you install Norton Antivirus 2001, for example, Symantec will not provide you with downloadable updates after the first period is past, whether you're willing to pay for them or not.

It's better to use one of the smaller anti-virus products, which have fewer features and thus place fewer demands on older PCs. The best of these is probably AVG Antivirus from Grisoft. Go to

www.grisoft.com. We've had it running on PCs going back as far as 1998, and while the performance hit is noticeable, It does not bring older PCs to their knees as Norton or MacAfee would.

The key is to install as few "extra" features as you can avoid. You're looking for virus protection. Limited firewalls, pop-up stoppers, cookie managers, and other extras only slow you down, and aren't generally the best for the purposes they claim to serve. If an anti-virus product offers you a list of things to choose from when you install on an older PC, choose only virus protection. That's really what you need.

Configure Internet Options

You have complete control over how secure your Web surfing is, how much of your private information is given to Web sites, and what content can and can't be viewed on your computer. You can even configure custom security zones to personalize the security options that you've selected.

In the following sections, you'll learn about security zones, how to configure trusted Web sites, and how to restrict what happens when you visit untrusted sites. You'll also learn how to keep your private information private, as well as the pros and cons of using strict privacy settings (including restricting cookies).

Configure Security Zones

The zones you can configure for Internet Explorer are shown in the Security tab of the Tools>Internet Options dialog box. You can view information on each zone by clicking it. Let's take a look at the zones you can configure and the ones that are set up by default. Here are the steps to follow:

1. Open Internet Explorer, click the Tools menu, and click Internet Options.

2. From the Internet Options dialog box, click the Security tab, shown in Figure 16-3.

3. Select an Internet zone to view its properties.

TIP: Figure 16-3 shows a Security tab with the defaults chosen. If you've made custom changes on the Security tab, yours will look a little different. If that's the case, simply click Default Level (grayed out in the figure) to see the defaults.

Figure 16-3
The Security tab in the Internet Options dialog box offers zones that can be configured for more or less security.

Internet Zone

By default, all Web sites fall into the Internet zone, and the security level for the zone is Medium. (The other zones require you to choose sites manually and place them in the zone yourself.) Medium security offers safe browsing while still being quite functional. With this setting, you will get a prompt before anything potentially harmful is downloaded. Medium security is appropriate for most users and Internet sites. You can change the security level for the Internet zone by simply moving the security slider up or down. When you move the slider, the information about the zone's security precautions changes.

Additional Zones

In addition to the Internet zone, there are three other zones: Local Intranet, Trusted Sites, and Restricted Sites. When you use these zones, you must manually place Web sites in them. Once a Web site has been placed in a zone, the site takes on the security measures for that zone.

In the Local Intranet zone, for instance, the default security level is Medium-Low. That's because any site you manually place in this zone should be a site on your local intranet; it should be a trusted and secure Web site maintained by your company.

In the Trusted Sites zone, the default security level is Low. This setting and zone are only appropriate for sites you absolutely trust, like your own. Low security provides minimal safeguards; for example, no prompts appear when ActiveX content is downloaded and run on your machine. Because all ActiveX content is run, it is only appropriate for sites you absolutely trust.

Finally, the Restricted Sites zone has a security setting of High. Place Web sites here that you do not trust. A security level of High reduces functionality, but you'll at least be safe while visiting!

Here's how to add a Web site to any of these zones:

1. Open Internet Explorer, click Tools, and click Internet Options.
2. Click the Security tab and select any zone other than the Internet zone.
3. Click Sites.
4. In the Sites dialog box, type in the Web address of the zone to add and click Add. Note that the URL for trusted sites will have to start with https://, a verification that the site is indeed secure. Figure 16-4 shows an example of a Web site being added to the Trusted Sites zone. When finished, click OK twice.

Figure 16-4

You can add sites you trust to the Trusted Sites zone.

Custom Zones

You probably noticed in Figure 16-3 that a Custom Level button is provided in the Internet Options dialog box under the Security tab. Clicking Custom Level here allows you to tweak the default security settings for a particular zone. For instance, if you want to use the Internet zone and the Medium security settings but you'd like to disable the option to have Desktop items installed (instead of the default of being prompted before they are installed), you can configure just that single option using custom settings. Here's how:

1. Open Internet Explorer, click Tools, and click Internet Options.

2. Click the Security tab.

3. Choose a zone to change—for instance, the Internet zone.

4. Click Custom Level.

5. In the Security Settings dialog box, shown in Figure 16-5, make changes as desired. You can use the Reset button to undo the changes if you decide to later.

6. Click OK twice.

Figure 16-5
Configure custom settings for more control.

As an aside, we'll discourage configuring your own custom settings. If you run across a problem and need tech support, perhaps a problem with access or with performance on a Web page, the solution can be difficult to uncover. This is especially true if you configured custom settings a year ago and the computer is only now developing problems.

Privacy Options

When you surf the Internet, Web sites you visit will pick up little tidbits of information from you, including information about your computer configuration, what version of Windows Media Player you use, your Internet connection speed, and maybe even your purchasing history at that site, your favorite topics, your favorite screen colors, or other items. While this might seem like it's on the edge of being intrusive and potentially harmful (or downright illegal), it isn't.

Before you panic, keep in mind that if you have the proper security settings and anti-virus, anti-adware, and anti-spyware software in place, a Web site can't easily uncover personal information about you unless you supply it yourself. The majority of information collected at Web sites without your knowledge is harmless data about your preferences when you visit. This information is stored as a text file, called a *cookie,* which is stored on your computer in the Cookies folder. Each time you visit, the Web site can give you more personalized treatment because of the cookie. Cookies can be used to remember your computer configuration (you use Windows XP, for instance) or a password you created at the site from which the cookie is sent, just to give you a couple of examples.

Information You Give Out

Most cookies that Web sites send out and use to make surfing more customized are generally harmless, but sometimes additional information is provided to Web sites unwittingly. Consider this: you purchase something online, and during the transaction you give out your phone number, address, full name, credit card numbers, passwords, and more. If you create a user account and/or password, you also give the Web site permission to collect information about you and your surfing habits while you are visiting. If you've configured any of the "My" pages from MSN, Yahoo!, or other service, these companies might know even more (but no more than you've told them). Have you created a customized home page at Yahoo! or a similar site? If you have, you might have also configured a "personal profile" and gladly provided information about your age, sex, hobbies, income, and even marital status. That information is public!

The point here is that any information you supply will be collected, stored, and used by someone. You need to be careful about handing out information at sites you don't trust. You should read the agreements you so eagerly accept when creating a password or sign-on name. With that bit of warning out of the way, and knowing that we can't control what information *you* give at Web sites, we can show you how to control what anonymous and/or personal information is collected from you without your knowledge or consent.

Understand Your Options

You have control over what cookies are placed on your computer. Open up the Privacy settings as follows, and let's have a look:

1. Open Internet Explorer, click Tools, and click Internet Options.

2. Click the Privacy tab.

3. If Default is not grayed out, click it, and configure the settings to Medium by sliding the security slider. See Figure 16-6.

4. Read the explanation for Medium security. If you'd like more secure Privacy settings, move the slider up; less secure, move it down.

Figure 16-6
You have the option to configure custom privacy settings.

As with zones, you can configure custom settings. You can override default cookie handling for a particular Web site by clicking the Advanced button. We'll say that for the most part, Medium (or Medium High) is the best choice for Privacy settings. Too low of a setting can make you vulnerable; too high, and your Web surfing will be extremely limited. You will find that you must have cookies enabled to enter many sites, so enabling cookies is generally a good idea.

GunkBuster's Notebook: More about Cookies

Recapping: Cookies are little bits of data stored as text documents that Web sites place on your computer when you visit. First-party cookies come from the site itself, and third-party cookies come from advertisers and other third-party vendors. Cookies are generally harmless, as long as you keep a Medium or higher level of security. Cookies are what allow Web sites like **www.amazon.com** to know that you enjoy gardening books and don't want to see books on motorcycles. They enable you to log on to a Web site without always having to type a password.

You can view and delete the cookies that have been placed on your computer by using Windows Explorer to locate Local Disk:\Documents And Settings\All Users\<*your user name*>\Cookies. Figure 16-7 shows a Cookies folder. If you look

Figure 16-7
Cookies are generally harmless, but you may have thousands of them.

closely at the names of the files, you'll see cookies from Expedia, ESPN, eWEEK, FedEx, Fidelity, and more. In our minds, these are harmless or are items we set up ourselves.

You can also delete the cookies stored on your machine from inside Internet Explorer by following these steps:

1. Click Tools, click Internet Options, and click the General tab.
2. Click Delete Cookies to remove all of the cookies stored on your machine.

This would be a good idea if you are selling or loaning the computer to someone, or if others share your computer and online accounts. (It's always best to format and reinstall the operating system before selling any computer, though.)

Enable the Guest Account

If you're planning on having guests anytime soon and they will want access to a computer for checking e-mail, surfing the Web, printing, or writing letters home, you'll want to enable a Guest account. A Guest account is the perfect way to give visitors the computer and Internet access they need while still keeping the computer and your personal files safe and secure. The Guest account should be configured to show on the Welcome screen so that guests have easy access to it.

Once configured, the Guest account has the following properties:

√ It provides access to the computer for anyone who does not specifically have an account on it.

√ It is not configured with a password.

√ Guests cannot install software or hardware.

√ Guests have access to installed hardware and software.

√ Guests cannot upgrade an account to Limited User or Administrator or join any group that has more privileges.

√ Guests cannot change the picture or make permanent changes to the computer.

√ Guests will have access to items in the Shared Documents, Shared Pictures, Shared Music, and Shared Videos folders.

TIP: For this section, we're going to assume that you have a computer that is not a member of a larger, corporate domain. Computers in these environments typically have restrictions on accounts such as this. This section is written for stand-alone computers or computers in a workgroup.

Enable and Configure a Guest Account

Once you've decided you need a Guest account, it's extremely easy to enable the default one. When your guests leave, though, you should disable the account immediately. An enabled Guest account is considered a liability and is not a good long-term security configuration.

To enable and configure the Guest account, follow these steps:

1.   Open Control Panel, and open User Accounts.

2.   Click the Guest account icon.

3.   On the User Accounts page labeled Do You Want To Turn On The Guest Account, click Turn On The Guest Account.

4.   Back at the User Accounts Page, click Change The Way Users Log On Or Off.

5.   Verify that Use The Welcome Screen is checked. Click Apply Options.

6.   Make sure to log off each time you are finished with the computer. When a guest accesses the computer, they'll go through the Welcome screen to log on.

Remember, guests cannot harm the computer by installing applications or hardware, and they will not have access to your private files.

A Look at Administrative Tools

Administrative Tools in Windows XP allows you to take even more control of your computer. These components allow you to set computer-wide local security policies that affect all users of the computer and contain computer management tools that enable you to monitor system events, create and manage shared resources, start and stop services, view device configurations, and more. Other administrative tools are available as well, but for the most part, these two features, setting computer-wide security policies and monitoring the computer, are the ones you'll use most often. Administrative Tools make good degunking partners because they allow you to set local user policies to prevent other users of the computer from doing harm. You can set rules for passwords and logon attempts to heighten the security of the computer. You can also view events like failed logon attempts. Any tool that gives you more control over your computer, who accesses it, and what they can do while at the computer is a great security asset.

Local Security Policies

A big part of degunking is securing your computer from new gunk, and whether that gunk comes from outsiders or from people you know, you need to have complete control over who can access what and how they can access it. Local security policies can be configured to secure your computer from the people who have access to it, including the night staff, additional users, or coworkers. You'd be surprised just how much damage someone can do in a short period of time, whether it's intentional or not.

In this section, we'll introduce you to some of the less-complicated policy settings and tools that can be applied through a local security policy change. By configuring these policies, you can prevent malicious access of your computer by locking the computer after a specific number of failed logon attempts, you can require users of the computer to use complicated passwords so they cannot be easily guessed, and you can require users to press Ctrl+Alt+Del to log on (just to name a few options).

Listed next are some of the more common security changes you can make. In the next section, you'll learn how and where to apply them.

Account Policies>Password Policies:

√ Enforce Password History: Used to determine how many days a password can be remembered in the password history. This is best left at 0 days, thus requiring each user to type in their password each time they log on. The default is 0. For maximum security, set a password and use it each time.

√ Maximum Password Age: Used to determine how many days a password can remain active until it expires and must be changed. The default is that the password never expires; however, this might need to be changed if other people have access to the computer and have time to try to guess a password. I set mine to expire every 15 days.

√ Minimum Password Age: Used to determine how many days a password must be kept before it can be changed. The default is 0 days, meaning the password can be changed immediately and at any time. This default is recommended.

√ Minimum Password Length: Used to configure how many characters must be in a password. The default is 0, but a password containing at least 7 characters is much more secure.

√ Password Must Meet Complexity Requirements: Disabled by default, this setting allows you to require complex passwords containing uppercase and lowercase letters, numbers, and symbols.

Account Policies>Account Lockout Policy:

√ Account Lockout Threshold: Used to configure how many logon attempts can be made before the account is locked. By default, no lockout threshold is set. For extra security, change this setting to 3 or 5 tries and configure the Account Lockout Duration setting.

√   Account Lockout Duration: Used to configure how long an account will be locked out if the account lockout threshold has been met. If an account lockout threshold has been set, the default is 30 minutes.

√   Reset Account Lockout Counter After: Used to configure how soon the Account Lockout Threshold counter will be reset after it is locked. Similar to the Account Lockout Duration setting, the default is 30 minutes. After 30 minutes, the user can try to log on again.

Local Policies>Security Options:

√   Accounts: Rename Guest Account: Allows an administrator to change the Guest account name.

√   Devices: Unsigned Driver Installation Driver Behavior: Determines whether unsigned drivers can be installed. To prevent unsigned drivers from ever being installed, choose the Do Not Allow Installation choice. The Warn But Allow Installation option is the default.

√   Interactive Logon: Message Text For Users Attempting To Log On: Allows an administrator to configure a message that each user, upon logon, will need to read.

√   Interactive Logon: Do Not Require Ctrl+Alt+Del: Allows you to define whether this key combination is required of users who log on. By default, it is not required.

Making Basic Security Policy Changes

If you share a computer with another person, or if your computer can be accessed by others, either at night or when you are away from your office, you should consider configuring some of the local security polices listed in the previous section to protect the computer and your users. Here's how:

1. Open the Control Panel, and if you are using Category view, click Performance And Maintenance. Click Administrative Tools. (If you don't see an Administrative Tools icon, use Start> Search, and search for the Administrative Tools folder.)

2. Open Local Security Policy. Expand Account Policies and click Password Policy, as shown in Figure 16-8.

3. Double-click any password policy to change. Figure 16-9 shows the Maximum Password Age Properties dialog box. Notice it's been changed from the default of 0 to 15 days. Click OK.

4. Repeat these steps to set account lockout policies and security options.

You can be sure with these settings that your computer is more secure and protected than ever. When you are finished configuring the settings, simply close the Local Security Settings window. Your changes will automatically be saved.

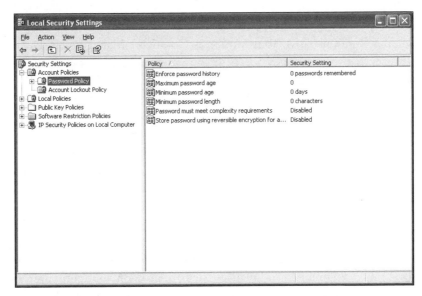

Figure 16-8

Set local security policies to further protect your PC.

Figure 16-9

Each policy has a settings box for configuring your own preferences.

Computer Management

Another Administrative Tools option is Computer Management. Degunking requires that you have easy access to computer management tools such as Device Manager and Disk Defragmenter, as well as the Properties dialog boxes for the hardware installed on your computer. The Computer Management console puts these items in a single place for easy access. Besides these degunking tools, though, the Computer Management console, like the Local Security Policy console, offers lots of advanced options for administrators. For instance, an administrator can use the Event Viewer to view security audits, which can inform an administrator of failed logon attempts and other security issues, system failures such as failed printing requests, failed connection requests, and similar errors and warnings. The Users folder shows all of the users configured for the computer and their properties (which can be changed from this console). You can also access Device Manager, view properties for removable storage devices, run Disk Defragmenter, and manage the hard disks on your computer, all from this single console. Figure 16-10 shows this console with a failed logon attempt security audit selected. Double-click the item to see additional information about the message, which is shown in Figure 16-11. As you can see from the Event Properties window, someone tried to log on at 12:10 P.M. on July 5th, with a bad user name or password. That was us, of course, but if it had not been, we would have had something to worry about.

The best way to become familiar with the Computer Management console is to browse through its options. Many will look familiar, including Disk Defragmenter, Device Manager, and Services:

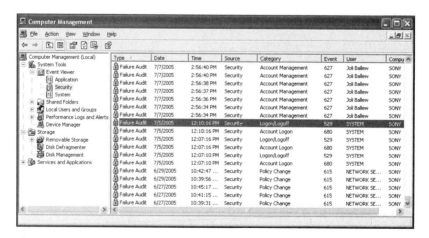

Figure 16-10

System Tools>Event Viewer>Security shows failure and success security audits.

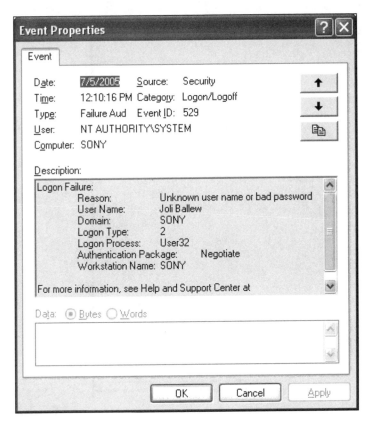

Figure 16-11

Double-clicking any audit reveals additional information about the event.

1. Open the Control Panel, and if you are using Category view, click Performance And Maintenance. Click Administrative Tools. (If you can't find this icon, perform a search for the Administrative Tools folder.)

2. Open Computer Management.

3. To view Event Viewer, Shared Folders, Local Users And Groups, Performance Logs And Alerts, and Device Manager, expand the System Tools tree in the left pane, and then expand and/or click any item in the list to access it.

4. Figure 16-10 showed how to access the Security log; access the Application and System logs similarly. Double-click any item to view more information about it.

5. Expand Local Users And Groups and the Users folder to view the users who have access to your computer. Double-click any users you've created to change the options and requirements for that user. In Figure 16-12, notice that we can change Jennifer's password requirements or disable the account. We can also see what group she is a member of (Member Of tab) and add her to another group or remove her from any group quite easily.

Figure 16-12
With the Computer Management console, you can manage users and groups.

6. Click Device Manager under the System Tools console to view the console and make changes to the computer's configuration.

7. Expand the Storage tree to view Disk Defragmenter or the Disk Management consoles.

If you become interested in setting up users and groups, configuring performance logs and computer alerts, or working with shared folders among computers on a workgroup, there are lots of help files on the subject. Simply click Help, and click Help Topics. In the Help window, choose Computer Management.

Firewalls

Firewalls are important products that protect computers from Internet intrusions, just as deadbolts on a door protect your home from intruders. Just as you would secure your home with locks and a security system, you should also secure your computer with a firewall *and* anti-virus, anti-adware, and anti-virus software.

Firewalls, even the most basic ones, offer lots of protection from trespassers and bad guys. Firewalls come in all shapes and sizes, but a determined hacker may still be able to break in. With that in mind, you should configure your system to thwart attacks by making it as difficult as possible for an intruder to get in and access personal data. There are several ways to do this, and the best one is to enable the firewall that comes with Service Pack 2 for Windows XP. If you don't have Windows XP and/or SP2, you can enable Windows XP's Internet Connection Firewall. You can also purchase a third-party hardware or software firewall, although SP2's firewall is pretty secure and is fine for most home users if you have it. If you have an always-on connection, you may already have a hardware-based firewall in the form of an external router.

No SP2? Enable Windows XP's Internet Connection Firewall

Windows XP initially shipped with a host firewall that you could enable called Internet Connection Firewall (ICF). ICF protects you pretty well from what can come into your system from the Internet. It's called a host firewall because it is created for use on a single computer (the host), like a desktop system or laptop. For the home user, Windows XP's ICF might suffice if you also have up-to-date anti-virus software, but keep in mind that it only offers the most basic protection.

Do this to enable ICF:

1. Click Start, point to Connect To, right-click your Internet connection (or choose My Network Places, View Network Connections, and then right-click your Internet connection), and choose Properties.

2. Click the Advanced tab.,

3. Under Internet Connection Firewall, check Protect My Computer And Network By Limiting Or Preventing Access To This Computer From The Internet. Click OK.

TIP: *ICF should be enabled on any Internet connection that is shared with other computers and any connection that is used on any computer to directly connect to the Internet. ICF should not be enabled on any connection/computer that does not directly connect to the Internet.*

As mentioned earlier, ICF combined with up-to-date anti-malware software protects the computer pretty well. This might be all you need for a single computer or laptop that connects to the Internet, but complete security isn't necessarily guaranteed.

If you want more protection or have sensitive and valuable data, extra protection is certainly available. First, upgrade to SP2. If you can't do that or don't want to, two of the most popular third-party host firewalls are Zone Alarm and Norton. These offer additional security features, including protecting your privacy, protecting against determined hackers, and other options not found in ICF or SP2's firewall. You can never go wrong purchasing a third-party firewall for extra protection, so if you can afford it, you should buy it! These products are extremely affordable and well worth the expense and peace of mind.

Windows XP and SP2's Firewall

Once you have downloaded and installed Service Pack 2 (SP2) for Windows XP, you should enable the new firewall available on your computer. As with the older ICF, you can do this from the Internet connection's Properties dialog box. This is shown in Figure 16-13.

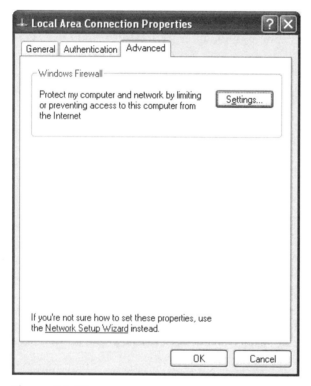

Figure 16-13

You can enable Windows XP and SP2's firewall from your Internet properties window.

You can also access and configure this firewall from Control Panel:

1. Open Control Panel.

2. Open Security Center.

3. Verify that the Firewall is turned on; if not, enable the firewall. See Figure 16-14.

For more information about SP2, refer to Chapter 10.

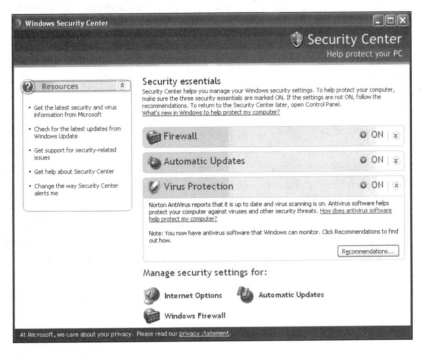

Figure 16-14

SP2 comes with a new firewall that you should enable.

Home Office and Business Firewalls

Business networks require more protection than a home computer because they generally are larger, internal networks and have valuable data that must be protected. Because of this, businesses may use a second type of firewall called a *network firewall*. Network firewalls can be hardware or software based and can range from fairly inexpensive to extremely expensive. One common large-business firewall is Microsoft's ISA Server, which watches traffic that enters and leaves the intranet and looks for uninvited or malicious data. Another popular firewall for businesses is the intrusion detection firewall that identifies attack patterns and uses routers to stop the connection to the source before harm can be done. These advanced firewalls offer protection that is far superior to the simple host-based firewalls like the one you get in SP2. You can get plenty of information about these different firewalls—their capabilities, pricing, and configuration—from your local computer store and from Windows XP's help files.

Get the Best Security for the Buck

One sure way to gunk up your computer is to allow a virus, adware, spyware, or worm to attack it! You want to have the most reliable software and system configuration possible, but how can you do that on a budget? If you have a single home computer that connects directly to the Internet and is not networked, you can probably get by fairly securely and cheaply using Windows XP's firewall and a good anti-virus software program. If you have an external hardware router, or if your anti-virus software program comes with its own firewall, you're in business! Zone Labs' excellent Zone Alarm Pro firewall comes in a free version with the firewall alone, or with some extra features for around $40 U.S., a good investment. (The free version is gentler on older PCs.) If you have two or three computers on a home network that uses Internet Connection Sharing, the same is true. It's also important to have firewalls if you have an always-on connection, although these days virtually all routers come with a very effective hardware firewall. The price on these has come down to the $50 level, and you can often get them for less on sale and with rebate offers. Your local computer store certainly carries at least a few of these software firewall products and a number of routers, and larger computer retailers like CompUSA offer a bewildering selection.

Summing Up

Improving security is a multilevel task and can be time-consuming and expensive. However, an unprotected computer can get gunked up beyond belief by a single worm or script attack—and the attack can occur scant minutes after you connect your PC to the net. Viruses will attempt to seize your PC and add it to "zombie" networks to do shadowy work behind your back. All attacks install Windows services, place files and change settings on your PC, all of which are designed to resist removal. In fact, you might not be able to recover fully from a virus or worm without reinstalling Windows completely, along with everything else you use. As detailed in this chapter, you must enhance security to avoid getting gunked up in the first place!

In this chapter, you learned to first repair any obvious holes in security using a security analyzer like Microsoft's MBSA tool. With the most basic security flaws repaired, you absolutely must purchase, install, configure, and keep up-to-date your anti-virus, anti-spyware, and anti-adware software. Following that, Internet options can be configured to customize and/or configure zones and privacy options.

Administrative actions for securing the computer include enabling a Guest account when company arrives from out of town (and disabling it when they leave), setting local security policies for computers with multiple users or those that are left in unsecured environments like unlocked offices, and configuring a firewall. There are many different types of firewalls, including the firewall that comes with SP2 and third-party hardware and software options.

Backing Up Precious Files

Degunking Checklist:

√ Use the Backup utility to back up important files and folders.

√ Learn what to back up and how often.

√ Store backups in a safe place.

√ Configure a scheduled task to run the Backup utility for added flexibility.

√ Learn how to use the Restore utility in case of emergency.

√ Burn to a CD-R as a backup option.

√ Manually drag and drop files to a CD as a backup option.

One of the most important tasks for a computer user to remember to do is to back up data regularly. And as you become more diligent about degunking your PC on a regular basis by using some of the degunking maintenance tasks outlined in this book, you'll need a good backup strategy. After all, degunking your PC properly involves deleting documents and programs as well as moving files around on a regular basis. If you have a regular backup strategy in place, you'll feel more confident about getting rid of files and programs because you'll be able to restore them if you later decide that you need them. The worst kind of degunker you can be is the "packrat degunker," which is the person who is afraid to throw anything away because they think that something valuable might be lost. Usually, this fear comes from having a lousy backup strategy!

Backing up data is especially important these days because we store everything—family videos, pictures, music, important documents, faxes, important records—all on a single hard drive. Imagine how much data could be destroyed by a single hard drive crash. A hard drive crash can be like a house fire or flood: every important picture, video, file, and fax would be lost.

In this chapter, you'll learn all about backing up data: scheduling a task and backing up automatically, configuring and using the Backup utility, and restoring when a crash occurs. You'll also learn what to back up, how often, and how to store your backups. In addition to using the Backup utility, you can back up files by manually dragging and dropping them to another drive, including a CD-R drive.

Perform Backups with the Backup Utility

You'll be a better degunker if you're comfortable with your backups. You'll know that you can restore from backups if you delete anything you decide you want to keep later. The Windows XP Backup utility offers an easy way to back up your data regularly. As you'll learn later in this chapter, you can combine it with the Scheduled Tasks utility to run backups automatically. The Backup utility can be run and configured via a wizard, but our suggestion is that you run it in Advanced mode because this mode offers so many more choices. In the following sections, we'll work with the Backup utility in various modes, discuss how to use it, and talk about what should be backed up and how often. In addition, I'll give you some strategies for storing your backups safely.

Getting Started

Using the Backup utility does not require you to have any special equipment, but it does require you to have some place to save the backup file. This can be a second hard drive, a USB flash drive, an iPod, or backup device like a Zip disk, or it can be on your own hard drive. If you use your own hard drive to save the backup, you'll need a CD or DVD burner to copy that backup file for safekeeping. With that in mind, the first step in configuring (and getting to know) the Backup utility is to open it in Advanced mode:

1. Click Start, point to All Programs, point to Accessories, point to System Tools, and click Backup. If you use Windows XP Home Edition, skip to step 2 to install this utility. If you use Windows XP Professional Edition, move ahead to step 3.

2. If you have Windows XP Home Edition, insert the Windows XP Home Edition CD-ROM into your CD-ROM drive. Browse to the \VALUEADD\MSFT\NTBACKUP folder and double-click the Ntbackup.msi file. Run the wizard. Return to step 1 to open the application.

3. If the Welcome To The Backup Utility in Advanced Mode opens, as shown in Figure 17-1, you're good to go. If the utility opens in Wizard mode, click the link to start Advanced mode.

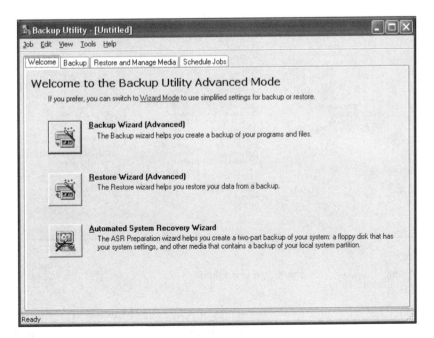

Figure 17-1

Open the Backup utility in Advanced mode.

4. Click the Backup tab, and on the Job menu, click New.

5. In the Backup Destination area, you can save the backup either as a file or to a tape device (if one is available). File is selected by default, and if no tape device exists, no options will be given.

6. Refer to the next few sections to decide what type of backup to perform and how to select the required folders. Once the folders are selected, you can either set advanced options (also detailed) or simply start the backup.

Creating a Simple Backup

So what's the next step and how do you decide what to back up? The answer to that is not a simple one. If you only want to do a minimal backup of your important data, you can click (not check) the drive that holds the data in the left pane and then simply check the appropriate folders in the right pane. In Figure 17-2, the D: drive is checked because that's the drive that contains the data to be backed up. (The C: drive holds the system files in this case.) In this example, only the My Documents, My Pictures, and My Videos folders will be backed up, and not system files, system state, or anything else on either drive.

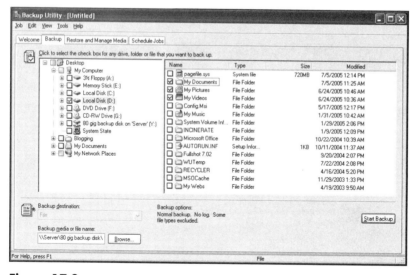

Figure 17-2
A simple backup only contains a few folders.

Once the appropriate folders are chosen, click the Browse button to locate the backup device (an external hard drive, tape drive, USB flash drive, Zip disk, or other removable media) or choose to save the backup as a file; then click Start Backup. You can't save a backup to a CD-R, CD-RW, or DVD-R, though, so don't even bother trying to choose any of those devices! (If you want to archive backups to a CD or DVD, you can always save the backup to your hard drive as a file and then copy that file to the CD. You'll learn how to do that in the section "Copy to CD or DVD as a Backup Option" later in this chapter.)

This "simple" type of backup is by no means a complete backup of the system and does not include important data like the system state, the Registry, drivers, and fonts. It also won't include programs, your Favorites list, cookies, and other important settings. To get a more complete backup requires a different approach.

Creating a Thorough Backup

To create a more thorough backup, we'll use the Advanced Backup Wizard. This wizard makes it fairly easy to define what exactly you want to back up and includes options to back up the system state.

NOTE: *When you back up the system state, you back up the boot files, system files, the Registry, and other important data.*

To use the Advanced Backup Wizard to back up anything or everything on your computer, including the system state and Registry, follow these steps:

1. Click Start, point to All Programs, point to Accessories, point to System Tools, and click Backup.

2. If the Welcome To The Backup Or Restore Wizard opens in Advanced mode, as shown in Figure 17-1, you're good to go. If the utility opens in Wizard mode, click the link to start Advanced mode.

3. From the Welcome tab, click the Backup Wizard (Advanced) button.

4. If prompted, click No to clear any previously configured backups, and in the Welcome To The Backup Wizard page, click Next.

5. In the What To Back Up page, you can choose Back Up Everything On This Computer; Back Up Only Selected Files, Drives, Or Network Data; or Only Back Up the System State Data. If you select the second choice, you'll be prompted to choose folders, as shown in Figure 17-2, before you can continue. If you choose either of the other two choices, the Backup Wizard will continue as described in step 6.

6. In the Backup, Type, Destination, And Name page, choose the backup type (File or Tape Device), browse to a place to save your backup, and type a name for the backup as shown in Figure 17-3. Click Next.

7. In the Completing The Backup Wizard page, shown in Figure 17-4, verify that the information is correct and click Back to change anything that is not. To complete the wizard and begin the backup, click Finish.

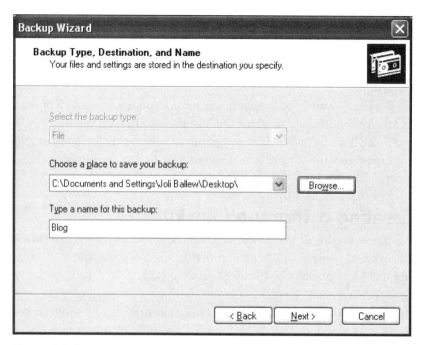

Figure 17-3

Configure where to save and what to name the backup.

Figure 17-4

Verify the description, contents, location, media, and other options by clicking Finish.

8. To set advanced options, click the Advanced button and work through the remaining pages. The Advanced button allows you to select a backup type, which is detailed in the following section. You can also decide if you want to append the data to an existing backup or not and whether to perform the backup now or later

GunkBuster's Notebook: Perform Backups Before Deleting, Installing, Moving, and Experimenting

You know you should create a system restore point prior to performing a risky task like installing a downloaded application from a third party or unreputable Web site, installing software from a file sharing Internet site, performing virus removal tasks, or installing an unsigned driver. But you might not know that there are other circumstances in which you should also perform a backup.

Although System Restore can often restore your computer successfully if something happens, sometimes it can't. (You'll learn more about the System Restore utility in Chapter 18.) This is especially true if a procedure such as removing a virus, editing the Registry, or installing some third-party software that has questionable code goes awry. You'll need a good, solid backup to recover from that. Create a backup before doing anything risky, including the following:

√ Installing software you've downloaded from the Internet

√ Editing the Registry

√ Making changes to the BIOS

√ Installing an upgrade

√ Creating a dual-boot system

√ Using partition-moving software to make major changes to the hard disk's configuration

√ Performing a virus removal procedure

√ Joining a file sharing Internet group

Use Different Types of Backups

There are several types of backups you can create, and you'll need to understand each type so that you can regularly create a good set of backups that are both efficient and effective. As mentioned in step 8 in the previous example, clicking the Advanced button offers additional options for creating the backup. The options for choosing a backup type are available from either the simple wizard interface or the advanced one, as well as from the Backup tab (after you've clicked Start Backup).

The five types of backups available are normal, copy, incremental, differential, and daily. Depending on the backup type you choose, you can also opt to append the data to the previous backup or overwrite the existing data. To decide what type of backup you should choose, read the following descriptions:

√   Normal: You'll generally choose this option the first time you create a backup file. This type of backup is the default. Your selected files are copied and marked as backed up.

√   Incremental: With this type of backup, only files created or changed since the last normal or incremental backup are copied and marked as backed up.

√   Differential: With this option, only the files that have changed since the last normal or incremental backup are copied, but they are not marked as backed up.

√   Copy: All selected files are copied but not marked as being backed up. This is useful if you want to back up files between normal or incremental backups but don't want to affect those normal or incremental backups.

√   Daily: All selected files that have been modified the day the daily backup is scheduled or run are copied. The backed-up files are not marked as backed up and thus do not affect other backups.

Combining backups and restoring from multiple backups and multiple backup tapes can get a little complicated. You have to fully understand exactly what each backup does and how it is used to restore a computer.

Recommendations for the Home User

Just in case you get gunked up with a virus or make a mistake while editing the BIOS or Registry, make sure you have good, solid backups. For the home user, we'll suggest creating a normal backup of the system state and a normal backup of the My Documents, My Pictures, My Music, and other data folders and then storing those backups on a CD, DVD, flash drive, or a separate hard drive. You might also back up the Fonts folder, other personal folders, the Unzipped folder (if you have one), and even a few program folders. You can then combine those normal backups with daily backups if so inclined. In addition, you should create a normal, full backup in case of an extreme emergency. Both can be used with the Restore utility, and you can decide which one to use depending on the situation at hand.

How Often to Back Up

You should develop a backup schedule based on how much data you can stand to lose. We perform a daily backup, but we make quite a few changes every day to the data stored on our hard drives and we consider our data quite valuable. We perform normal backups once a week. If, however, you only log on twice a week to send a few e-mails, there's certainly no need to create a backup schedule like this one. Table 17-1 briefly outlines common backup strategies.

Table 17-1   Back Up Regularly

If you are a...	Perform a normal (daily) backup ...	Perform a full backup ...
Casual user who only turns on the computer twice a week to e-mail a friend	Once every two weeks or anytime anything is created that cannot be lost	Twice a year
Home user and access the computer daily	Two or three times a week or anytime anything is created that cannot be lost	Four times a year
Home user and digital media enthusiast or if you work from home	Once a day, at the end of each day	Once a week or twice a month
Home user and run a home-based business	Once a day, at the end of each day	Once a week

Regardless of how much you use your computer, you should have at least one full backup at least a couple of times a year. You should perform normal backups combined with daily backups as you deem necessary. We think, for most people, backing up important (and changed) documents at least once a week is a good habit to get into.

About Storing the Backups

A spilled soda that lands on your computer and then spills over onto your backup device will destroy both, so placing your external hard drive (with your backups on it) on top of your tower doesn't make much sense. In the same vein, a lightning strike that gets by your surge protector will likely destroy anything that's plugged into it, so even having the backup device in the same room can offer up problems.

Consider creating a backup on an external drive and then burning that file to a CD or DVD once a month or so. Then you can store the CD in another room, in a safe deposit box, or at another location for safekeeping. You might also back up to an external drive and then unplug and remove it to protect it from power surges, viruses, spilled coffee, or other catastrophes. Data stored on computers has certainly become *that* valuable; pictures, videos, and some data simply can't be replaced or re-created.

TIP: Treat your backups as you would your most precious photos or videos. You want to keep them in a safe place where flood, fire, or theft won't be a threat.

Scheduling a Backup Using the Backup Utility

Although you can use the Scheduled Tasks utility, as you'll learn later in this chapter, to remind you to back up your data daily, weekly, or monthly, you can also schedule a backup using the Backup utility itself. Using the Backup utility is more comprehensive and a better choice because you can change the backup type, what's backed up, and where it's stored for each job you create while creating the scheduled task.

Here's how to create a scheduled job using the Backup utility:

1. Open Backup in Advanced mode as detailed earlier.

2. Click the Schedule Jobs tab and choose a day to create the backup job, as shown in Figure 17-5.

3. Click Add Job, and click Next in the Welcome To The Backup Wizard page.

4. Continue working through the wizard to create the job as detailed earlier.

Figure 17-5
Use the Schedule Jobs tab to create a scheduled backup.

You certainly can't have too many backups or back up too often. Configure backups to run at least weekly, store the backups in a secure location, and use the Restore utility if a restoration of data is necessary.

Schedule Backups with the Windows Scheduled Tasks Utility

The Scheduled Tasks utility in Windows XP allows you to schedule almost any task to run automatically whenever you choose so that you don't have to remember to perform the tasks yourself. Scheduled tasks can include running a program like Outlook Express every morning at 8 A.M., running the Backup utility every other day at 5 P.M., running Disk Cleanup once a week at noon on Monday, or having Windows Media Player open each night at 9 P.M. so that you can listen to music or Internet radio when you go to bed. You might even configure System Restore to create a restore point every Sunday afternoon, just before the workweek starts. The tasks can be fun, useful, or necessary, but the task must involve a program, script, or document that is either in the Scheduled Task list or can be browsed to. Scheduled tasks, once configured, run in the background, although some require user input to be run.

You might already have some scheduled tasks configured if you've set your anti-virus program to check for updates or to scan your computer daily or weekly. Figure 17-6 shows a sample Scheduled Tasks window, which can be opened in Control Panel (under Performance And Maintenance if you use Category view).

Configuring a Scheduled Task

Configuring a scheduled task is as easy as clicking Add Scheduled Task (shown in Figure 17-6) and following the prompts from the Scheduled Tasks Wizard. In this example, we'll schedule the Backup utility to run automatically as often as you desire, but you can configure just about any program or task to run by browsing to it instead of the Backup utility we'll schedule here.

To schedule the Backup utility to run automatically on a specific schedule, follow these steps:

1. Open Control Panel, and if you use Category view, click Performance And Maintenance. Click Scheduled Tasks.

2. Read the first page of the Scheduled Task Wizard and click Next.

3. In the second page of the Scheduled Task Wizard, click Backup as shown in Figure 17-7. Click Next.

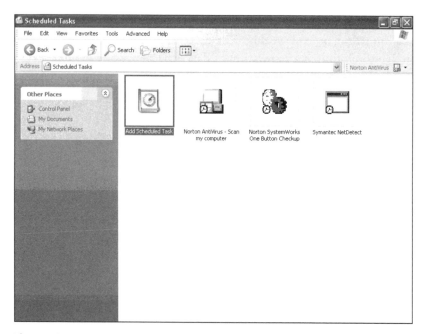

Figure 17-6

You can view scheduled tasks from Control Panel>Scheduled Tasks.

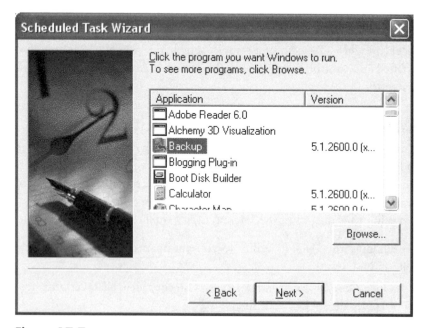

Figure 17-7

Choose the program you want to schedule from the application list.

4. Continuing with the Scheduled Task Wizard, type a name for the task (you can keep Backup if you like), and choose how often to run the task. We'll choose Weekly. Click Next.

5. Schedule the time (and day if applicable) for this task to run. For backups, disk cleanups, and other maintenance tasks, choose a time when no one will be using the computer but when the computer will be turned on. Click Next.

6. Many tasks must be run using an administrator's account, and Backup is one of them. Enter the name of an administrator as well as the password. Confirm the password and click Next.

7. Check Open Advanced Properties For This Task When I Click Finish. Click Finish.

8. In the task's Properties box (Backup is shown in Figure 17-8), type in comments on the Task tab, verify the schedule on the Schedule tab, and configure any advanced settings on the Settings tab. Advanced settings can include starting the task only if the computer is idle, awakening the computer to perform this task, and more. Generally the defaults are fine. Click OK.

Figure 17-8

Tell Backup how to perform the scheduled task.

With the Backup utility configured to run, you'll need to configure it so Windows will know what you want to back up and to where.

TIP: *Make sure the scheduled task is run under an administrator's account and that it also has a password assigned. If you have problems with the task running as scheduled, check this first by right-clicking the task in the Scheduled Tasks window and clicking Properties.*

Using the Restore Utility

If you've decided you need to restore data because it has become corrupt, because you accidentally deleted it, or because you purchased a new computer and want to transfer the backed-up files to it, you can do so easily with the Restore utility in Backup. You can also use the Restore utility if you've so seriously gunked up your computer that you've had to reinstall everything! Restore can be run in Wizard mode or Advanced mode. Restoring in Wizard mode is the easiest, and the wizard even goes to the trouble of locating the saved backups for you! Figure 17-9 shows an example of how the restoration option works.

Figure 17-9

Use the Backup Or Restore Wizard to restore files, folders, system state, and more.

Follow these steps to restore from backup:

1. Open Backup and choose the Wizard mode. Although you can use Advanced mode or the Restore tab, this is easiest. Click Next to begin.

2. When prompted at the Backup Or Restore page, choose Restore Files And Settings. Click Next.

3. In the What To Restore page shown in Figure 17-10, locate the backup to restore with and click Next.

Figure 17-10

Select a backup to restore.

4. In the Completing The Backup Or Restore Wizard page, click Advanced. You can chose to restore the files to their original location, an alternate location, or a single folder. Click Next.

5. In the How To Restore page, choose how to restore the files. You can choose Leave Existing Files (Recommended), Replace Existing Files If They Are Older Than The Backup Files, or Replace Existing Files. In most instances, the first option is the best choice. Click Next.

6. In the Advanced Restore Options page, leave the defaults and click Next. Click Finish to begin the restoration.

TIP: *When restoring to a new computer, you might choose to alter the default settings and restore the files to a single folder. This way, you can place the files you've restored into the exact folders you'd like them to go in.*

Restoring is a great way to put things back where they were before the computer got really gunked up. Restoring allows you to put back into place data such as valuable pictures, music, movies, and documents, as well as the system state, fonts, and even permissions, audit entries, and ownership settings.

Copy to a CD as a Backup Option

Archiving unneeded data is a great way to keep your computer gunk free. If you only have a few specific folders to back up, if you don't have a device to save a backup to, or if you have created a backup file that you'd like to burn to a CD for archiving, you can use the CD Writing Wizard to burn a backup CD via Windows XP. CDs make great archiving tools and allow you to keep copies of important data in a separate location easily. As you know, the Backup utility can't be used to burn directly to a CD.

In this section, we'll show you two ways to burn data to a writable CD, such as a CD-R. In the first example, we'll show you how to create a backup file and save it to your hard drive and then how to copy that backup file to the writeable CD. This is the perfect backup arrangement for those who do not have a backup device such as an external hard drive, tape device, USB flash drive, or Zip disk but who do have a CD-R drive. In the second example, we'll show you how to drag and drop any folder using Windows Explorer, bypassing the Backup utility altogether.

Here's how to burn a backup to a CD:

1. Create a backup and save it to your hard drive.

2. Browse to the folder holding the files. Hover the mouse pointer over the folder to select it, and notice the option to copy this file in the left pane.

3. Choose Copy This File from the File And Folder Tasks pane, and put a CD-R disk in the CD drive.

4. From the Copy Items dialog box, browse to the location of the CD drive and click Copy.

5. Wait while the files copy, and when the CD is ready, browse to it and choose Write These Files To CD from the CD Writing Tasks pane.

6. Name the CD and click Next in the CD Writing Wizard.

You'll probably find this option a quick and easy way to get around not having a backup device. Unfortunately, you might also find that your CDs won't hold all of the data you'd like to back up, especially if you're trying to back up your entire system. If that's the case, you'll either have to create the backup manually, being careful to choose a limited number of files to burn for each CD, or manually drag and drop the folders you want to copy to the CD, keeping track of how much you're putting in there along the way. Of course, you can always burn a DVD; DVDs hold almost 5 GB of data. (If you decide to go that route, we'll suggest using your DVD burner's software.)

To drag and drop files and folders and copy the data to a CD-R, follow these steps:

1. Place a CD-R disk in the appropriate drive.
2. Open My Computer and select the CD drive. Position the window so that it takes up only half the screen.
3. Right-click the Start button, and choose Explore. Browse to the folder to copy, and then right-click and drag it to the CD-R folder.
4. Once the folder has copied, hover the mouse pointer over it to see its size. As you can see in Figure 17-11, the Cookies folder is only 34.3 KB. The CD can hold 702 MB, so there's plenty of room for this folder and then some. Continue adding files and folders to copy until the disk is 95 percent full.

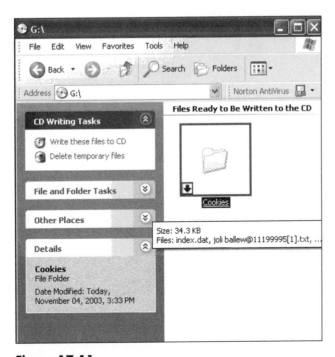

Figure 17-11
Know how much you're adding to a CD so it will all fit and you can get the most out of each CD.

5. When you are ready to write the files to the CD, click Write These Files To CD in the CD Writing Tasks pane.

Whatever way you decide to go, backing up is certainly a necessity and worth the time it takes to perform the task. It doesn't have to be anything elaborate; just a simple backup of your pictures and documents will generally suffice. Choose a backup program that you can live with, and then stick with it!

Summing Up

Good backups promote good degunking habits. If you know you have a backup of your important data, you're more likely to experiment with the degunking techniques introduced in this book. Besides that, though, it's important to keep up-to-date backups for the pictures, videos, Web sites, and other data stored on your computer, because losing all of this data could be potentially devastating. Windows XP comes with a Backup utility just for this purpose and offers several different types of backups. Besides backing up manually, you can schedule backups using Scheduled Tasks or you can configure Backup to run at specific intervals. Once the backups are created, you should store them in a safe place in case they are ever needed.

Last Resort Degunking Techniques

Degunking Checklist:

√ Check your system for incompatible hardware and uninstall these devices using the Windows XP CD-ROM.

√ Solve problems with drivers by installing new drivers and using the Device Driver Rollback utility when necessary.

√ Configure and prepare System Restore in case it's ever needed.

√ Recover from a computer problem or minor crash using System Restore.

√ Use the Repair option on the Windows XP CD-ROM to repair your computer.

√ Upgrade to Windows XP if Repair can't be used.

√ If you decide to reinstall and format your drive, gather all the critical information on settings, configurations, and applications.

√ Perform a clean installation only if you really, really have to.

Degunking does have its limits. At some point, you might experience problems with your computer that become so bad that degunking and normal troubleshooting just won't work. Don't panic just yet because we still might be able to help you. Perhaps you installed a new driver recently and your computer blue-screened, or maybe you deleted some necessary files and your computer now produces errors on boot-up. You also might discover that your computer mysteriously shuts down while running applications or it simply won't get past the loading of system files during the boot process. If errors like these occur, you can employ some specific techniques for getting your computer working properly again.

In this final chapter, you'll learn how to solve some common (but tricky) problems by locating incompatible hardware and using the Device Driver Rollback and System Restore utilities, two excellent programs for correcting serious errors. You'll also learn how to replace missing files needed for booting and for starting Windows XP by using the Windows XP CD's Repair option and sfc / scannow, a command line utility. Finally, you'll learn how to upgrade to Windows XP if you can't access the Repair option and how and when to perform a clean installation of Windows XP. Installing a new version of XP is certainly a last resort; however, if all the other degunking strategies you learned in this book no longer work for you, the smartest thing to do is to install a clean version of XP.

Locate Incompatible Hardware

You might at first feel helpless if you are having recurring and unexplainable problems with your computer, problems such as those listed here:

√ Your system crashes randomly.

√ Programs that you use regularly lock up without warning.

√ Your computer freezes up when performing tasks like printing files.

√ A new device you've recently connected to your computer, such as a scanner or a printer, is causing your computer to lock up and exhibit other strange behavior.

You've probably tried a number of things to solve one or more of these problems, including asking everyone you know who knows anything at all about Windows. You've also probably tried to play detective and duplicate the cause of the problems. Often in situations like this, the problems might not be with your computer or the operating system files. They might be created by the hardware that you've added to your computer.

Before panicking and reinstalling the entire system, you should run a compatibility check. If such a check finds anything that's not compatible, it'll tell you right away. Uninstalling the problem device or locating a new driver for it might solve all of your problems.

Here's how to check system compatibility:

1. Put the Windows XP CD in the CD-ROM drive. It should start automatically. If you don't have an XP CD, you might try the disk that came with your computer. If you can't find your XP CD or if you don't have one, you're out of luck here, unless you can borrow one from a friend.

TIP: *If you know your product ID number (also called your product key) but can't find your own XP CD, you can borrow a CD from a friend or colleague for repairing or reinstalling Windows. This only works if you can produce your own product ID, though.*

---

2. From the choices on the What Do You Want To Do? page, select Check System Compatibility. On the next page, select Check My System Automatically.

3. If prompted, choose to let XP get updated system files from Microsoft's Web site.

4. Once the process is complete, you'll receive a report about any incompatible hardware or software.

The compatibility report offers quite a bit of information if incompatible hardware or software is found. For instance, it will list the name of the incompatible device or program and allow you to view details regarding it. If you find out that you have some hardware that is not compatible with Windows XP, read the details to see what can be done to remedy the situation. Incompatible drivers are a common issue. Therefore, you'll generally search for a newer driver first, before scrapping the hardware altogether. If you can't find a signed one, seriously consider uninstalling the device and removing it from your system. (If that ever happens, look around—there may be a similar device from another manufacturer that is compatible with XP and also includes a signed driver.) From our experience, an incompatible device can cause major problems, but once it's removed, the system will generally perform normally.

Fix Problems with Hardware Drivers

If you've ever installed a newer driver for a piece of hardware like a camera, printer, or modem and then had problems after installing it, you know firsthand how dangerous bad drivers can be. Installing an incorrect driver for a device doesn't just affect the hardware for which you're installing the device. It can also wreak havoc on the entire system, causing unexpected blue screens or causing applications to shut down for no apparent reason. If you suspect a newly installed driver has caused a system problem, you can remove that driver and replace it with a different one. You can also use the rollback feature of Windows and instruct your system to use an older version of a driver. We'll show you how to do this in the next section.

To solve a driver-related problem, follow these steps:

1. Isolate the hardware device that is causing problems for your computer. This can be a little tricky if you have recently installed more than one hardware device, such as a camera and a scanner. If this is the case, disconnect all of the hardware devices that you have installed recently and then connect each device, one at a time, and test to see if you can find the device that is causing problems for your system.

2. Once you find the problem device, you should reinstall the hardware driver for it. Use the installation disk that came with the hardware device and follow the instructions carefully. It is possible that device driver files became corrupted and reinstalling them can solve your problem.

3. If you have an Internet connection, you may want to visit the Web site of the company that produces the device for which you are reinstalling the driver. Many companies offer driver updates for free, and their Web sites are likely to have the most recent drivers. Find the driver you need, download it, and install it.

4. After you successfully install the new driver, reboot your computer to ensure that the new driver gets initialized properly.

TIP: When trying to diagnose your driver problems, don't forget to use the Web. If you are having a problem with a hardware device, it's likely many other users are having the same problem. Companies who produce hardware devices often post troubleshooting sections on their Web sites to make it easier for you to play detective and solve tricky problems.

Return to Older Versions of Drivers Using the Device Driver Rollback Utility

If you are having a problem with a hardware device that you have been using for a while and have installed different drivers for it, you can easily use the Device Driver Rollback utility to return to an older version of the driver. When hardware manufacturers issue new versions of their drivers, usually the new drivers help fix problems that have been detected in the past by other users. In some situations, new drivers will create problems that didn't exist before. If this happens, your best bet is to use an older version of the driver. This is easy to do because Windows provides a built-in feature for managing driver versions.

To use Device Driver Rollback, follow these steps:

1. Right-click My Computer and click Properties.
2. Click the Hardware tab, and then click Device Manager.
3. Locate in the device tree, shown in Figure 18-1, the device whose driver needs to be rolled back.
4. Double-click the device, and in the device's Properties dialog box, click the Driver tab. Figure 18-2 shows this tab and the available options.
5. Click Roll Back Driver, and click Yes to roll back to the previous driver.

Figure 18-1

Use Device Manager to access a hardware driver's details.

Figure 18-2
Use the driver's Properties dialog box to roll back or update a driver.

If, after rolling back the driver, you are prompted to restart the computer, do so. If a problem occurs with the rolled-back driver, run Device Driver Rollback again. If problems still occur, consider System Restore, detailed later in this chapter.

TIP: As you can see from Figure 18-2, you can also update or uninstall the driver from this dialog box.

Use System File Checker

If you can't pinpoint any specific problem, be it a driver, software gone bad, hardware, or adware or spyware, you may have a problem with your Windows system files. You can almost always fix problems with system files by performing a repair installation of Windows XP as detailed later, but that takes some time. A faster way, and a better option for diagnosing and repairing unknown problems, is to use the System File Checker utility. This utility comes with Windows XP, will check your computer for required system files, and will replace any that are missing. To run System File Checker, click Start, point to All Programs, point to Accessories, and choose Command Prompt. Type *sfc /scannow*. Wait while the utility runs.

Return Your System to an Earlier State with System Restore

One special trick that many Windows XP users aren't aware of is that they can restore their computer to the state it was in prior to its present state. Why is this important? Let's say that over the past two weeks you hooked up a few new hardware devices, installed hardware drivers, and loaded up a few new applications. After this was done, your computer really started to act up. You tried some of the critical degunking tasks outlined in this book—such as installing new drivers and removing gunk off of your hard drive—but your machine still won't run as it did a few weeks back. With the help of a seemingly magical tool called System Restore, you can return your computer to the state it was in before you made all of your changes. The best part is that you can restore your computer without losing any recently added items like documents, Internet Favorites, e-mail messages, or your Internet History files. If this sounds like the next best thing since time travel, you're right! Once your system is restored, you can add back your hardware and software one at a time, testing for problems and rebooting after installing each.

TIP: *The System Restore feature provides a good approach for backing up important system-level data, such as the Registry. We recommend that you use this feature before you consider making any changes to the Registry. This technique is covered in Chapter 17.*

In order for the System Restore utility to be able to perform its magic, you must make sure that it is first enabled. (It is likely enabled on your system by default.) Once enabled, it operates by creating what are called *restore points*.

These restore points keep track of the different states of your computer over time as you make changes. You can think of them as bookmarks. Depending on how much space is reserved for System Restore, you can have up to three weeks worth of restore points available, and they are created almost daily. While this data takes up some space on your hard drive and uses some system resources, it is vital to recovery. You should configure and use the System Restore feature.

Configure System Restore

Take a look at how System Restore is configured on your computer, and verify that it is running, so that you can be sure to have the maximum amount of protection against computer glitches, failures, and errors:

1. Right-click My Computer and click Properties.

2. Click the System Restore tab, shown in Figure 18-3.

Figure 18-3

Verify that System Restore is enabled.

3. Verify that Turn Off System Restore On All Drives is not checked and that all available drives are being monitored. (System Restore won't work if you have less than 200 MB of free space on your computer's hard drive.)

4. Click a drive, and click Settings. In the Settings dialog box, verify that ample space is provided for System Restore to store its data. We keep ours at about 1000 MB, but we have a huge hard drive. You'll have to decide how much space you'd like to share: 10 to 12 percent of the hard drive's available space is fine, but depending on the size of your hard drive, this could mean 7000 or 8000 MB of space. At least keep 1500 MB of space reserved for System Restore to allow for optimal protection. Click OK.

5. Check any additional drives for System Restore settings. Click OK to exit.

Now, if you ever need to restore your computer to an earlier time—say, before you installed that last driver, last downloaded Internet application, last screensaver, or that piece of hardware that blew out the system—you can do so quite easily.

Create Restore Points Manually

Restore points are created automatically by System Restore whenever the program is enabled, once a day or so. They're also created when you install specific applications and programs. Windows XP creates them when you install unsigned device drivers, when you install automatic updates, and when you use the restore operation. Anytime you use System Restore, the restoration process is absolutely reversible. However, if you know that you are planning on doing something risky or something that might make your computer unstable (such as installing that screensaver you're so fond of), you can create a restore point manually.

Creating a restore point manually is incredibly easy:

1. Click Start, point to All Programs, point to Accessories, point to System Tools, and click System Restore. The initial System Restore page is shown in Figure 18-4.

2. Select Create A Restore Point and click Next.

3. In the Create A Restore Point page, type a description of the restore point. Click Create.

4. The new restore point will be created. Click Home in the Restore Point Created page.

5. To see the new restore point, back at the Welcome To System Restore page, click Restore My Computer To An Earlier Time and click Next.

The new restore point will be selected and visible, as seen in Figure 18-5. You can now use this restore point if your risky installation doesn't go well. In this

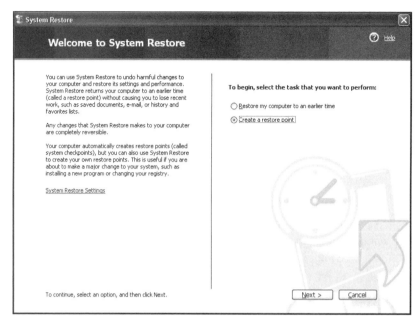

Figure 18-4

The System Restore Welcome page allows you to create a restore point as well as restore the computer to an earlier time.

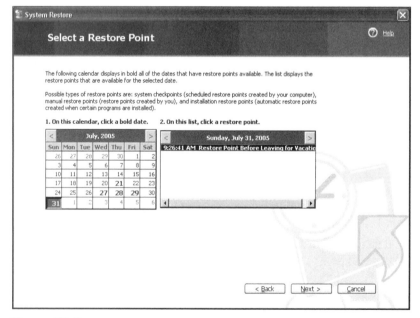

Figure 18-5

If you need to choose a restore point, choose one from a date you knew the computer was working properly.

figure, we've created a restore point on a laptop, just before leaving for vacation. If something goes awry at the hotel's Internet hot spot, we have a good place to restore to.

Using System Restore

If you've decided you need to use System Restore, it's just about as easy as rebooting, and if you aren't happy with the results, you can switch back. System Restore creates its own restore point before it uses one you've selected, so you're safe using it whenever you feel it's necessary. The restore process will restore your computer to an earlier time, any that you choose, and the computer will act like it did on that date. This is the perfect way to solve minor problems with applications gone bad, downloads gone wacky, or drivers gone crazy. It can also be used if you are suddenly having difficulty diagnosing computer problems, problems with applications, or problems with hardware. Simply use System Restore to return to a date when the computer was working properly.

Here's how to use System Restore:

1.   Click Start, point to All Programs, point to Accessories, point to System Tools, and click System Restore.

2.   Select Restore My Computer To An Earlier Time and click Next.

3.   Select a restore point. Restore points are marked with a dark blue font. Locate the restore point; use the arrow to return to a previous month if necessary. Click Next.

4.   Click Next in the Confirm Restore Point Selection page to begin the process. The computer will reboot, and you'll be prompted on startup that System Restore is reversible.

System Restore is the first thing you should try before running more time-consuming tasks like the Repair option or upgrading using the Windows XP CD. These are also better choices than performing a clean installation.

Repair XP with the XP CD-ROM

Before using the Repair option with the Windows XP CD, you should have tried the following:

√   Employed the critical degunking techniques outlined in this book

√   Run System File Checker at the command prompt

√   Downloaded and installed the latest and critical Windows updates

√   Used Device Driver Rollback to switch back to earlier versions of device drivers for your hardware

√ Attempted to solve your current computer problem with System Restore by restoring your system to an earlier state

If you are still having problems with your PC, you can try to solve your problem with the Repair option on the Windows XP CD. The Repair option is a powerful tool and can fix startup problems, problems with system files, and more, all automatically.

CAUTION! We highly recommend that you try the Repair option before you install a clean version of Windows XP. Always remember that installing a clean version of XP should be your last resort.

To repair your system with the Windows XP CD-ROM, make sure you have a valid product key before starting. You can locate the product key from the Windows XP CD's packaging materials.

What If I Don't Have an XP CD?

If you purchased a computer that did not come with a Windows XP CD and you want to use the Repair option, you are probably out of luck. Perhaps you purchased the computer secondhand and it didn't come with a disk, or your new computer came with a restore CD instead of a Windows XP CD. Either way, you can't use the Repair option if you don't have the disk! (If you've broken or lost your disk and have a valid product ID, you can get a replacement from Microsoft.)

Unfortunately the missing disk phenomenon happens to a lot of buyers, and the restore CDs that many people receive with their computers will only reformat the drive and revert the computer back to the state it was when the computer was purchased. If this has happened to you, the installation files might be stored on your computer or restoration CDs. We'd suggest calling the computer manufacturer's technical support line to inquire. If worst comes to worst, and it probably will if you only received a restore CD, you might want to purchase an XP CD from your local computer store or online dealer.

If none of these solutions works, do a complete backup of all of your files, settings, and system state; use the restore CD to reformat the computer; and then use the Backup And Restore utility to restore your data to the newly installed computer.

TIP: To protest the missing CD phenomenon, make sure you insist your next computer comes with a real XP CD. If all computer buyers insisted, we'd all have the CDs we need!

How to Boot to the CD

If you use the Repair option, your computer will have to be configured to boot to the CD. Chances are good it already is configured that way, so before you go messing around in the BIOS, pop in the Windows CD and reboot the computer. If you see an option during boot-up telling you to "Press any key to boot to the CD" or something similar, follow the instructions to do so. If you do not see that option and you cannot boot to the CD, you'll have to make a change in the computer's BIOS.

Changing the BIOS

Entering the BIOS requires you to press the right key combination or the correct function key at the right time during boot-up, and it isn't always that easy. Computer manufacturers would rather you not fiddle around in there, and they don't make it that easy to find. If you don't know your key combination and it isn't listed at boot-up, try pressing the F1, F2, F3, or similar key at the splash screen. If that doesn't work, you might have to visit the Web site of your computer maker and search through its knowledge base.

Once you can access the BIOS, browse through the pages using the arrow keys and locate the page that offers a listing of the boot-up sequence. Use the arrow keys and follow the instructions listed to change the boot sequence to include the CD-ROM drive as the first option. Exit the BIOS saving the changes, and continue on to the next section.

Repair XP Without Doing a Clean Install

You can repair XP without doing a clean installation. This option is the first one you should try if you've been having serious problems with startup errors, boot errors, or hard-to-diagnose problems that no other degunking technique has been able to solve. Here's how to perform a repair:

1. Put the Windows XP CD in the CD-ROM drive and reboot the computer.
2. When prompted to boot to the CD, perform the required steps. Generally, this is achieved by pressing any key during the boot process.
3. Wait while Setup loads the files. At the Welcome To Setup screen, press Enter to select the option To Set Up Windows XP Now.
4. Press F8 to agree to the terms. At the next screen, use the arrow keys to select the partition that contains XP's current files.
5. Press R on the keyboard to start the repair process.

CAUTION! *Do not press Esc because this will start a clean installation of Windows XP and will format the drive.*

6. Wait while the drive or drives are examined and follow the prompts as you work through the repair task.

7. The computer will reboot. Do *not* choose to boot to the CD again; the process will simply start over. Let Windows reboot on its own.

8. When prompted, set up Regional and Language settings and type in the product key located on the XP packaging.

9. After the installation is complete, work through the activation pages.

We've found that the Repair option works really well in solving operating system problems, and on boot-up, errors are usually gone and the system is fully functional. With a repair, you don't lose any existing files, data, applications, or settings, so it's one of your best options as a troubleshooting technique.

Upgrade to Windows XP

If you can't boot to the CD, you won't be able to use the Repair option. If this is the case, you can perform a repair by reinstalling Windows XP using the Upgrade option. Upgrading preserves your installed programs, data files, and computer settings and does not format the hard drive as a clean install would.

TIP: The Upgrade option does the same thing the Repair option does but generally takes 60 to 90 minutes, in comparison to the 40 minutes or so a repair takes.

If you can't configure your computer to boot to the Windows XP CD but you'd like to use the Repair option, you'll have to work through the process this way:

1. With the computer running, put the Windows XP CD in the CD-ROM drive.

2. At the Welcome screen, choose Install Windows XP.

3. In the Windows Setup dialog box, choose Upgrade and click Next.

4. Accept the license agreement and click Next.

5. Type in the activation code and work though the setup process.

6. After installation is complete, finish by working through the activation screens.

Performing an upgrade or a repair installation will fix many common problems with the operating system because it recopies the operating system files and puts everything back in the proper place. Performing an upgrade does not cause you to lose any data, pictures, music, or e-mails and is a good way to get a gunked-up system running again.

Do a Clean Install but Only If You Really Have To

If you've given up all hope of repairing your computer on your own, if tech support has told you that reinstalling is the only option, or if you are going to sell your computer (or give it to someone) and want to erase all of the data on it, you should perform a clean installation of Windows XP. But beware! A clean installation will format your drive, which means all of the data you have saved on the computer will be erased. You'll want to make careful backups of everything you've created before moving forward.

GunkBuster's Notebook: When to Perform a Clean Installation

Performing a clean install of the operating system should be a last-ditch effort to save the computer from the trash heap. Your computer needs to be so severely gunked up that you simply can't stand to look at it, or it needs to be so unresponsive that it hangs up regularly and causes loss of data (and headaches). You can do a clean install for good reasons too, though, like when you're selling the computer to someone else to buy a new one! Here are a few telltale signs you need to reinstall clean:

√ You want to sell the computer and don't want your data to go with it.

√ The computer hangs when printing documents.

√ You get DLL errors on boot-up that a System File Checker, an upgrade, or a repair doesn't solve.

√ The computer blue-screens or hangs more than once a week.

√ The computer is severely slow, even though it has a fast processor and plenty of RAM.

√ You've tried all of the degunking tasks in this book.

√ You're beginning to hate your computer and/or sometimes slam the mouse on your desk.

The #1 cause of systems that require a clean installation are certain really vicious varieties of spyware. Some spyware is so persistent and clever that if it finds that any part of itself has been damaged (i.e., removed by you or by an anti-spyware utility) it will go back to hidden files that it stuffed away somewhere on your hard drive and repair itself. If you get the sense that that's what's happening, a clean installation may be the only way out.

Gather Your Critical Information

Since the computer's drive will be reformatted, you'll want to take special precautions not only in backing up all of your data to a disk or CD, but also in writing down the settings for your ISP, the phone number you dial, your broadband configuration, network settings, and other critical information. You'll also need to gather up all of the applications you use, including their product or activation keys. There are other things you should make a note of too: printers, cameras, scanner drivers, software you've purchased from the Internet, downloads that you don't have on disk, and screensavers you dearly love.

Before you begin, sit down and make a list of everything you can think of that will need to be reinstalled and see if you can locate them either in your desk or on your computer. If they're on the computer's hard drive, locate the program folder and burn a CD of the files.

Although this is not a complete list of things you should locate and/or back up, Table 18-1 will help you get started. For a more complete list, refer to the form in Appendix A.

Table 18-1   Clean Installation Checklist

Items to Acquire and Back Up	Check Here Once Acquired
System folders, including My Documents, My Pictures, My Music, My Webs, and My Videos	
Any personal folders you've created	
Program files for downloaded applications that you do not have on disk	
Anti-virus disks and activation codes	
The Windows XP product key	
Service packs on disk if you have them	
ISP phone numbers, Web sites, and settings	
E-mail account information	
E-mail address book	
Hardware drivers and software disks	
Computer name and workgroup name	
Favorites, bookmarks, and cookies	
E-mail messages	

You can acquire some of this information by browsing through the settings for your Internet connection, viewing Outlook or Outlook Express settings for accounts and options, and viewing the Properties dialog boxes for codes and activation keys. Other information such as product activation keys can be retrieved from a disk's packaging materials or from e-mails you received when you purchased the software. Figure 18-6 shows an example of where to find information about incoming and outgoing e-mail server settings. (In Outlook Express, click Tools, click Accounts, and click Properties.)

Figure 18-6

Sometimes you have to drill down into the menu options and configuration settings to find the information you need.

TIP: There is a nice free utility called the Belarc Advisor that, when run, will print out a summary sheet with as many of your critical Information items as it can find. If your PC is still functional, you can install it before reformatting the hard drive and let it do some of the sleuthing for you. It's free and you can download it from www.belarc.com.

With the required information in hand, reinstalling Windows XP is pretty easy:

1. Put the Windows XP CD in the CD-ROM drive and reboot the computer.

2. When prompted to boot to the CD, perform the required steps. Generally this is achieved by pressing any key during the boot process.

3. Wait while Setup loads the files, and at the Welcome To Setup screen, press Enter to select the option To Set Up Windows XP Now.

4. Press F8 to agree to the terms, and at the next screen, use the arrow keys to select the partition that contains XP's current files. Make a note of the partitions and their size.

5. Read the directions for deleting or creating partitions. Either tell XP to install over the partition that holds the system files, or delete and re-create the partitions as desired.

6. Continue with the installation, setting the regional settings, time and date, network configuration (if necessary), and any additional settings, as required.

7. When the installation completes, work through the activation process. Once you've done so, you'll be ready to reinstall each of your programs.

Reinstall Everything

With a clean slate, you can really do things right! As you copy and import your backed-up data, make sure to put it in the right place the first time. As you reinstall hardware, make sure not to install any unsigned drivers. Reboot between each installation, and then use the hardware to verify that no problems occur because of it.

As you reinstall applications, make sure to activate them immediately so problems can be solved immediately.

If you do decide to install something risky, like an unsigned driver, third-party screensaver, or incompatible device, do so slowly. Create a System Restore point. Install the device and its unsigned driver on Monday, and wait until Wednesday or so to see if the computer acts as it should. If it does not, uninstall it or use a System Restore point.

A freshly installed computer should not have issues unless you cause them. If you discover a few days after installing that cheap Web cam that the computer is sluggish, generates blue screens, or has similar problems, uninstall it, remove it from your system, and then use System Restore to return to your system's state before it was installed for extra protection.

Maintain the Computer

Finally, remember to use Disk Cleanup and Disk Defragmenter to keep your computer clean. Remember to perform simple maintenance tasks like empty-ing temporary files once in a while and deleting cookies that can build up on your computer. Above all, keep your anti-virus and firewall software updated. You can have a nice, smooth, fast, and efficient computer; you just have to know how to treat it right!

Summing Up

Sometimes, problems occur that are so bad, specific actions are necessary, such as using Device Driver Rollback or System Restore, reinstalling Windows us-ing a repair or an upgrade, or performing a clean installation. Windows XP makes it pretty easy to do these things, and often only a single System Restore is needed to get your computer working flawlessly again. When troubleshoot-ing, work through the techniques described in this chapter in the order given, and save performing a clean installation as a last resort.

Performing a Clean Windows Install

In Chapter 18, we discussed when you may need to perform a clean install of Windows XP. Because a clean install will format your drive, all of the data that you have saved on your PC will be erased. This includes documents, pictures, movies, music files, and more. You will also lose all of your configuration settings for items such as e-mail, Internet connection properties, network properties, printers, applications, and so on. To help you compile all of the settings and information you will need after you perform a clean install, we've created the form provided in this appendix. We suggest that you use the form as a checklist as you save all of your personal data and gather all of your critical settings and write them down.

You will also need to gather up all of the applications you use, including their product or activation keys. Don't forget to compile the registration numbers for products that you installed directly from the Web, such as FTP clients or other utilities. You might find these codes in old e-mail correspondence. The hardware drivers that you use to support devices such as printers, digital cameras, scanners, PCMCIA cards, Wi-Fi hardware, and so on are also very important. It's likely that you have these drivers stored on the CDs that came with the devices you installed. If you installed newer drivers from the Internet, make sure that you back up copies of these drivers. You should also make sure that you back up your e-mail files so that you have copies of your personal inbox and outbox e-mails. One thing that never hurts is to create—even in longhand—a paper summary containing all of your registration keys and other data needed to install all those applications you've paid for.

TIP: *To back up any driver, you must know where it is located on the hard drive. Often, it's in the C:\Windows\system32\drivers folder. You can get more information about any driver from Device Manager, which can be opened from Control Panel>System>Hardware. Device Manager shows all devices on the system and offers information about their status, driver, and physical location.*

If you follow the guidelines suggested here, you will have a good record of all of your settings, along with the data that you need to save. This will save you much time and aggravation when you need to perform a clean install. One of the most difficult and time-consuming aspects of reinstalling Windows involves reconfiguring your PC so that it will operate as it did before you did the reinstall (minus the gunk, of course!). The settings and data that you compile before you start the reinstallation process will save you from having to perform a lot of detective work after the fact.

Settings Needed for Reinstalling Windows

Personal Data to Save:

My Documents: ☐

My Pictures: ☐

My Music: ☐

My Webs: ☐

My Videos: ☐

Any personal folders you've created (check all hard drives):

Hard Drive Configuration:

FAT 32 or NTFS: _____

Drive configuration/format (C: drive only or C: and D: drive): _____

_____

Internet Connection Properties:

Phone number dialed: _____

Dialing options: _____

Security settings: _____

Custom settings (if used): _____

TCP/IP protocol properties: _____

Type of dial up server: _____

Any special ISP settings: _____

FTP addresses and passwords (if used): _____

Hardware configuration of cable modem, router. and other hardware:

_____

Static IP addresses if applicable: _____

Technical support phone number for ISP or broadband provider:

_____

E-Mail Settings and Data:

Account names: _____

Tools>Accounts settings: _____

Tools>Options settings: _____

User information (name and password): _____

Server URL for any HTTP servers: _____

Incoming and outgoing POP3 and SMTP servers: _____

_____

Connection settings: _____

Advanced settings:

E-mail address book: _____

Saved e-mail messages: _____

Network Configuration Settings:

Workgroup or domain name: _____

Computer name: _____

Passwords: _____

Local area network authentication settings: _____

Application Disks and Activation/Product Keys:

Operating system: _____

Microsoft Office (if used): _____

Internet browser (if applicable): _____

Disks needed to install hard drives (if applicable): _____

_____

Anti-virus programs: _____

Firewall program (if applicable): _____

Other application software: _____

_____

_____

_____

_____

Other utility software: _____

_____

_____

_____

Drivers and Software:

Printers: _____

Scanners: _____

Cameras: _____

Other hardware: _____

Other:

Third-party software downloaded to the computer but not stored on disk:

All of your data using the Backup utility and burned to CD: _____

Service packs (if applicable): _____

Tips on Locating Personal Data and Configuration Settings

Most of the personal data components that you'll need to save (and later re-store) when reinstalling Windows are relatively easy to locate. You just need to spend a little time and think about all of the folders that you have created on your hard drive(s). Here are a few tips to help you gather your data:

√ Hard Drive Partitions. Review how your hard drive is partitioned and formatted. For example, do you have a single drive (C:) or more than one drive (C: and D:)?

√ E-mail. Look in the directory where your e-mail program (Outlook or AOL, for example) is stored to locate the e-mail client's main data files. It's important that you back up the files that store your actual e-mails and your address book, if you use one.

√ Applications. If you have special applications that store data in the folder where the application itself is stored, make sure you view these folders and back up any critical data files. If you use older applications, you'll find that that they often store their main data file in the default directory where the program is stored. For example, a program such as Quicken would probably store its main data file in the directory C:\Programs\Quicken.

√ User Data. If you have multiple users who access the computer, make sure each person has ample time to back up their own data, write down their own settings, and agree to the reinstallation.

The configuration settings that your computer uses are a little trickier to locate, but with a little detective work, you can find them. You can acquire some of the information you need by browsing through the settings for your Internet connection, viewing Outlook or Outlook Express settings for accounts and options, and viewing the Properties dialog boxes for codes and activation keys.

Other information, such as product activation keys, can be retrieved from a disk's packaging materials, or from e-mails you received when you purchased the software. The following sections include some specific tips to help you locate the settings that are more difficult to find.

Locating Hard Drive Configuration Settings

To determine how your hard drive is set up:

1. Double-click on My Computer from the Desktop. The My Computer window opens.

2. Scan the window to locate the Hard Disk Drives section. You should see at least one disk drive listed. Note the number of drives that are available.

3. Click on one of the drives to select it (select the C: drive if present), right-click, and select the Properties option from the menu that appears. This opens the dialog box shown in Figure A-1.

Figure A-1

Know what type of file system you have.

4. Look for the label "File system." This section will tell you how your drive is formatted. You should see the text "FAT 32" or "NTFS" to indicate if your drive is formatted as FAT or NTFS. This information is important because you'll likely want to keep the format of your drive the same when you reinstall Windows.

TIP: You can view advanced information from Start>Run>MSinfo32, including the paths to applications, Internet settings, and hardware components.

Locating Your Internet Settings

The Internet settings you need to record (and later restore) will depend on whether you connect to the Internet by a dial-up modem or a high-speed broadband connection. If you use a dial-up modem, you'll need to save the phone number(s) and passwords that you use to connect. If you have a broadband connection, you can locate the settings by following these steps:

1. Click on the Start menu and select Settings and then Control Panel.

2. From the Control Panel window, double click the Network Connections icon.

3. Right-click the Internet connection you use and click Properties. You will see a screen showing your connection settings.

4. Finally, make a note of how your modem, router, and other hardware are positioned and connected.

Locating Registration Information for Software You Download

If you have software that you've downloaded, registered, and installed, you likely won't have installation CDs with the registration information for the software. When you reinstall Windows, you'll need to redownload and reinstall this software. The easy way to locate your registration information is to run the software and try to locate the Help menu for the program. Most programs provide an About option that displays information about the program, including your name and registration number. This is the information that you should record.

You can also use Windows Explorer to locate downloaded installation files. There is a folder called Downloaded Installations in C:\Windows\Downloaded

Installations. Figure A-2 shows an example. You can see that there are several installation packages, all of which could be backed up to a CD or DVD and reinstalled later. (You can check other folders, too; you'll be surprised what you find.)

Service Packs and Updates

Finally, if you've been using XP for a while, you'll have lots of Windows XP updates on your hard drive. If you want to see just how many, open Control Panel>Add Or Remove Programs>Change Or Remove Programs and check Show Updates. Figure A-3 shows an example. If you perform a clean install, you'll have to download all of those updates again.

If you have dial-up, acquiring all of these updates could take a while, especially if you have to reinstall SP2 or obtain upgrades to Movie Maker or Media Player. If you wanted to, you could try to back up these updates to CD or DVD before you perform the reinstall.

To see if this is a workable solution, using Start>Search, perform a search for "security update." As you can see from the results, there are lots of files stored in lots of different folders. While you might be tempted to copy and then try to

Figure A-2

If you can locate the installation packages, you can back them up.

Figure A-3
You have lots of updates on your computer.

reinstall the C:\Windows\ServicePackFiles folder on your new machine, we're going to advise against it. There may be newer or more reliable updates, you might not get all of the files you need, and other problems may arise. To avoid gunking up your new machine, then, we'll suggest you simply turn on Automatic Updates after reinstalling and leave your PC connected to the Internet as much as possible.

Recovering from a Corrupted Registry

Believe it or not, just as we were putting the finishing touches on this book, one of us encountered a problem with the Windows XP Registry. This problem kept the computer from booting. In Chapter 13, we explored the Registry in some detail and showed you how to clean and tweak the Registry. This degunking task should help to keep your machine running well, but if you ever encounter a problem with the Registry, you could suffer from the same fate that happened here.

In this appendix, we'll outline a course of action to recover from a Registry problem that keeps your PC from booting. With a little bit of knowledge and patience, you can quickly recover from such a problem and get your PC back up and running.

Using Microsoft Support for Help

If you encounter a problem with your Registry that prevents your PC from booting, the first thing to do is check with Microsoft support services. They provide an excellent service that helps registered Windows users fix critical problems, such as booting problems with the Registry. Don't feel that you have to be a hero and fix your own Registry problems. As you learned in Chapter 13, the Registry is very complicated and requires specialized knowledge to repair, especially if the Registry is corrupted to the point where your PC will not boot.

The information that Microsoft provides for fixing a corrupted Registry can be found on a Web site that Microsoft provides for customer support: **http://search.support.microsoft.com/kb/c.asp?fr=0&SD=GN&LN=EN-US**

When you get to this site, search for article number 307545, "How to Recover from a Corrupted Registry That Prevents Windows XP from Starting."

How to Know When You Have a Registry Boot Problem

While working at home one day or traveling on a flight for a business trip, you might boot up your computer, only to discover the following error message that tells you Windows can't start:

Windows XP could not start because the following file is missing or corrupt:

\WINDOWS\SYSTEM32\CONFIG\SYSTEM

The error message might also contain information about a specific Registry key or hive that is damaged.

Fixing Your Corrupted Registry

Although the Registry involves a set of various files, as we learned in Chapter 13, there are five critical files that will likely need attention if your computer won't boot due to a Registry problem:

√ System

√ Software

√ Sam

√ Security

√ Default

Each of these files is stored in the directory C:\Windows\System32\Config. To fix a corrupted Registry problem, you basically need to replace each of these files. But if you replace one of these files, you must replace them all—that's the law—of the Registry.

Replacing the Registry files might sound simple, but there are a few catches. First, because your computer won't boot, you can't simply get on the computer and replace the files. The second catch is that even if your computer could boot under Windows, you can't simply copy over the files because Windows is always accessing the Registry files while it is running, and while files are being accessed they cannot be copied over. (For more information about how the Windows Registry operates, see Chapter 13.)

Fortunately, Windows provides a tool called the Recovery Console (good name, right?) that you can use to access your system and replace the corrupt Registry files with default repair versions. You can do this because the Recovery Console doesn't need to run under the full Windows operating system. You'll then be able to boot up Windows and access your archived copies of the Registry files that were created by the System Restore feature, which is built into Windows XP. (The System Restore feature was covered in Chapter 18.) Once you locate the proper files, you can rename them so that you can later use them and move them to the proper directory.

For the third major task, you can use the Recovery Console again to move the Registry files to the C:\Windows\System32\Config\ directory so that Windows can access them. Finally, you can re-boot Windows and, if you did everything correctly, your PC should be restored.

NOTE: *In the remaining sections of this appendix, we'll show you how to briefly perform the Registry recovery tasks just outlined. Because Microsoft provides very good technical information on this process, we suggest you either call Microsoft for technical support or obtain the Microsoft Knowledge Base Article introduced at the beginning of this appendix.*

Task 1: Use Recovery Console to Set Up Replacement Registry Files

One little-known secret is that Windows stores replacement or "repair" copies on your computer of the five Registry files that you can use to get your PC to boot. So for our first step, we will use the Recovery Console to locate these files and move copies into the C:\Windows\System32\Config directory. Keep in mind that these Registry files are only "repair" files and they won't fully restore your computer to run as it did, with all of your settings, before you encountered problems. To perform this task, follow these steps:

1.   Locate your Windows XP Setup CD-ROM.

NOTE: *If you don't have an XP Setup CD-ROM, you won't be able to run the Recovery Console. If you have a computer that came with XP installed and thus the Setup CD-ROM was not provided, you may need to purchase a copy of the Windows Upgrade CD. (Often many computers that have Windows XP Home edition installed do not ship with Setup CD-ROMs.) The advantage of purchasing this CD-ROM is that you will then become a registered Windows user and you can call Microsoft support for help. You may not be happy about spending additional money, but this is a relatively inexpensive way to go if you have a system crash and the Upgrade CD-ROM can get you up and running again. It also ensures that you can get ongoing support from Microsoft in the future.*

---

2. Boot up from the XP Setup CD-ROM. (The detailed instructions for doing this are presented in Chapter 18.)

3. Run the Recovery Console, which provides you with a command-line prompt. (This prompt will look similar to the prompt you see when you use DOS.)

4. Make a temporary directory by typing in this command:

   md temp

   Make sure to press Enter after each command you type in.

5. Next, you'll need to make backup copies of the existing Registry files. You do this by issuing each command shown next for each of the five Registry files:

   copy c:\windows\system32\config\system c:\windows\temp\system.bak

   copy c:\windows\system32\config\software c:\windows\temp\software.bak

   copy c:\windows\system32\config\sam c:\windows\temp\sam.bak

   copy c:\windows\system32\config\security c:\windows\temp\security.bak

   copy c:\windows\system32\config\default c:\windows\temp\default.bak

   Remember to press Enter after each command.

6. Delete the Registry files using these commands:

   delete c:\windows\system32\config\system

   delete c:\windows\system32\config\software

   delete c:\windows\system32\config\sam

   delete c:\windows\system32\config\security

   delete c:\windows\system32\config\default

7. Copy the "repair" Registry files to the directory where they need to be so Windows can boot:

   copy c:\windows\repair\system c:\windows\system32\config\system
   copy c:\windows\repair\software c:\windows\system32\config\software

   copy c:\windows\repair\sam c:\windows\system32\config\sam

   copy c:\windows\repair\security c:\windows\system32\config\security

   copy c:\windows\repair\default c:\windows\system32\config\default

8. Quit the Recovery Console by typing in exit. Your computer should re-boot automatically.

Task 2: Locate Replacement Registry Files

Task 1 allows you to boot Windows temporarily so that you can now get in there and locate your archived Registry files, which you will use to replace the repair files. This is an essential task because the repair files you just set up do not contain all of your Registry settings, such as the configuration settings for your applications, desktop settings, and so on. In fact, your computer might look a little different to you right now—but don't panic!

NOTE: *You must log in as an administrator to perform the steps presented in this section. You might also need to boot your computer in "Safe" mode. The easiest way to do this is to continue to press the F8 key while your computer is booting. This should display a screen of boot options. Select the Safe Mode option and continue with the boot process.*

Follow these steps to locate and rename the archived Registry files:

1. Start Windows Explorer.

2. Select Tools and then click Folder Options.

3. Click the View tab to display the file and folder settings.

4. Using the setting window, select the Show hidden files and folders option and deselect the Hide protected operating system files (Recommended) option, as shown in Figure B-1. This step is necessary to unhide the system level files and folders that you will need to locate.

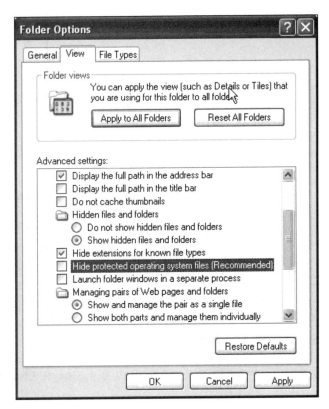

Figure B-1

Selecting the options to unhide files and folders.

5. When the dialog box is displayed confirming that you want to unhide files and folders, click Yes. Click OK to close the Folder Options dialog box.

6. From your Desktop, locate the hard drive where Windows is installed (likely the C: drive), and double click on the drive to obtain the list of folders stored on the drive. Open the System Volume Information folder. You should see a screen like the one shown in Figure B-2.

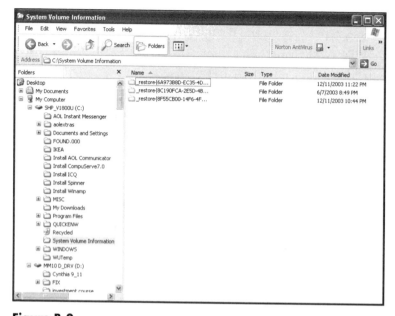

Figure B-2

Viewing the System Volume Information folder.

7. In this folder, you should notice a set of folders that start with the label "_restore ...." These folders represent the different restore points or "snapshots" that have been saved on your computer. Open the folder that has the latest date and time. Don't open the one with the current date and time, if present.

8. Open one of the restore points folders you see (look for the name "RP...") and then open the folder named Snapshot. This folder, as shown in Figure B-3, contains the actual Registry files you'll need to copy and move.

9. Look for the files labeled, REGISTRY_MACHINE_SECURITY, REGISTRY_MACHINE_SAM, REGISTRY_MACHINE_SOFTWARE, REGISTRY_MACHINE_SYSTEM, and REGISTRY_USER_.DEFAULT, and copy them.

Figure B-3

Locating the Registry files in the Snapshot folder.

10. Paste copies of these files in the directory C:\Windows\Temp.

11. Rename the files copied as SECURITY, SAM, SOFTWARE, SYSTEM, and DEFAULT.

This is as far as we can now go with these files because Windows is currently running and accessing the versions of the Registry files that are stored in the C:\Windows\System32\Config directory. We can now use the Recovery Console again to delete the temporary repair files and replace them with the versions that we just obtained from the Snapshot folder.

Task 3: Use Recovery Console to Set Up Archived Registry Files

Your repair Registry files have done their job, so it's now time to replace them with the real Registry files. We'll use the Recovery Console to move over the files that are now stored in the Temp directory we created. To perform this task, follow these steps:

1. Boot up from the XP CD-ROM.

2. After you boot from the CD-ROM, run the Recovery Console.

3. Delete the Registry files stored in the C:\Windows\System32\Config directory:

    del c:\windows\system32\config\system

del c:\windows\system32\config\software

del c:\windows\system32\config\sam

del c:\windows\system32\config\security

del c:\windows\system32\config\default

4. Next, you'll need to move over the archived Registry files from the Temp directory. You do this by issuing this set of commands:

copy c:\windows\temp\system c:\windows\system32\config\system

copy c:\windows\temp\software c:\windows\system32\config\software

copy c:\windows\temp\sam c:\windows\system32\config\sam

copy c:\windows\temp\security c:\windows\system32\config\security

copy c:\windows\temp\default c:\windows\system32\config\default

5. Quit the Recovery Console by typing in exit. Your computer should re-boot automatically.

If you follow all of these steps, your PC should now be fixed.

Appendix C

Troubleshooting Your PC with Degunking Techniques

If your PC is currently gunked up and you are having specific problems that are slowing you down or keeping your PC from running, we can show you how to apply some degunking techniques to solve the most common problems you are likely to encounter. This appendix will help you if your time is limited and you can't take the time to degunk your entire PC by following our twelve-step degunking program (see Chapter 2). The Degunking Sheet we presented in the first part of the book can also help you perform different degunking tasks, depending on the amount of time you have.

To get the most out of this appendix, we suggest that you first identify the problem (or locate the one listed in this appendix that is most similar to your problem) and then perform the corrective action we recommend. You'll be surprised at the number of problems that you can fix by referring to this list and simply performing the right degunking tasks. After you solve a specific problem, put a little time aside later to more fully degunk your PC. For example, if you encounter the problem of not being able to save a document file because your hard drive is full, and then you fix the problem by deleting a few large files, we suggest that you later return to this area and perform the degunking tasks covered in Chapter 3. That way you can get rid of a lot of files and keep the "full disk" problem from occurring again. Our experience shows that if you encounter a problem, it will likely continue unless you put some type of maintenance plan in place.

Operating System Problems

Problem: Your PC boots slowly, or the boot process sometimes stalls and you need to re-start your machine.

Windows may be having difficulty loading one of its system-related files, or you may have too many programs that are trying to be loaded into the System Tray (also called the Notification Area) at boot-up. To speed up the boot process, we recommend:

1. Remove some of the programs that get loaded when Windows starts (see Page 89).

2. Clean the Registry using a registry cleaning utility (see Page 226).

Problem: You recently installed new applications or made changes to the Windows Registry and your PC is having difficulty booting or is running very poorly.

It's likely that something occurred while you were installing new programs or making changes to the Registry. Rather than try to find the actual problems, which can be really difficult, we recommend that you use the System Restore feature to return your system to an earlier state (see Page 329).

Problem: Your computer won't boot and you receive an error message that you have a corrupt or missing file in the directory C:\Windows\System32\Config.

One of your Registry files may be missing or corrupted. You can fix a problem such as this by following the instructions provided in Appendix B.

Problem: Your computer freezes up when performing tasks like printing files, or you notice that your computer crashes randomly.

Problems like this could be created by the hardware that you've added to your computer. You should run a compatibility check of your hardware and drivers to see if there are any problems (see Page 324).

Problem: You are having serious problems with startup errors, boot errors, or hard-to-diagnose problems that no other degunking technique has been able to solve.

You can still possibly repair Windows XP without having to do a clean install by using the XP Setup CD-ROM (see Page 333).

Problem: You get an "error report" message, and your system asks you if you want to send the report to Microsoft.

Microsoft likes to track system errors so that they can better help their customers. By clicking OK and sending the report to Microsoft, you can possibly help other users down the road. You don't need to worry about any security or privacy issues because of sending the report to Microsoft.

File Management/Hard Drive Problems

Problem: Other users who have used your PC have left files and folders on it that you want to get rid of, and you aren't sure how to access those files and folders.

You'll need to log into your computer as the Administrator and then use the Control Panel to see which users have accounts on your computer. You can then use a Control Panel component called User Accounts to delete an account and the associated files (see Page 47).

Problem: You use multiple computers and you are having difficulty synchronizing your files and folders.

The best way to synchronize your files and folders is to use a third-party utility. You can find freeware and shareware on the Web with the tips and tricks introduced in this book (see Page 272).

Problem: You have too many temporary files on your computer, and you are concerned about how to find all of them so you can delete them.

You can locate and delete most of the temporary files on your PC by using Disk Cleanup, the utility that is provided by Windows XP (see Page 43). You can also delete other temporary files that Disk Cleanup doesn't find by applying some smart searching operations (see Page 44).

Problem: Your hard drive is just about out of free space and you are having trouble running your applications.

You need to first manually delete as many personal files and folders as you can (see Chapter 3). Then you need to uninstall all the programs you no longer use (see Chapter 4). When all of the unnecessary files and programs have been removed, empty the Recycle Bin (see Page 78). To finish your work, you should run the Disk Defragmenter utility (see Page 81). After you complete these steps, you should check your hard drive to make sure that you have created enough free space.

Application Problems

Problem: While using an application such as Word or Excel, you receive an error message indicating that a file you are working on can't be saved because your hard drive is full.

You need to quickly free up some space on your hard drive. We suggest you:

1. Look in your default folder for old files you don't need (see Page 24). Pay particular attention to large files.

2. Remove all of the temporary files on your system (see Page 41).

3. Once you are able to save your data from the application, we suggest you close all of your applications and perform the other file cleaning tasks presented in Chapter 3. Make sure you run the Disk Cleanup utility (see Page 42).

Problem: An application freezes, and you can't close it or work with it.

If the application freezes often, there may be a problem with how the application was installed. In such a case, we recommend you remove the application and re-install it:

1. Remove the application by utilizing the application's uninstall options (see Page 51). If the application does not have an uninstall option, you should remove it using the Control Panel (see Page 52).

2. Once the application has been uninstalled, you can re-install it using any setup software that you have. If you are uninstalling and then reinstalling an application that you have previously downloaded from the Internet, make sure you first take note of the application's registration information before you un-install it.

3. You can also configure the program to run in Program Compatibility Mode, a feature that gives older applications their own virtual space on the hard drive.

Problem: It takes forever to load an application.

If you encounter this problem, the application could be installed incorrectly or the setup information about the application could be stored incorrectly in the Registry. To solve such a problem:

1. Try cleaning the Registry using a Registry cleaning utility (see Page 226).

2. If cleaning the Registry does not improve the problem, remove and then re-install the application using the techniques presented for the previous problem.

Problem: You can't find applications you need on the All Programs menu.

You can easily add an application to the Start menu so that it shows up in the All Programs list by following the steps presented on Page 93.

Problem: An old program that you used with a Windows 98 computer installs but it doesn't work right.

If you find that an older program that worked fine on your Windows 98 machine doesn't run so well on your Windows XP machine, you can tell Windows to run it in Program Compatibility Mode (see Page 61).

E-Mail and Web Browsing Problems

Problem: When you try to send an e-mail, it just sits in your Outbox and doesn't go anywhere, or it takes forever to send a two-line e-mail.

Your e-mail system might be so overloaded with saved e-mails that it can't send out or receive e-mails. To fix this problem, you should clean up your e-mail gunk by following the instructions in Chapter 8.

Problem: You have only one e-mail address, and you are getting so much spam that you are having difficulty getting to important e-mail.

You should set up different e-mail accounts to reduce the spam you receive (see page 110). You should also set up a spam filtering utility to help reduce the spam you receive (see Page 120).

Problem: After installing Service Pack 2, you can no longer open attachments, view images embedded in e-mails, or, click links in e-mails when using Outlook Express.

You should tweak Outlook Express' security settings. These are changed during the installation of SP2.

Problem: You send e-mail messages to some of your friends or business associates but they don't receive them.

You may be including items in your e-mails that are triggering other people's spam filters (see Page 131).

Problem: Your e-mail program takes an exceptionally long time to start up.

It's likely that your combined set of e-mail inboxes and outboxes have gotten too large. You should follow the instructions in Chapter 8 to clean up your mailboxes. Pay special attention to the task of eliminating the attachments that might be gunking up your mailboxes (see Page 141).

Problem: When you visit Web sites, you get deluged with annoying pop-up messages.

Windows doesn't currently have a global built-in setting for controlling pop-up messages, but you can use a third-party utility such as Pop-Up Stopper Professional to block the pop-up messages (see Page 272).

Problem: You can't save images from the Internet using the Save As command.

You can solve this problem by cleaning out your temporary Internet files (see Page 44).

Problem: You can't load a Web page because your system indicates cookies aren't enabled.

Configure your browser to allow cookies to be used (see Page 289).

Problem: While using your browser to access the Web, you get errors indicating that you are in a restricted zone and you can't view the Web page.

Your browser is limiting your access to the Web because of the security and privacy settings that have been configured. To reconfigure the privacy and security settings, see Page 284.

Security Problems

Problem: You think that intruders have been getting into your computer and possibly accessing your data or leaving unwanted files.

You should enable Windows XP's firewall (or install a third-party firewall) on your PC (see Page 300).

Problem: Your anti-virus program doesn't run automatically any more.

Keeping your anti-virus program running and up-to-date is crucial because you don't want viruses to sneak onto your machine. If your anti-virus program is no longer running automatically, your registration might have expired. Many anti-virus programs are set up to run for a specific amount of time. You also should check to make sure that your ant-virus program is set up in the System Tray so that it will load when you start Windows (see Page 89). Additional anti-virus configuration information is provided on Page 282.

Problem: You're concerned that your kids are accessing adult-only Web sites or other sites you don't want them to visit.

You can easily set up Internet security zones by using your Web browser (see Page 284).

Problem: You're concerned that Web sites are gathering too much information about you when you visit these sites.

You can control the amount of information that Web sites gather from your computer by using Windows' privacy settings (see Page 288).

Hardware and Peripheral Problems

Problem: You don't have enough memory to run an application, run multiple applications at the same time, or open an attachment.

You'll need to add additional memory to your PC. You can do this by following the instructions presented in Chapter 14. If you are not sure of the type of memory to add to your PC, there are a few ways to determine the type and amount of memory you'll need (see Page 237).

Problem: You've recently installed a new hardware device, such as a digital camera, printer, or scanner, and your computer is running poorly or crashing when you use the hardware device.

You may have a bad or incorrect driver installed. If you suspect a newly installed driver is causing a system problem, you can remove that driver and replace it with a new one (see Page 325).

Problem: You are having trouble typing on your keyboard because some of the keys keep sticking.

You can really improve the performance of your keyboard by cleaning it with compressed air.

Media Problems

Problem: The Media Player and Movie Maker interfaces don't look the ones shown in this book.

You need to get upgrades for both from Microsoft's Web site. They are free (see Page 180).

Problem: You have problems playing music in your Media Player playlists, and keep getting errors about missing files or licenses.

You need to work through some degunking tasks including checking for valid licenses, verifying the tracks are still on your hard drive, and possibly recreating your media library (see Chapter 11).

Problem: You have a lot of duplicates in your Windows Media Player library.

Either delete the files manually or recreate the media library (see Page 181).

Problem: You've never backed up the licenses for the music you've downloaded from legitimate music sharing sites.

Use Media Player's Manage Licenses utility to back up (and restore) licenses (see Page 188).

Problem: You have a million files in the My Movies folder, and you can't seem to even find what you need.

You need to degunk that folder by learning what source files, project files, and movie files are, and how to delete them safely (see Page 192).

Problem: When you create a movie, it's too large to do anything with.

Learn how to use advanced Save Movie options in Movie Maker to make smaller files with the same data (see Page 192).

Appendix D

The Future of Degunking

Degunking your Windows PC is a complicated business. You have to uninstall abandoned software, dodge spyware and viruses, clean out your Registry and lots of other things, one piece at a time. Sometimes it seems like you spend half your life picking gunk out of Windows. Wouldn't it be great if you could click one button…and have a sparkling clean Windows install again?

Soon, that "one click" degunking will be a reality. As our PCs become more powerful and Windows becomes more capable, new degunking techniques become possible. We've already hinted at one in this book: Windows XP System Restore (see Chapter 18). With System Restore, you can "roll back" a failed software install or registry tweak that has damaged part of Windows, so that it's like the damage never happened. As good as it is, System Restore has its limitations, and some damage (from spyware or viruses, especially) is beyond its ability to heal.

In this final section of the book, we're going to show you what degunking will be like in just a couple of years—and if you're technically sharp and have a powerful PC, we'll show you how you can start experimenting with tomorrow's degunking technologies right now.

Making Windows Virtual

A new technology called *virtualization* is reinventing PC computing. Most simply put, virtualization allows an operating system—like Windows or Linux—to create a sort of artificial PC in software. This artificial PC is called a *virtual machine* (VM). To you, a VM looks like a Windows window. Inside that window, you can "boot up" the VM, and then install software to run on it—software that includes other operating systems like Linux, BSD Unix, or Solaris, or even Windows itself, along with anything that runs under Windows.

Running a second copy of Windows in a window sounds like a neat trick, but what good is it? The real magic has nothing to do with running Windows inside a window. (Most of the time, you run a VM "zoomed" so that it controls your entire display.) The magic begins with the ability to save the entire VM—including everything installed in it: Windows, your applications, your data—*everything*—to a single (large) disk file.

You can save this image (which we call a VM *snapshot*) to another hard drive, or burn it to a DVD for backup storage. You can send it to a backup server over a network. The snapshot represents a complete, bit-by-bit record of the state of your Windows installation running in the VM. You can bring back a snapshot of a VM in only seconds, and it will be running just as it ran when you took the snapshot.

What I've described so far can also be done (with care and a little fussing) with a few other software utilities like Norton Ghost. However, aside from being a great deal faster than Ghost and similar utilities, virtualization is much more powerful. Each VM is *extremely* well isolated from other VMs and from the underlying PC. Software running in a VM has no way to get out of the VM and affect the underlying copy of Windows. A snapshot can be taken on one PC, then moved to and run on another. The technology is extremely versatile.

The best way to demonstrate this versatility is to give you some scenarios.

Instant Degunking

The simplest scenario is one-click degunking. In this scenario, you create a VM, install Windows in it, and then install all of the software that you use day-to-day. After configuring Windows and all your software just the way you like to use it (but before you actually *do* use any of it), take a snapshot of the VM. That snapshot is your "clean" copy of the VM, including Windows and all your software. Store the clean snapshot somewhere safe.

After you take your snapshot, the VM becomes your daily, workaday copy of Windows. When you boot your PC in the morning, you don't just jump into the "real" Windows and begin doing your work. Instead, you launch your Windows VM, zoom it so that it uses the full display, and go on using it as your working desktop.

If during the day something goes wrong (spyware, a virus, a piece of software that installs badly and makes Windows unstable), you back out your data, bring up your VM's *virtual machine manager* (the "boss" program that controls Windows virtualization) and "revert" to your clean copy. In about ten seconds, the virtual machine manager loads the clean copy of the VM and runs it. One click, ten seconds, and the damage to Windows is simply gone, as though it never happened at all. Bring your data directories back and you're in business.

With some virtualization technologies, you don't even have to back out your data. Your data can be stored independently of the VM copy, on a folder elsewhere on your hard drive. You can revert to your clean copy and your data will still be there in the independent folder, right where you saved it.

Trying Out Software

Suppose you want to get serious about digital photography and acquire a photo editor. You look around: There are a lot of them. Many allow you to download the full product and "try before buying" for a limited time. Unfortunately, as most people eventually discover, installing and uninstalling a lot of software is a great way to build up gunk in your system folders and the Registry, and if you do it enough (and if you install carelessly written software, or software that comes with spyware and adware) you can make Windows unstable very quickly.

Virtualization makes it easier. You begin by taking a snapshot of the current state of your Windows VM. Then you install the first photo editor package. You run it, and...uh-oh, there's a bar of animated ads and your network port is suddenly very busy. Adware! No problem. Bring up the virtual machine manager, and revert to the snapshot you took before you did the install. In ten seconds, the installed photo editor is gone, along with the adware and spyware that rode in with it. Gone here means *really* gone. There is *absolutely no trace* left of anything you did to the VM after you took that first snapshot.

Dust off your hands and install the next photo editor package. This one looks good, so you work with it for awhile, but after an hour or so it still seems clunky. Bring up the VMM, revert to the snapshot, and ten seconds later this one is gone too. Bring on the third one. What pitiful garbage! Revert. It's gone. Bring on the fourth one and try again.

With virtualization, trying software packages is like trying on sweaters at Penny's—except that sweaters sometimes leave fuzz on your shirt. When you revert to a snapshot, an installed product leaves behind nothing at all.

Virtual Projects

This is where it gets interesting. When you take a snapshot of a VM, the snapshot captures not only all your files and program settings, but also the "state" of all running software. In other words, if you take a snapshot of a VM with six open windows in various parts of your screen, all running various applications and utilities, the snapshot captures the location of each window, the utility running in the window, and whatever dialogs, menus, or edit screens happen to be active in the utility when the snapshot is taken. It's a "freeze-frame" for the current state of the work you're doing. It even includes data on the clipboard! You can shut your physical PC down, go to bed, and the next morning, you can launch the snapshot of your VM, and your project is suddenly right there in front of you. You don't have to remember what page you were editing, what mode you were in, or anything else. The project is literally there in front of you, *precisely* as it was before you went to bed.

Many busy people work on several major projects at once. Virtualization allows you to change projects in ten seconds without having to remember where you left off or how to set up several programs before you begin. Even the relative positions of the applications on your screen are the same. Taking a snapshot is like lifting the entire Windows project and throwing it in a file folder, from which you can retrieve it the next day, or from somewhere else. Because the snapshot is just a file (albeit a *big* one) you can burn the file to a DVD or send the file over a network to another PC running the same virtual machine manager. In other words, if you have to get home but need to keep working, you take a snapshot of your project on the VM at work, save it to DVD or store it on a network server, and then when you get home you can retrieve it from DVD or from the server and launch it on your home PC. It's there just as it was when you left the office.

Safe Surfing

Every time you turn around, it seems like there are new Web browser security flaws coming to light. The bad guys are trying very hard to create situations in which surfing to a tainted Web site will automatically install software on your PC and take it over, to send spam or launch "denial of service" attacks. Apart from being hazardous, such software is hard to detect before you encounter it, by which time it's too late.

With virtualization, you can create a VM that you use only for Web surfing. You open a browser window in the VM and take a snapshot. Then go on and wander the Web. No matter what happens out there, when you're done, you back out your bookmarks and revert to the clean snapshot. No matter how evil an exploit might have been planted on your VM by a Web site, when you revert to the clean copy, it's history.

What Makes Virtualization Work

Windows XP alone does not handle virtualization. You need an entirely separate piece of software called a *Virtual Machine Manager* (VMM) or *hypervisor*. This installs under Windows just as a word processor or photo editor would. However, the VMM has special powers over the PC's hardware and memory. It can partition your memory so that two VMs can run at once, each thinking it has all the memory there is.

The copy of Windows that you have installed normally on the PC is called the *host operating system*. When you create a VM and install Windows, Linux, or some other operating system inside the VM, the operating system in the VM is called a *guest operating system*. The virtual machine manager can create several VMs and run them all at once if you need them, and you can jump between them with one click. The next generation of CPUs from both Intel and AMD will contain special machinery to make virtualization even faster and more bullet-proof.

The VMM provides another service that may be a little hard to understand: It creates a standard virtual hardware environment for each VM it creates. Your VM can display graphics, make sounds, and transfer data through serial ports and removable disk drives. This sounds like the VMM allows all the VMs to share the physical hardware in your PC, and while true, that's not the whole story. The VMM creates a "virtual video adapter" for each VM. This virtual video adapter responds to program commands just as a physical one does. The virtual adapter belongs only to the VM it was created for. Other VMs each have their own separate virtual video adapters, and none of the virtual adapters interfere with or "know about" any of the others. The VMM is "boss" and manages the process by which all the virtual video adapters share space on your physical screen. Each virtual video adapter believes that the screen belongs to it alone. The same can be done for network adapters, sound adapters, printer ports, and removable disk drives. A VM really is a virtual PC, right down to the hardware!

Virtualization's Limitations

It's still very early in the desktop virtualization game. (Most virtualization technology is currently being used for servers.) The technology is advancing rapidly, but it has some limitations and complications:

√ Virtualization requires a fast machine and a lot of memory. The VMM imposes a burden on your PC, of both memory and CPU cycles. The more you have the better, and virtualization enthusiasts recommend PCs with a 3 GHz CPU and at least 1 GB of memory.

√ Virtualization software is still relatively expensive. The category leader, VMWare Workstation, costs about $200.

√ Today's PCs were not designed with virtualization in mind. Toward the end of 2005, Intel and AMD will release new CPUs and support chips designed to make virtualization much faster and more reliable. The PC you buy next year will likely handle virtualization much better than the one you have now.

√ The virtual hardware created for a VM is "least common denominator." Even if you have a ramcharged, multiprocessor 3-D accelerated graphics board in your PC, a VM will only see a very generic superVGA. Sound support is similarly standardized on a simple, Sound Blaster-compatible virtual adapter. If you have software that requires fancy graphics or fancy sound, it will not run inside a VM.

√ You cannot install a second display adapter or specialty hardware unknown to the VMM and expect a VM to "see" it and use it. Your VM only sees the virtual hardware that comes standard with the VMM.

√ For arcane technical reasons, no VMM yet allows you to burn CDs or DVDs from within a VM. To make optical copies of things, you'll have to copy data to a shared folder on a physical hard drive and burn the disk from the host OS.

√ A VM is an entirely new machine from the perspective of Windows XP. If you install a copy of your Windows XP OEM CD into a VM, it will demand to be authenticated, and it will appear to Microsoft to be a pirated copy, even if it's physically just a region of memory inside a legitimate, activated XP installation. To run XP in a VM, you'll need to buy a whole additional copy of XP. Software licensing hasn't quite caught up with virtualization's peculiarities.

You'll have the best chance of success by doing relatively ordinary things within a VM: Office suites, Internet suites, databases, page layout, and photo editing (video can be a problem). Games beyond simple puzzle games often do not work at all. Digital lab equipment with PCI bus add-in boards (like DVMs and oscilloscopes) will not work because the VM cannot see the add-in boards.

Because Ethernet hardware is so highly standardized, networking applications actually work very well.

All of this will improve in years to come, but for now you have to keep such things in mind.

How to Get Started

As you can see, virtualization is still a sort of wild and woolly beast. Unless you're a PC enthusiast and understand things like MAC addresses, DHCP servers and leases, memory usage, and so on, virtualization will be a lot to take on and we recommend against it. It's still not as plug-and-play as Windows itself, though the products get better all the time.

Your first step is to buy a virtualization package and study it carefully. By far the best is VMWare Workstation 5. It can be installed under Windows 2000/XP/2003, or under certain high-end distributions of Linux, especially Red Hat and SuSE. Look for articles or forum postings on the Web from people who have created a configuration (say, Windows XP hosted on Linux, or Windows 2000 hosted on Server 2003) like the one you're planning. Learn as much as you can. It's all new.

Make sure your PC has enough memory and disk space. You can run a single VM with 512 MB, but everything will work better if you have at least 1 GB. Virtualization is disk-intensive. Snapshot files can be *gigabytes* in size. If you're going to keep a lot of them over time, plan on having 100 GB available to store them. (And getting rid of snapshots you've abandoned or don't need anymore will become a whole new type of degunking!)

Make sure you have a separate, legal copy of Windows XP (assuming you'll be using Windows) for installation in a VM.

VMWare Workstation installs from CD like any software package. After you have it installed, you can run Workstation's VMM, and use the New Virtual Machine Wizard to create a brand new VM. Creating a new VM involves allocating a (large) block of space on your hard drive and creating some additional files. After the VM is created, it's just like a naked PC without an OS: It will go through its virtual BIOS but will not boot into anything. You have to separately install an OS, either from physical CDs or from .ISO files ripped from the CDs.

As soon as you finish installing an OS in a VM, *take a snapshot of the VM immediately*, before you install anything else or do anything to it. Store it somewhere safe; that's literally a backup of the entire virtual machine, right down to the hardware! You can always "start fresh" by reverting to that pristine copy.

VMWare Workstation has a brilliant snapshot manager screen (see Figure D.1), which plots your snapshots in relation to one another, so you always know which "parent" snapshot gave birth to which "child." Learn it thoroughly. This is central command & control for the VMM, allowing you to take snapshots and revert to them. The snapshot currently running is always marked "You Are Here" so you never have to wonder what state your VM is in.

Figure D.1

The VMWare Workstation Snapshot Manager always lets you know where you are in the snapshot hierarchy.

Once you're comfortable with the system, *try things*. Think about what you can do with snapshots and how they can improve your work environment. Nobody knows "what's best" yet. This is the future, and it's wide open. You can make it up as you go along.

And somehow, we think that against a VMM, gunk just doesn't have a chance!

Index